CW01667105

The

Growing Business Handbook

BARCLAYS
OPEN FOR BUSINESS
Unpaid invoices getting you down? We'll take the weight.
Expanding a business can be a balancing act. On the one hand, you need to pay your suppliers. On the other, you have to wait for your customers to pay up. With our range of specialised services, Barclays could play a pivotal role. Our sales ledger financing provides you with cash as soon as you've raised your sales invoices. And, unlike an overdraft, the level of available finance grows with your sales ledger. For more details, contact your local branch or call 0800 418 418.

The Growing Business Handbook

Strategies for Planning, Funding and Managing Business Growth

Consultant Editors:
Richard Willsher
Adam Jolly

KOGAN PAGE

in association with

CBI The Confederation of British Industry

and

KPMG

Publisher's note
Every possible effort has been made to ensure that the information contained in this handbook is accurate at the time of going to press, and the publishers cannot accept responsibility for any errors or omissions, however caused. All liability for loss, disappointment, negligence or other damage caused by the reliance on the information contained in this handbook, or in the event of bankruptcy or liquidation or cessation of trade of any company, individual or firm mentioned, is hereby excluded.

Published in 1997

Apart from any fair dealing for the purposes of research or private study, or criticism or review, as permitted under the Copyright, Designs and Patents Act, 1988, this publication may only be reproduced, stored or transmitted, in any form, or by any means, with the prior permission in writing of the publishers, or in the case of reprographic reproduction in accordance with the terms of licences issued by the Copyright Licensing Agency. Enquiries concerning reproduction outside those terms should be sent to the publishers at the undermentioned address.

Kogan Page Ltd
120 Pentonville Road
London N1 9JN
kpinfo@kogan-page.co.uk

© Kogan Page 1997

British Library Cataloguing in Publication Data
A CIP record for this book is available from the British Library
ISBN 0 7494 24753

Typeset by Barratt Word and Data Processing, Studley, Warwickshire
Printed and bound in Great Britain by Thanet Press Ltd

CBI
The Confederation of British Industry
Small and Medium Enterprise Unit
Tel: 0171 395 8238

Contents

8 OUT OF 10
TOP COMPANIES
VALUE STAFF
IN THE
RESERVE FORCES.
Letting your colleagues train with the Reserve Forces doesn't just contribute to the country's defence. It also develops qualities of leadership, motivation and initiative in your staff that are so vital in helping to drive business forward. The importance of our Reserve Forces has now been recognised by new legislation which will govern them beyond the millennium. The new Reserve Forces Act, which came into force in April 1997, contains specific provisions, developed in consultation with employers, to assist business. For a free copy of our explanatory leaflet, fax us on 0171 218 4888 or write to: NELC, Duke of York's HQ, Chelsea, London SW3 4SS.
NELC
Source: 'Times 1000' 96
THE VOLUNTEER RESERVE FORCES. BRITAIN'S BEST KNOWN BUSINESS SECRET.
Issued by the National Employers' Liaison Committee on behalf of the Territorial Army and the Volunteer Reserves of the Royal Navy, the Royal Marines and the Royal Air Force.

Foreword

The challenges facing business have altered dramatically over the past decade. Change is everywhere around – often driven by the advances in information technology and the increased expectations of customers. So businesses must respond to the challenges, or find their markets collapsing, their ability to service their markets impaired and their best people leaving to join competitors.

It is no longer good enough to rely on traditional ways of doing things, and growing businesses must address and resolve their changing business issues, if they are to thrive and grow. And it is at the needs of these growing businesses, that this handbook is addressed.

The chapters in this handbook cover a wide variety of management topics, written by people who have proven track records, and are well qualified to author each section. In addition, a number of well-known business leaders have also contributed chapters, and shared the secrets of their success.

I would like to thank my colleagues at KPMG, and all those who have contributed to this handbook. I hope that it will provide a ready source of reference to the entrepreneurs running growing businesses, and will be an invaluable addition to their bookshelves.

Peter Mamelok
Lead Partner, Owner Managed Business Group
London

Preface

We decided to produce *The Growing Business Handbook* because, as far as we could see, there was no other on the market that took a practical approach to the issues encountered by fast-growing businesses.

There are plenty of books on starting your own business, setting up as a sole trader or making a fortune from your back bedroom. But there are not many designed to help those businesses with an established position in their market, which may already have a substantial turnover and which are having to soothe and solve the growing pains of their own cleverly wrought success.

This is no management school tome. We have included articles from people like Sir Tom Farmer of Kwik-Fit and Charles Dunstone of The Carphone Warehouse. These are people who write from firsthand experience and whose businesses have become role models for a generation of entrepreneurs. We also have articles from businesses in high-technology fields, such as computer suppliers Dell and software group Symantec.

Our contributors include specialists, advisers and consultants. These are first-class firms such as our sponsor, KPMG, who have worked alongside a variety of different growing businesses and so have a broad base of experience to draw on.

We are very grateful to all of our contributors for sharing their time, effort, expertise and experience. Of course, they are interested in growing their own businesses even further and reaching new clients or customers. That is why we have included contact details for all of them in an appendix. We are interested in promoting new businesses development as much as they or any growing business would be.

We hope that our readers will find *The Growing Business Handbook* of value and of practical use. If there is some aspect of growing businesses that we have overlooked then please e-mail us, so that when we update the book we can make it even more relevant to the growing businesses of today and of tomorrow.

Richard Willsher
100337.27@compuserve.com

Part 1

The Challenge of Growth

1.1
Growing Complexity

Charles Dunstone
Managing Director, Carphone Warehouse

The Carphone Warehouse has grown from a single store, set up on an initial investment of £6000, to one of the UK's fastest growing private companies, with over 100 branches, a staff of over 600 and an annual turnover of £120mn. One of the secrets behind our success in the management of this increasingly complex structure has been to **keep it simple**.

When we started the Carphone Warehouse back in 1989, our ambition was to build a company unlike any other. Today, our desire to give people the service they really want at prices they can afford, to pioneer new concepts in service and to restore a sense of pleasure to the purchase of mobile communications continues to remain our foremost goal.

Most phone retailers do things more or less the same way. Right from the start we knew we were going to do things differently. And when people told us it couldn't be done, we wouldn't take no for an answer. Our readiness to challenge the conventions of the communications industry is central to what we stand for.

While we never compromise on quality of service, we do everything to give our customers a unique experience.

Every business should create a philosophy and mission it can support. By following this philosophy, many complex problems and difficult decisions are often overcome or negated. At Carphone Warehouse we created a retail philosophy to which we remain true to this day (see Table 1.1.1).

In addition to a philosophy, we have created a set of rules, which every member of staff can follow and which applies to everyone in the company, from the chairman down. These are posted throughout the stores on mes-

Table 1.1.1 The Carphone Warehouse retail philosophy

Rational proposition	Emotional proposition
Impartiality	Young
Range	Enthusiasm
Choice	Unconventional
Knowledge	Fast growing
Meaningful guarantees	Friendly
Integrity	Customer focused
Recognisable brand	Innovative

sage pads, at head office on computer screensavers and even on the back of our business cards. They are:

1 If we don't look after the customer, somebody else will.
2 Nothing is gained by winning an argument, but losing a customer.
3 Always deliver what we promise. If in doubt, under promise and over deliver.
4 Always treat customers as we ourselves would like to be treated.
5 The reputation of the whole company is in the hands of every individual.

A major challenge for our business has been to ensure that the quality standards, put in place while the company was small and London based, are upheld as the Carphone Warehouse expands across the country. Within the retail environment, and I suspect across the majority of businesses, the company is only as good as the staff who work for it. At Carphone Warehouse, the staff *are* the company's greatest asset.

One of the most complex issues we have tried to simplify is recruitment. The majority of our staff come to us through personal recommendation and staff are rewarded for introducing successful candidates. This means that people recommend their friends, family and people like themselves, leading to a consistency which would be hard to replicate by any other means. Wherever possible, we promote from within, highlighting the opportunities available to even the most junior members of the team, which helps provide stability and continuity to the style and culture of the company. Finally, we try to avoid stereotypical backgrounds and recruit on the basis of enthusiasm and communications skills rather than academic qualifica-

Solving the Year 2000 Problem
JAMES KEOGH

This book will give a brief description of what the Year 2000 Problem is and how it came about. It will examine what it will cost to correct the problem and the dangers of not correcting the problem at all. It will also discuss what to look for and where to look for it as well as solutions to the problems. Overall, the book will offer a five step process to handle the change to the Year 2000.

Key Features
- A list of service vendors that will assist an organization in finding and correcting the date fields in their code and data files
- A list of tools that will allow an organization to analyze and code their data files
- A list of tools that will assist in correcting code and data files
- A list of tools that will assist in testing and validating code and/or systems

Hardback, c. 320 pp. Published February ISBN: 0-12-575560-0 £21.95

AP Professional http://www.europe.apnet.com/approfessional
Academic Press 24-28 Oval Road London NW1 7DX

tions. Incidentally, we never employ people who have worked in mobile communications retail before: too many bad habits to overcome!

After recruitment, we have to ensure quality standards and, importantly, that our staff retain the enthusiasm and commitment for which they were first employed. We invest over £4000 per head on training and I give a presentation to everyone joining to explain our aims and goals; we pay well above the industry average and in consequence have one of the lowest staff turnovers in the business; we have a Benefit Trust, which helps support staff through difficult times and provides loans for cars and other aspirational things within reason; we have plenty of fun, with regular Friday night parties, two semi-educational company days and an annual ball to ensure that everyone gets the chance to meet up; and finally, we have a company structure which is flat, where fiefdoms and empire builders are discouraged and which provides effective channels for complaints and grievances so that they can be logged and dealt with quickly.

However, you have to provide people with the right tools with which to do the job properly. This ranges from finding the right sites for new branches — a problem which we have overcome gradually as the reputation of Carphone Warehouse has grown and our presence on the high street is increasingly welcome — to a huge investment in IT to provide the tools and speed to allow the completion of nearly every task without reference to anyone else. Our need for sophisticated software outgrew every available system, so we have created our own, at vast expense, which will see us well into the millennium.

Evaluation is key in every business. We employ an independent consultancy to 'mystery shop' every brand and every customer-facing department each month; we send out a satisfaction questionnaire to every new customer and analyse the results; we produce regular attitude questionnaires for staff to hear what they have to say about the company; and our customer care department holds a hitlist tracking every complaint or problem experienced, whether the problem stems from our company or from the service of our suppliers, the networks and handset manufacturers.

And finally, the directors and senior staff need a very close understanding and feel for the day-to-day needs of the company. We all still help out in the stores on a regular basis and are able to assess the efficiency of the processes and systems at first hand. However, the most important part of the exercise is keeping in touch with the needs and demands of the customers whom we aim to service. If we do it right, we are in business — it's that simple.

Charles Dunstone set up the **Carphone Warehouse** and it is now the UK's leading independent communications specialist retailer with over 100 branches throughout the UK and Eire. In 1996, the Carphone Warehouse was recognised by a major national survey in the *Independent on Sunday* as Britain's fastest-growing private company.

S·T·C
STRADLING TRAINING & CONSULTANCY

For The Holistic Approach To
Management Guidance & Training

SWAN HOUSE
54 STATION LANE
HORNCHURCH,
ESSEX RM12 6NB

PHONE: 01708 473075
FAX: 01708 478064

1.2
The Route to Growth

Nigel Clothier-Brunning
KPMG's Owner Managed Business Group

Finding a successful route to growth is probably the most difficult task facing directors and managers in Britain today. The Japanese post-war economy highlights the culture that is needed to achieve widespread supergrowth, having accomplished much through creative imitation, as well as the willingness and ability rapidly to exploit management techniques and new technology as it becomes available.

The first digital watch was produced by the Swiss. However, with so much invested in traditional watchmaking, they decided on a gradual introduction of quartz-powered watches. Meanwhile, the Japanese Hattori company, a small Japanese watchmaker, saw the opportunity for the digital watch to become the mass-market timepiece of the future. With rapid application of new technology and product development, its Seiko watches soon became the world's leader. Likewise, the transistor was invented by Bell Laboratories in 1947, but the Americans only intended to convert from valves to transistors around 1970. At that time Sony was not even involved in the consumer electronics industry and was unknown outside Japan. Akio Morita, the head of Sony, bought a licence for the transistor from Bell Laboratories for $25,000 and within two years had produced the first portable transistor radio, weighing one-fifth less than conventional radios and costing less than one-third. Rapid domination of the worldwide market soon followed.

These examples represent growth in high-tech areas, yet both illustrate the need continually to assess the business opportunities available and emphasise the benefits of rapid deployment of resources and commitment once a strategy has been decided on. A company that is unwilling to push its existing boundaries or take decisions that are outside its comfort zone is unlikely to achieve steady growth. Gary Hamel and CK Prahalad once said: 'Any company that can't imagine the future won't be around to enjoy it'.

On a company-by-company basis, there are a number of simple routes to growth that businesses can look at and usually a combination of some or all of these will be used:

- increasing the value and frequency of sales of existing products to existing customers;
- selling new products to existing customers;
- selling existing products to new customers;
- all of the above plus selling new products to new customers.

Of these, the last route is undoubtedly the one with the highest risk and yet can provide some of the largest returns. A new product requires resources to develop it and to update it once it has been introduced to the market. With a revolutionary product, marketing may be needed to promote the concept of the product and in all cases some form of advertising is needed simply of the company as the purveyor of the product. When done effectively, the generic product name can become synonymous with the manufacturer, as with the Hoover, the Biro or the JCB.

Of the recent successes, The Body Shop illustrates the benefits of capitalising quickly on a good idea. Having identified a range of new products in the form of environmental and animal friendly cosmetics, the first shop turned out to be a huge success. The basic idea was very simple and had to be rolled out quickly if others were not to capitalise on the initial achievement. Deciding that it was in the business of retailing, The Body Shop subcontracted the manufacturing in order to concentrate on rapid expansion of the retail chain. With little capital to finance expansion it used franchising to achieve a rapid national coverage of shops and establish itself as a household name.

Selling new products to existing customers should arise from a perceived demand for that product from the current client base. Often new products will be complementary to established ranges and may lead to an opportunity to increase sales of these mature products. A new product will still require the commitment of resources to develop and maintain it, although publicising the product should be relatively straightforward. Salesforces will have established personal contacts with customers and should be able to convince buyers to try a new offering if the company already has a good reputation. Likewise, a database of customer addresses already exists to include details of a new product with an existing mailing.

Undoubtedly the route to growth that most businesses are considering is selling existing products to new customers, especially when they are in a mature industry. Often companies will be restricted geographically in terms of their customer base and it may be necessary to set up a distribution chain in separate geographical markets in order to achieve this. It is at this stage that the skills of management can be tested, requiring control to be maintained while motivating the new team, perhaps with a degree of autonomy for the staff who run it.

A very simple way of achieving growth through increasing the value of transactions is to see which of your products you could sell to existing customers but are not doing so already. By preparing a grid of each feasible combination of products and customers, it is soon possible to identify specific opportunities. Although extremely straightforward, this technique can prove extremely effective in highlighting areas for potential expansion.

Acquisition is just another method of accomplishing these strategies; in effect an acquisition is merely a purchase of new products, new customers or both. Although this method of growth may appear the most expensive, handled correctly an acquisition may be more cost effective than new product development and the associated launch, especially when the latter is linked to a large-scale advertising campaign. To handle an acquisition well, however, requires both funding and management capacity.

In all routes to growth, care must be taken to avoid the spectre of overtrading, while still maintaining the impetus for expansion. So often a business with profitable commercial operations will falter due to insufficient available funding to support its expansion. Overtrading can apply equally to management resources as to funding. The Body Shop achieved rapid growth through franchising, which requires little capital. Oasis, another recent example of retail supergrowth, continually managed the number of outlets it opened every year according to the cash generated from profits, as well as the management time needed to control growth successfully. All of these factors are developed in later chapters.

Whatever route to growth you are pursuing, do not let your existing horizons limit your ambitions. As Mao Tse Tung said: 'The frog in the well say, "The sky is no bigger than the mouth of the well".'

KPMG's Owner Managed Business Group which is the UK's market leader in advising mid-corporate owner-managed businesses. The staff in the group have a proven track record of assisting companies and their owners achieve their business and personal goals with innovative business solutions, employing industry and technical expertise. For more information on KPMG's OMB group in your locality, call Peter Mamelok on 0171 311 2858.

The Key to Business Growth...

Effective telecommunications are vital in today's increasingly competitive environment.

Independent surveys have shown efficient communication with your customers can hold the key to business profitability.

Not only does the telephone provide the means to keep us in touch, but it can also assert a positive influence on how your customers perceive both your products and services - making it a powerful asset to your company's image.

While it is imperative not to be left behind, it is essential for a business to make the right investments in technology.

The Britannic Telecom Company is a dynamic and service orientated company with a total commitment to providing the right solution to your needs - quickly, efficiently and with the utmost integrity.

As a fully authorised dealer for both BT and SDX Business systems, and a fully accredited Systems Maintainer, Britannic provide unrivalled levels of support and account management to all their customers...

We are making a special offer in conjunction with the publication of the CBI Guide to Business Growth...

Send now for a free copy of our guide to unlocking your business potential through effective customer communications, at the address opposite

or call us on 01732 - 747576 to find out how we can be of service.

...through effective customer communication.

BRITANNIC TELECOM COMPANY

Britannic Telecom Limited
(Business Telecommunications Guide)
3 Victoria Road, Sevenoaks,
Kent TN13 1YD.
Tel: 01732 - 747576

SDX Business Systems

Authorised Dealer for BT

Britannic Telecom - *Excellence on Call*

1.3

Adapting Ownership and Control

Peter Mamelok
KPMG's Owner Managed Business Group

Recent surveys show that over two-thirds of businesses in Britain consist of only one or two people and often the second person is the spouse or a close family member. Furthermore, almost 97 per cent of firms employ fewer than 20 people, 99 per cent fewer than 100 and only 9000 employ 200 or more. It is undoubtedly true that the organisation and management of a growing business are some of the most difficult elements to achieve successfully.

As a business develops, not only are new management skills required, but also new attitudes and personal qualities. This places great demands on the owner-managers and their team. They need not only to develop and adapt themselves, but typically they will also need to bring in outsiders at an appropriate stage.

The owner-manager of a growing firm needs to adapt from being a 'doer' to being a manager. This involves delegating certain tasks and decisions. It is this delegation that is at the cornerstone of the organisational route to growth. Owner-managers often find delegation difficult as they fear losing control and do not trust others to do as good a job as they themselves would. Delegation necessitates tolerating mistakes, supporting and protecting staff as they grow into their jobs and rewarding successful initiatives. Without delegation there can be little or no growth. Sir John Harvey-

Jones's advice to managing directors was: 'Do only that which no-one else can do.'

A distinction needs to be drawn between delegation and abdication of responsibility. Merely giving someone a major task and then reviewing the results after it has been completed is not effective delegation. By that stage, the outcome, good or bad, has already been decided. Effective delegation involves giving someone responsibility for a certain task while providing them with the training and support to achieve it. It also entails maintaining some element of control over the final decision, while giving the person the opportunity to make recommendations as to what that should be. As a level of trust and proven ability is established, then greater responsibility for decisions can be transferred.

The strong desire for control, often exhibited as an autocratic and dominant management style, can lead to 'overcontrol', a desire to let no one else have any authority. This can lead to staff being 'infantilised', expected to feed all information on decision making through the owner-manager who desires to be involved in all aspects of the business. This is incredibly demotivating for staff, hindering their training and personal development. It slows their progress towards becoming the managers of the future who can continue the growth of a business and is inefficient. Above all, a business run in this way will in time become a group of 'yes men', surrounding their leader, with little or no capacity to adapt to change, most especially if the group loses its leader.

Priorities should also change from operations to planning and control, which can be difficult as many owner-managers enjoy the operations aspect, with its immediate tangible successes and failures. More time should be given to thinking strategically, giving leadership and direction to the increasing number of staff. Time should also be set aside for developing a cohesive management team that will be able to continue to drive the business forward in the coming years.

However, an owner of a successful business may not feel comfortable with becoming a managing director or believe that they have the best skills to take the company forward. They may wish to concentrate on the operational side of the company, feeling that this is the area where their particular strengths lie. Such a policy is not unusual and can relieve the owner of considerable stress, with growth maintained by a professional manager employed to attend to the stewardship of the business and its efficient organisation. Additionally, as any organisation becomes larger, it is important to take a number of different opinions and the recruitment of experienced non-executives can add this extra dimension as well as enhancing the credibility of the business.

As a business grows, the informal 'face-to-face' style of communication becomes more and more difficult to sustain. Written reports, memos and e-mails replace informal chats and the old hands-on style of management is no longer possible. Formal management and directors' meetings should be planned constantly to monitor the trading and strategic position. Formal lines of responsibility and communication should be established and it may be appropriate to split the business into separate cost/operational centres with a particular manager responsible for each.

With further expansion and diversification into differing areas, it may become appropriate either to divisionalise the business or to separate it into a group structure, with each distinct line of business operating as subsidiary to the principal business. During this process the organisation should continually be focusing on its desired position and not merely expanding for expansion's sake. So often you hear of businesses refocusing on their core activities after forays into less profitable areas.

Perhaps one of the most difficult routes to expansion is acquisition, particularly into unfamiliar geographical territory. Unless this is well planned to ensure that adequate management resources exist to absorb and deal with the resultant change, the result can be devastating to the original core business as its own key managers are 'sucked in' to resolve issues in the new business.

Throughout the growth process, the owner-manager needs to be flexible and adaptable and willing to acquire new skills and patterns of behaviour as the business expands. Above all, the owner-manager must be willing to accept change and relish the challenge that goes with managing it. When any problem presents itself, the owner-manager needs to think through the way to change and accept that some devolution of authority is necessary. Finally, there should be a willingness to discuss ideas with members of staff and others where appropriate, and the owner-manager should not be afraid of seeking the help of external advisers.

KPMG's Owner Managed Business Group which is the UK's market leader in advising mid-corporate owner-managed businesses. The staff in the group have a proven track record of assisting companies and their owners achieve their business and personal goals with innovative business solutions, employing industry and technical expertise. For more information on KPMG's OMB group in your locality, call Peter Mamelok on 0171 311 2858.

Adding *value* to your *business*
Small and medium size enterprises can add value to their business by using the expertise of Chartered Management Accountants in professional practice. Trained in the key principles of management and sensitive to the vital functions of an enterprise, these CIMA Accountants operate within a professional standards framework which encourages best practice and high quality services. They have a hands-on, highly focused approach that yields results.
With more than 100,000 members and students, CIMA is the leading management accountancy professional body worldwide.
CIMA has listings of Chartered Management Accountants in professional practice operating within your area.
Contact the Professional Standards Department of the Institute today for full information.
Access the power of management accountancy
phone: 0171 917 9294
facsimile: 0171 580 2493
e-mail: pstandards@cima.org.uk
CIMA
The Chartered Institute of Management Accountants

1.4

Family Firms and Succession

Mike Coughtrey
KPMG's Owner Managed Business Group

'All happy families resemble one another, but each unhappy family is unhappy in its own way'

Leo Tolstoy

These opening lines to *Anna Karenina* could equally be applied to family businesses. When the scale of family business is considered it can be seen just how important it is to the British economy that family firms run efficiently. A recent survey shows family businesses to be among Britain's biggest employers and estimated to contribute about half the country's gross domestic product. There are just under three million family firms in Britain, employing more than half the country's workforce. Many are household names such as Littlewoods and Clarks.

A well-run family business has a number of advantages compared to a public or alternatively funded private company. There is a greater degree of instinctive loyalty felt by family members and this is likely to engender a harder work ethic. It should also be easier to canvass opinions from shareholders and make rapid decisions over the strategic direction of the business. As with all owner-managed businesses, there will also be less pressure for results from external shareholders such as City institutions or venture capitalists. The problems often arise in sustaining these benefits over different generations.

It has been said that 'the first generation builds the business, the second helps it to grow and the third kills it off'. However, only about 30 per cent of family businesses actually survive to the second generation and only 13 per cent are still being run by the same family come the third generation, proving how difficult it can be to hand a business down to children and grandchildren.

The entrepreneurial spirit and drive that are found in the originators of successful family businesses can often be diluted in following generations. Staff may become disgruntled because they think that a less qualified family member has been promoted due to family ties rather than their business proficiency. Lack of desire or ability within the extended family can also limit the roles that younger members of the family grouping will take. This will often eventually lead to positions within the top management team being taken by people from outside the family on the basis of competence rather than kinship, although this change can bring with it unwelcome complications.

Market research by Transitions, a specialist supergrowth consultancy, shows that the most effective teams are those that develop an 'inner team', which for family companies often form naturally. However, this can be disturbed when a professional manager is appointed to a senior position within the company. Instead of being adopted to the 'inner team' and playing their full part in decision making, they may be kept at the boundaries of the team. This can potentially cause frustration for all involved, particularly the manager concerned. It also means that full advantage is not taken of the manager's particular skills and experience, which were the reason for their initial recruitment.

While the control of the day-to-day running of the company may move outside the family group, the shares in the business are frequently divided between a number of the founders' children and grandchildren, expanding the shareholder base and diluting the individual shareholdings. The management of the company will continually push forward, making the difficult strategic decisions that are required of a successful business, while often the shareholders are poorly acquainted with the detailed trading position and may have a risk averse stance that means that necessary difficult decisions are not taken or deferred. By then some members of the family will have little or no commitment to the ongoing development of the business and the principles of the founding fathers. Balancing the conflicting interests of passive family members who wish to maximise their immediate returns with those of management who want to plough profits back into the business is a continual problem.

Shoe manufacturer and retailer Clarks, which is 70 per cent family owned and has over 400 family shareholders, is a good example of a large business which has seen substantial conflict and change over recent years. When Berisford International mounted a £184mn takeover bid in 1993, it was eventually rejected, but only after considerable family debate. Part of the family lobbied for the company to be sold so they could realise the value of their holdings and eventually negotiated a promise that the company would float within five years. Solving these problems is not easy under any circumstances, but with an integrated company like Clarks, involved in manufacturing, wholesaling and retailing, the task is especially difficult. With many competitors reversing out of this vertically integrated position, Clarks is a large and complex business to drive forward. After the Berisford vote, the family influence on the board was reduced by cutting the number of directors from 13 to 8 and by the creation of a new 15-member shareholder council. Both of these measures helped alleviate the effect of differing family opinions and enabled the management to concentrate on positioning Clarks as a growing, profitable company to put before City investors.

Problems often arise from a simple lack of communication and understanding between family members, or the failure to get to grips with an issue because managers are concentrating on the day-to-day running of a business, rather than strategic direction. As Sir John Harvey-Jones said: 'It seems to me abundantly clear that family businesses have all the problems of running a business, with an extra overlay of specific and different problems which have to be managed to boot.'

KPMG's Owner Managed Business Group which is the UK's market leader in advising mid-corporate owner-managed businesses. The staff in the group have a proven track record of assisting companies and their owners achieve their business and personal goals with innovative business solutions, employing industry and technical expertise. For more information on KPMG's OMB group in your locality, call Peter Mamelok on 0171 311 2858.

1.5
Leadership Skills

Philip Sadler CBE
Partner, Philip Sadler Associates

In recent years it has become accepted that successful enterprises are created through effective leadership as well as sound management.

Management guru Charles Handy attributes the current emphasis on leadership to an underlying change in the way we think about organisations. He suggests that in the past we thought of organisations as pieces of engineering, 'flawed pieces maybe but capable in theory of perfectibility'. Thus organisations were things to be designed, planned and *managed*. Today, however, we use a different kind of language when talking about organisations — a language which uses such terms as vision, mission, commitment, culture and shared values. This, Handy argues, is the language of *leadership*, not of management.

Professor John Kotter of the Harvard Business School argues that management is about dealing with complexity, whereas leadership is about coping with change. Management brings order and consistency to complex organisations. It involves planning and budgeting. Leadership is about setting a direction, developing a vision of the future and strategies for achieving the vision. Management is about controlling and problem solving, while leadership is about motivating and inspiring. It follows that leadership calls for skills which are quite different from those involved in management.

If leadership is to be effective it must win the acceptance of those who are to be led. Whether or not people will follow a particular leader depends on their perceptions of his or her personal qualities and/or actions. In respect of other types of authority, legitimacy derives from position power — we accept the authority of the public official or the works manager or the doctor or the proprietor because of the position they hold. No pharmacist when filling a prescription wants to know more about the doctor who signed it beyond the fact that he or she is properly qualified. A directive from head office is enacted if the managing director has signed it, even if the people at the receiving end have never met the managing director. Leadership, however, is *personal*. We accept leadership or refuse to accept it on the basis of judgements we make about the person offering leadership; these judgements will be based to some extent on what we perceive as his or her personal qualities and on his or her observable behaviour. Effective leader behaviour involves the exercise of a set of learned skills in just the same way as does effective performance in sport or the performing arts. In each case, some basic aptitudes are necessary, but aptitude by itself is not sufficient: the development and practising of skills are essential ingredients of success.

The Skills of Successful Business Leaders

The skills exercised by successful business leaders in recent years have been the subject of a great deal of research and there is a growing consensus as to what these skills are. (The most well known and respected of these studies are included in the recommended reading at the end of this chapter.)

The critical skills for success in a leadership role in today's business environment fall into seven clusters and are briefly described below.

Goal-setting skills

The effective leader must be capable of creating a clear vision of the desired future of the organisation and must be skilled in articulating that vision in such a way that people find it motivating and involving. The creation of a vision calls for the exercise of imagination and the ability to think outside the boundaries of one's past experience. A good example is Colin Marshall's vision of British Airways as 'The world's favourite airline'.

Motivating skills

Effective leaders have learned how to motivate people, both as individuals and in groups. They understand people's needs to feel involved, the motivational power of participation in decision making, the importance of modelling the behaviour one is trying to promote in others and serving as an example. Among twentieth-century business leaders, Bill Hewlett and Dave Packard, founders of Hewlett-Packard, stand out as great motivators, having created a hugely successful organisation of truly committed people.

Interpersonal skills

These include the ability to establish rapport, the skill of active listening, coaching and mentoring skills and team-building skills. As chairman of ICI, John Harvey-Jones was superbly skilled at building warm, trusting relationships with people at all levels.

Implementation skills

Effective leaders get things done through their abilities to delegate and truly empower people and to keep in close touch with events through walking the job and practising 'visible management'. Percy Barnevik of ABB exemplifies this group of skills as head of what is probably the world's most decentralised global corporation.

Representational skills

The ability to represent the group and defend its interest calls for such competencies as negotiating skills and public speaking ability. There is no better illustration of this than the defence and advocacy of Jaguar's reputation by John Egan a few years ago.

Situation-specific skills

Some types of situation require the leader to be highly skilled in the actual task if he or she is to command the respect of others. Bill Gates, founder of Microsoft, provides a classic example.

Self-awareness and the capacity for self-criticism

In the opinion of some commentators this is the most critical of all the skills — the ability to come to terms with one's own strengths and weaknesses, to accept and encourage objective feedback, to play to one's strengths and above all to continue learning so as to remedy weaknesses. It is hard to point to a good example of this, since by its nature it is a skill that is not visible to the observer. Thomas Watson of IBM does, however, serve as a useful role model. He created IBM's well-known 'Speak-up' programme which encouraged people from the lowest organisational levels to direct questions and criticism publicly to members of top management, including Watson himself.

A list of skills of this kind can be daunting to the would-be leader, but, as the examples indicate, what is important is to develop strong skills in one or two areas and then play to one's strengths.

Further Reading

Syrett, M and Hogg, C (eds) (1992) *Frontiers of Leadership*, Blackwell, Oxford.
Kotter, JP (1988) *The Leadership Factor*, Free Press, New York.
Harvey-Jones, J (1989) *Making it Happen: Reflections on Leadership*, Fontana, London.
Sadler, Philip (1997) *Leadership*, Kogan Page, London.

Philip Sadler CBE was for 20 years chief executive of Ashridge Management College. He is currently a non-executive director of the Williams Lea Group, United Engineering Forgings and the Centre for Tomorrow's Company. He has written several books on management, including *Managing Change* (Kogan Page, 1994) and *Leadership* (Kogan Page, 1997).

1.6
Staff Motivation at Kwik-Fit

Sir Tom Farmer CBE
Chairman and Chief Executive
Kwik-Fit Holdings plc

First of all, there are no 'staff' at Kwik-Fit, nor are there any 'senior management'. The terms 'human resources' and 'personnel' are redundant. Strictly speaking, there is no 'head office' either.

We prefer the more accurate term 'Kwik-Fit people'.

This is not simply a question of language or current business jargon. The distinction is of crucial importance, so that everyone within the company understands their role — their relevance to what Kwik-Fit is all about.

There may be no 'staff', but there is plenty of motivation. We take the view that if we are not employed at the front end of the business, then our only role is to support the actions of those who do work there. That point where the customer meets the company, that interpersonal relationship, is the only relevant junction within the entire operation.

Our reasoning is simple, although I would not pretend that the achievement of everything that Kwik-Fit stands for in the marketplace today has been easy. But plainly we live or die by our ability to offer customer satisfaction at a more exacting level than the competition.

Nobody wakes up in the morning with the feeling that they want to pop along and have a new exhaust fitted to their car. We deal in distress purchases — up to 12,000 a day in our 1020 centres throughout the UK, Ireland, the Netherlands and Belgium. We have 6000 people whose primary task is to ensure that those customers continue to return to Kwik-Fit, happy in the knowledge that service levels will be uniformly high.

And they do appreciate us. Each day our call centre at Tannochside in Lanarkshire contacts 5500 recent customers, simply to say: 'Thank you for your business. Were you happy with the service you received?'

A staggering 98.2 per cent of those we call report complete satisfaction. The others will comment on everything from the condition of the waiting room facilities to the appearance of the fitters themselves. There are very few complaints, and those are acted on immediately.

We do not go to such lengths for nothing: it is simply good business to do so.

It is not for nothing that in the earlier days I took Marks & Spencer as a model for Kwik-Fit. We realised very early that a high emphasis on service would be the key to success, especially in a trade which had a poor image at the time.

In those early years we in 'management' took direct responsibility for the strategy. Our network was small enough for us to remain 'hands-on'. We travelled around the country every week, talking to the people in the centres, sharing information about this car or that model, how to do things and so on.

The situation changed drastically in 1980, when we acquired two companies in England. The company jumped from 50 to 200 centres almost overnight, and so did our responsibilities.

These acquisitions had not been well managed. The people resented the old management. There was distrust. None of this was good for business.

We knew then that we had to institute education programmes right across the company. Motivation — really the encouragement of self-motivation — was the key. The subsequent investment which has made Kwik-Fit's name synonymous with high-quality training provided a platform for all the growth we have achieved.

We have what we call the 'profit hour'. That hour is the last hour of the day when someone who is well motivated will not turn late customers away because he or she cannot be bothered, or wants to close up and head home. The interaction with the customer is crucial to Kwik-Fit.

If someone is not adequately rewarded for their work then they are not motivated. That is very true of pay, but it is true also of the more intangible elements of working life.

Very often we will invite a group of people who have left the company to come for a meal and ask them: 'So why did you leave?'

The answers are fairly typical: 'It was time to move on', or 'a new opportunity came up'. Sometimes it is domestic or personal. What I am listening out for is whether anyone expresses any dissatisfaction with the way they were managed during their time with Kwik-Fit. People must know that their colleagues care about them, and are interested in their lives away from the 'shopfloor' itself.

I know that if we find a centre returning a mediocre performance, a change of people can push business way up. The core of the business is its people, and how they interact with each other and their customers.

After 1980 we applied the basic principle much more seriously. We invested heavily in training and, since there were no 'off-the-shelf' packages to be had, we designed many of the education programme ourselves. We have won many awards, and even have equity in a Training for Advancement School at Stoke-on-Trent.

We recruit people not by their educational background, but by their attitude: it must be one of 'can do'. The rewards are good for them, and when it all works there is an immense difference in profitability as a whole.

There is no traditional command chain within Kwik-Fit. We tell our people that they do not move 'up'; instead they move 'along'. So a tyre-fitter becomes a brake-fitter, then one, two or three star manager, partner and so on.

Three of our UK divisional managers joined as fitters, and today they are running businesses with sales of £80mn or more. Our operations director was a fitter. Many of those who moved on found excellent jobs or founded companies of their own, because new employers and investors know that someone who has progressed quickly through Kwik-Fit has a very good grounding indeed.

The strategy pays off every day. Kwik-Fit has grown during a period when customer expectations have risen spectacularly. I believe that is because people today are better educated, have travelled more widely and want value for money. They know their worth.

I am very impressed with standards of service in the UK today. Things have improved greatly during the last 20 years or so, and I believe Kwik-Fit has played a part in that.

The thing to remember is that you can have the world's safest jet flying 200 people, but if one tiny cog fails those people will not come home. Business is like that too — all of us are vital to a company's success.

Kwik-Fit GB, founded in Edinburgh in 1971, is the UK's largest independent automotive parts repair and replacement specialist, operating more than 500 centres throughout the country. The company has added a fleet division, mobile fitting service and car insurance operation to its business. Kwik-Fit is an Investor in People company, and received 20 major UK awards for customer service during the 10 years to 1997.

Part 2
Growth Mechanisms

Where can you find:
Excellent transport links to the City, West End and Europe?
Well-established business support services and local labour hire?
Cost-effective premises and sites?
Customised training for current and prospective employees?
Access to regeneration funding and project partnerships?
A wealth of leisure and living options?
Stratford & Temple Mills, on London's east bank.
We're open for business - are you?
Ring 0181 519 7790 for available premises or sites.
STRATFORD & TEMPLE MILLS. YOUR STRATEGIC CHOICE.
Change
IN EAST LONDON
Regeneration

2.1

Don't Just Grow your Business . . . Make it Explode![1]

Derek Williams
Managing Partner
and
Steve Pipe
Founder, Stephens & Co

There are only four ways to grow any business — including yours. They are to increase:

- the *number* of customers;
- how *much* customers spend;
- how *often* customers buy;
- the *effectiveness* of your key processes.

Thinking about these four levers will give you powerful new insights that will help you to develop exciting new growth strategies and tactics. *Using* them will give you whatever growth rate you want.

1 This chapter is based on an article that originally appeared in the March 1997 edition of the international trade magazine *Party Times*

Use any one of the levers and your business will grow steadily. Use all four and your business will explode. The choice is yours!

Increasing the Number of Customers

There are literally thousands of ways of getting new customers. Unless you're already getting all the customers you want, you probably need to try some new options. How many new ideas have you tried this year? For example:

- Have you set up a system for getting a steady flow of referrals from your best customers?
- Do you get and use testimonials from every satisfied customer?
- Have you used benchmarking to borrow the best 'outside the box' sales and marketing ideas from other industries?
- And, above all, have you recognised that the new customers you are attracting must be of the type you really want?

Once you recognise the importance of only working with customers of the type you really want, you will be ready to implement a simple master strategy for business growth. Start by identifying the type of customers you really want (presumably the profitable ones!). Then organise your business and your sales and marketing efforts specifically to attract that type of customer. And finally, take a long hard look at your existing customers — and get rid of any that are unprofitable or unduly troublesome.

Increasing How Much Customers Spend

Getting customers to spend more is not an optional extra. It should be a central part of your strategy. One of the keys, therefore, is to systematise the entire selling process so that nothing is left to chance.

Some of the areas which these systems should cover include:

- *cross-selling* — persuading them to buy additional products or services;
- *up-selling* — persuading them to trade up to a bigger or better product or service;
- *out-selling* — persuading them to buy another company's complementary products or services.

At McDonald's, for example, every one of its thousands of restaurants uses the company's extraordinarily successful selling system. They up-sell with simple questions like: 'Are those large fries, sir?' and cross-sell by asking: 'Would you like a Coke with your Big Mac, sir?'

Those simple questions have been exhaustively tried and tested. They frequently double the amount of money customers spend. And they have helped McDonald's to create more millionaires than any other business in history.

Of course, you're probably not in the hamburger business, so your selling system may not be quite as simple as that for McDonald's. But you *must* have a selling system. A system that finds out what customers really want — and then helps them to get it. A system that builds up-selling, cross-selling and out-selling into every sale.

How good is your system, and how much have you invested in testing and improving it this year?

Increasing How Often Customers Buy from You

The third way to grow your business is to make your customers buy from you more often. By far the best way of improving customer loyalty is to make your service so incredible that customers keep coming back over and over again. As Tom Peters put it, the best-kept secret in the business world is that 'when your service is awesome you get so stinking rich you have to keep buying new bags to carry all the money home'.

Consistency is another key to repeat business and loyalty. McDonald's has got it right here too. Every aspect of its service is systematised so that it can be of a consistently high standard. Wherever you are in the world, you know exactly what you're going to get at McDonald's. It's not *cordon bleu*, but it's perfect for its market. And so the customers keep coming back to McDonald's more often than any other fast-food chain.

Increasing Your Effectiveness

The final way to grow your business is to increase your effectiveness at converting inputs into outputs. The trick is to identify all your key processes (especially those for converting sales leads or enquiries into sales). Understand how they work and what they deliver. Decide whether you need them. And, if you do, experiment with ways to improve them so that you get more output from every input.

But even experimenting with new ideas isn't enough, because you won't know whether the experiment (or 'test') has been a success unless you measure it. So the final moral is simple: *what you can measure you can test, and what you can test you can improve.*

And that brings us very nicely to an action plan that will help your business explode with growth:

Your action plan

- Measure where you are now. In particular, how many customers you have, how often they buy from you, the average amount they spend and how many enquiries you convert into sales.
- Think of what you can do to improve each and every one of these key measures (because, of course, by doing so you will be addressing all four of the ways to grow your business).
- Generate further ideas by systematically asking your customers what it is they really want.
- Borrow ideas from other successful businesses — especially those in different industries. They don't all have to be original or revolutionary. The best ideas are often the simplest and the smallest. As Jan Carlzon of SAS said, it's not about doing one thing 100 per cent better, it's about doing a hundred things 1 per cent better.
- Test your new ideas — ie try them one at a time.
- Measure the results.
- Use the best — and reject the rest.
- Build the best ideas into your systems so that they are used every single time.
- Don't rest on your laurels. There is always a better way. So carry on measuring and testing, and carry on finding better ways to do everything.

Derek Williams is the managing partner and **Steve Pipe** the founder of multi-award-winning business development specialists **Stephens & Co**. Based in Hertfordshire, between them they have written more than 150 training videos and the book *101 Ways to Make More Profits*, which is published by Kogan Page and on sale around the world in six languages.

API

INVEST IN YOUR FUTURE GROWTH

If you wish your **Chemical** or **Pharmaceutical** company to grow over the next five years take some time to invest in that future.

Applied Planning International have teamed up with KPMG's Pharmaceutical Division to offer an unrivaled combination of experience and knowledge designed to make project management work for you.

Project management can provide the catalyst that brings together diverse aspects of your business, enabling tighter control and improved performance.

Applied Planning International (UK) Ltd.
The Churchill Business Centre,
2 Sopwith Crescent,
Wickford Business Park,
Wickford, Essex. SS11 8YU

API have experience with project management in a variety of other industries including:

- ★ Construction
- ★ Computer
- ★ Petro-Chem
- ★ Automotive
- ★ Engineering

☎ **01268 769000**

http://www.api-europe.com

Contact us for more information

KPMG

Applied Planning International and KPMG: Putting project management to work

2.2

Buyouts and Buyins and how they can act as Engines of Growth

Tom Lamb
Director, BZW Equity Ltd

Since the early eighties, the buyout (used here as a general term for both MBOs and MBIs) has become an established organisational form and an essential tool of corporate restructuring in the UK. According to statistics[1] issued by the Centre for Management Buy-Out Research at Nottingham University (CMBOR), the total value of UK buyouts in 1996 was £7.8 bn in 610 transactions. This represents an astonishing 50 per cent by number and 20 per cent by value of UK Take-over Activity.[1]

The continuation of buyout activity at such high levels suggests that financiers and management teams must be expecting to continue to earn acceptable returns; for venture capital investors this is typically quoted as an internal rate of return of 20–30 per cent pa. A recent survey of buyout fund performance published by the British Venture Capital Association[2] has confirmed that UK buyouts, as an asset class, do in fact produce superior returns for investors over the long term. Over a ten-year period, large and middle MBO Funds, which probably account for the substantial majority of all UK buyout activity by value, have generated returns of 25.8 per cent pa and 15.7 per cent pa respectively against 14.2 per cent pa for the FT All Share Index and 11.9 per cent on UK Pension Funds Total Assets over the same period. Furthermore, these buyout returns are understated as they are measured 'net' after all costs and fees whilst the comparator returns are measured 'gross' before associated fees and costs. Interestingly this outperformance continues post flotation, well after the leveraged financial structure from the original buyout has been unwound. Since its inception in 1990[1], the CMBOR index of quoted (former) buyouts has outperformed the FT All Share Index by almost 50 percentage points.

Buyout returns are driven by three fundamental factors: P/E ratio arbitrage (being the difference between the entry and exit P/E ratios), profits growth and leverage. Changes in P/E ratios and profits together determine changes in enterprise value whilst leverage merely magnifies, for the ordinary shareholders, any such positive or negative change in enterprise value between entry and exit. Thus the outperformance of buyout returns implies an overall outperformance in the growth in the enterprise values of the underlying buyout businesses versus the comparator universe. This is principally due to an outperformance in profits growth rather than simple P/E arbitrage. Although P/E arbitrage can be a significant factor in the growth in enterprise value, particularly where the exit is via flotation or sale to a strategic trade buyer, above average P/E ratios can only usually be obtained for businesses which have achieved, and expect to continue to achieve, above average rates of profits growth. What then are the characteristics in buyout businesses which produce such above average profits growth?

The structuring of a buyout involves the introduction of significant equity incentives for the managers concerned, commitments to servicing external funding (including high levels of debt as well as institutional equity) and active monitoring by those external financiers. High levels of debt place pressure on management to restructure and improve performance over both the short and long term in order to generate the cash flow necessary to service the debt. The equity incentive ensures that management is ultimately rewarded for meeting its financing commitments.

Many studies regarding post buyout performance changes have concentrated on the first two to three years after the transaction, during which time there is usually a process of initial restructuring. For example, research on US LBOs[3] indicates improvements in revenues, profitability, cash flow, productivity, working capital and return on capital measures over this period. Often this involves rationalisation of product ranges, shedding of excess labour and disposal of non-core assets and activities. CMBOR[3] reports that the buyout managers involved are not wholly driven by their financial incentive and the financing commitments, but also regard 'ownership' as allowing them to perform their tasks more effectively by simplifying the decision-making process.

To a large extent these benefits from the initial restructuring post buyout can be regarded as a one-off. However, CMBOR[3] has analysed 156 buyouts completed between 1983 and 1985 and tracked their subsequent performance. CMBOR concluded that, on average, buyouts outperform their industrial sectors, by reference to comparable non-buyouts, for up to five years after the transaction on both 'return on total assets' and 'profit to employee' measures. This may be somewhat surprising as the classic MBO typically occurs in a mature market with a stable product base and thus, it could be argued, there is limited scope for investment opportunity. However, even in the classic buyout scenario, products may have limited life cycles and, therefore, investment in acquisitions and new product development may be required to maintain or improve the competitive position of the business providing a platform for future growth. Also, many buyouts over recent years do not conform to the classic buyout situation outlined above; there are numerous examples of high-growth businesses which have successfully gone through the buyout process. However, the common feature of all buyouts, whether in growth or mature sectors, is that, even after the initial two- to three-year restructuring period, the combination of the managers' equity incentive and the external financing commitments tends to ensure strict control is maintained over the allocation of excess cash flow. In basic terms, excess cash flow is used for advancing debt reduction, thereby enhancing equity values unless there is a strong financial case for investment. This acts as a powerful self-discipline which can often be absent in comparable non-buyouts.

References

1 CMBOR Quarterly Review, Spring 1997.
2 British Venture Capital Association – Performance Measurement Survey 1996 by the WM Company.
3 CMBOR Occasional Paper No. 60 – The Longer Term Effect of Management-Led Buy-Outs.

Tom Lamb is a director of **BZW Private Equity Ltd**, part of the Barclays Group and a leading investor in UK Buy-Outs. Recent significant transactions include the £220mn IBO of New Look, a ladieswear retailer, and the £33mn IBO of W Vinten, a specialist aerospace defence contractor.

2.3

What is Due Diligence?

Tony Fry
and
James Anderson
KPMG Corporate Finance

Due diligence is the process whereby the directors of a company satisfy themselves that a proposed transaction is only entered into after due and careful enquiry.

This process includes satisfying themselves that all significant financial matters have been assessed and all relevant regulatory and/or legal requirements have been properly complied with. There is no generally accepted definition of required procedures for this purpose; however, it is customary to instruct a firm of accountants to carry out a tailored review into the target's financial position and operating/commercial activities as part of the directors' due diligence process.

Due diligence assignments, due to their specialist nature, require someone of requisite skill and experience to carry out the work. In many cases a company's auditors, because of their detailed knowledge and understanding of the client's business and processes, are appointed as the investigating accountants and will undertake the work. However, the leading accountancy practices have departments specifically dedicated to providing a range of specialist services relating to corporate transactions and may be best placed to undertake the role of investigating accountant on larger or more complex transactions.

The cost of getting a transaction wrong can be high and it is therefore essential that the investigating accountants have the relevant transaction and industry expertise.

What is the Objective?

The objective is to assist the decision-making process of the client, who may not have the resources to look carefully into all areas in the time available, by identifying and discussing risks and opportunities of agreed aspects of a proposed transaction. The findings of the accountant will usually be set out in a formal report.

Naturally the decision as to whether to proceed with a transaction always rests with the principal.

Scope of the Work

To achieve this objective, having agreed the scope of work with the client, the accountant will make enquiries and perform analysis based on information made available by the client or target. The nature and scope of work undertaken on such assignments may vary significantly depending on the client's needs and on the type of issues arising on a particular transaction. Areas of particular concern may well need to be investigated in greater depth. The scope of work to be performed is normally documented in a formal engagement letter.

The nature and extent of work will be limited to the agreed areas and not all significant matters about a target will necessarily be revealed. It is therefore critical that the scope of work agreed with the investigating accountant is adequate to cover the perceived risk areas.

When is Due Diligence Undertaken?

The following includes some of the circumstances when due diligence may be required:

- Proposed acquisition, merger, joint venture.
- Prior to flotation, when a report on a potential applicant is prepared to facilitate the sponsors' understanding of the company.
- Proposed financing arrangements on behalf of a lender, for example on management buyouts or venture capital transactions.
- On disposals where independent due diligence is conducted prior to disposal for the benefit of potential purchasers, but commissioned by the vendor.

What Sort of Procedures will be Adopted?

Due diligence is not merely a review of historic financials; it involves investigation of both the commercial and financial aspects of a business. The commercial and financial aspects of a business are closely linked. Only by understanding the commercial drivers behind profit and cash-flow patterns can the right decisions on valuing a business be made.

The key commercial areas that may be covered on an investigation assignment might include some or all of the following:

- key assets and operations, including production/manufacturing processes and facilities;
- relationships with key customers and suppliers;
- commercial strategy;
- the marketplace in which a business operates;
- management reporting, controls and information systems;
- growth constraints, eg productive capacity, sourcing constraints etc;
- the adequacy of information technology and its impact on the business;
- the quality of management;
- environmental risks and liabilities.

The areas covered above, and indeed below, will often require a multidisciplinary team to be involved with accountants, tax specialists, pensions and environmental experts etc.

The financial side of due diligence typically includes the analysis of past and present financial performance, the purpose of which is to:

- seek to identify maintainable profits and cash flows;
- comment on financial strengths and weaknesses of the target business;
- identify potential 'black holes' or deal breakers;
- compare financial performance with industry benchmarks;
- seek to understand the exposure to tax liabilities and how those exposures are managed;
- consider the current funding and status of any pension schemes.

A review of the past is often undertaken in order to be able better to understand and comment on the financial projections of a business.

Financial due diligence would normally include detailed commentary on the assets and liabilities of a target. Particular attention would be paid to any specific areas of concern. For example, where the target may be materially affected by contingent liabilities, emphasis would be placed on enquiring about contingent liabilities which may not be recorded. Examples could include:

- product warranty liabilities;
- product liability;

- potential or actual litigation;
- additional tax exposures;
- under/self-insurance;
- off-balance-sheet items (hedging, foreign currency, leases etc).

Access to and Reliability of Information

The quality of the output from due diligence will depend on the quality of the information available to the accountant. Due diligence reports will normally indicate the sources of information within the report, but due to the time and costs involved will not usually seek to establish the reliability of those sources by reference to independent evidence. Due diligence is therefore not the same as an audit.

As part of the decision-making process, somebody intending to undertake some form of transaction will seek information from many sources, one of which will often be due diligence undertaken on their behalf by accountants. As will be seen from this chapter, this is often far more wide ranging than just a consideration of financial issues and will involve a wide variety of specialists from within an accounting practice.

Tony Fry is a partner and **James Anderson** a senior manager at **KPMG Transaction Services**. KPMG Transaction Services offers a range of services on corporate transactions, including providing advice on acquisitions and disposals, flotations and share issues, management buy-outs, private equity and venture capital transactions.

2.4
Legal Due Diligence

John Hutchinson
Partner, Pitmans Solicitors

The process of carrying out legal due diligence continues from the time that lawyers are instructed on a proposed acquisition until the acquisition completes. It includes ensuring that all legal requirements of a particular acquisition are satisfied, but also involves assessing aspects of a target company or business to ensure there are no legal considerations affecting the target's value.

It is important in any acquisition that all advisers work together. A well-compiled accountants' report will assist considerably in highlighting areas that are likely to cause concern and which will form a focus for legal due diligence. For example, a financial analysis of the target may reveal provisions for claims on product liability or environmental issues.

Legal due diligence will be needed to supplement the due diligence already undertaken by accountants in certain areas and to cover the extensive concerns that fall outside those considered by the acquirer's accountants. Information will be obtained either directly through searches of public registers or enquiries of the target. The types of enquiry will vary depending on whether the target is a business or a shareholding in a company, and the emphasis of due diligence will depend, amongst other things, on the size of the target and business sector on which it operates:

- *Property related enquiries* – these need to be addressed early and thoroughly. Property frequently forms a significant proportion of the value of a target. It is vital to ascertain any potential defects in title of freehold properties or relevant features of occupancy of leasehold premises at an early stage.

- *Environmental liabilities* arising from occupation or use of properties that the target now owns or previously owned and the likely impact they have on the true value of the target must be considered. Depending on the impact of environmental issues, outside consultants may need to be brought in to undertake an environmental audit of property owned or used by the target.
- *Pensions* – as with property, if due diligence is not commenced promptly it is easy for a transaction to be delayed, simply because of the complexities of analysing pensions issues that may emerge from initial due diligence. Once again, co-ordination is needed between legal and other advisers. Bearing in mind the new obligations and sanctions created by the Pensions Act 1996 (much of which came into effect in April 1997) thorough due diligence in this area is crucial.
- *Employees* – the introduction of increasing amounts of legislation governing employees rights, much of it emanating from Brussels, has meant that acquirers must undertake a thorough analysis of obligations arising from the target's workforce. The obligations to consult trade unions or worker representatives and the potential costs of restructuring a workforce, post-acquisition, need to be considered in the light of the most recent legislation and case law. Legal due diligence in this area has, on occasions, been complicated by the imperfect application of European Directives by the UK government.
- What *intellectual property assets*, for example trademarks or patents, contribute to the value of the target or are needed to enable it to operate? Intellectual property rights impact on many aspects of the conduct of transaction. Yet intellectual property assets have historically been neglected or unappreciated by target companies or businesses, as have the requirements to obtain licences to use other parties' intellectual property rights. As the value of an increasing number of businesses resides in their intellectual property this is an area that must be carefully explored. Extensive early investigation is often required, both through enquiries of the target but also through searches at, for example, the Trade Mark Registry.

Typical areas that would be the subject of due diligence are:

- The corporate constitution of the target. For example, are there restrictions on a company entering into a sale transaction contained in its memorandum or articles of association?
- Are any third parties consents needed for the transaction?
- Is appropriate tax clearance being sought?
- What banking arrangements affect the target? In particular, what charges exist over a target company and/or a target business and assets.

Are there any personal or corporate guarantees given by the target or in support of the target's obligations?
- What contracts are material for the conduct of the target? Assignability and competition issues are obvious relevant points when considering their significance.
- Have details of all current, pending or threatened claims or proceedings been disclosed and thoroughly investigated?
- Does the target have the benefit of, or is it subject to, any agreements restraining trade and, if so, are they legally enforceable?
- Are there any matters affected by the law of jurisdictions outside the UK? The opinions of foreign lawyers may have to be obtained. If so, early co-ordination by the English legal adviser must occur.

This is not an exhaustive check list, merely an indication of the types of investigation required.

The process of due diligence continues through to acquisition as a result of matters that emerge from initial enquiries and also from the process of agreeing warranties under the sale and purchase agreement for the acquisition of the target. It is almost always the case that in agreeing the warranties or in considering disclosures made against them, further relevant information is provided about the target that will modify or intensify the enquiries that need to be made. The significance of information revealed by any due diligence may only become apparent when it is being considered by other advisers within the acquirer's team – heightening the need for good communication between the acquirer's lawyers, accountants, pension advisers, insurance brokers and others who work closely together.

Immediately pre-completion of any acquisition, a final review of due diligence should be undertaken and, in particular, final searches and enquiries made with the Registrar of Companies and the Companies Court to ensure that the state and condition of the target is consistent at completion and when the exercise of due diligence began.

Legal due diligence is an essential part of ensuring that a potential acquirer obtains the value for the target that he legitimately expects. It is up to the legal adviser to ensure that all relevant information is obtained and, just as importantly, that the various strands of enquiry are brought together into a comprehensive and comprehensible form for the acquirer.

Pitmans is a leading Thames Valley law firm offering advice on acquisitions, disposals, management buyouts and management buyins, private acquisition and venture capital transactions.

Part 3
Marketing and Sales

3.1
Market Research

Elaine Asbridge
Associate Director, Research International UK

Since its modest beginnings in the mid-1950s, the UK market research industry has burgeoned into one worth some £750mn, and its annual growth continues today at an average of 11 per cent.[1] So, what has made it such a successful phenomenon?

To start with it might be useful to define the market research function and how this fits into the wider marketing context.

> Marketing sets out to provide products and services to a predefined market in a manner which will hold the greatest appeal; the nature of the product or service itself, its price, packaging, promotion and method of distribution all come into play.
>
> The role of market research is accurately and usefully to inform this design. This is achieved in a structured fashion, generally deriving the required information from relevant, targeted sections of the population.

Market research is therefore often essential before a product or service comes to market, in order to make sure that the optimum marketing design and execution are adopted, but also throughout the life of the product.

1 AMSO 1996 figures

Thus, the insight which research provides can be invaluable to a business of any size and at any stage of its development.

Below are just some of the areas in which market research can provide valuable marketing information at different stages in a product's or company's lifecycle.

Sizing new markets

No matter how good the product, its sales potential is zero unless there is a market willing to buy it! Accurate market sizing needs to take into account a variety of complex factors:

- identification of the target market and its incidence and location in the general population;
- propensity to purchase;
- probable frequency and quantity of purchase;
- amount willing to spend;
- most effective method of distribution;
- degree of promotional activity which the company is able to undertake.

Research companies are able to call on a number of techniques to obtain the necessary information, ranging from straightforward analysis of demographic data through to simulated test markets. The latter has the advantage of being able to test the appeal of potential products before much of the expense of product production or service implementation has been borne. With the advent of virtual reality and the computer-administered interview, potential customers can even be exposed to 'virtual purchase' scenarios where new products are shown literally up against any existing competition.

Understanding existing and potential competition

To what extent do competitors have a hold on the market? What are their strengths/weaknesses? To what extent can their customers be lured away and how?

Optimising new concepts, products, services with potential customers (NPD work)

Once it has been decided to pursue a product's development, it can be tested in greater detail either in concept form or as it moves into later stages of initial production. Qualitative (small numbers of respondents spoken to in depth to elicit a detailed reaction) and quantitative (large numbers of respondents questioned to generate statistically robust data) research techniques can be used at this stage.

Research: the key to effective business growth

by Dr. Andrew Brown
(Director of Research & Analysis, Gallup UK)

All executives understand the importance of financial information. It would, of course, be difficult to explain a profit or loss situation to shareholders without supporting data; or to convince managers that productivity was down using only anecdotal evidence. And this is why companies use leading accounting firms to audit the financial performance.

However, for businesses wishing to improve their performance, there are a number of other "audits" which need conducting if real growth is to be achieved. Based on over 60 years of research, Gallup has surveyed three key audiences for business which need researching so that expansion can take place (see Figure1). These audiences are:

1. Customers

Customer satisfaction tracking has been the backbone of much market research in the UK for over twenty years. Gallup's research suggests that a quality of service or product quality audit can be as important to corporate performance and growth as financial accounting. Ultimately, it is customers who determine which companies will prosper in the decade ahead.

A quality of service audit or QSA focuses a company on three key business outcomes (see Figure 2): i) current customer retention; ii) expansion of sales to current customers; and iii) attraction of new customers. The model assumes that the ultimate goal of any business is to increase profits and that organisations are interested in doing so by delivering products and services to the market which are highly valued by their customers. Gallup has helped a huge number of businesses world-wide to begin measuring the key elements of the model using customer surveys.

Usually administered by telephone, an individually designed questionnaire is used to ascertain customer ratings on the various aspects of service outlined. The

FIGURE 1:

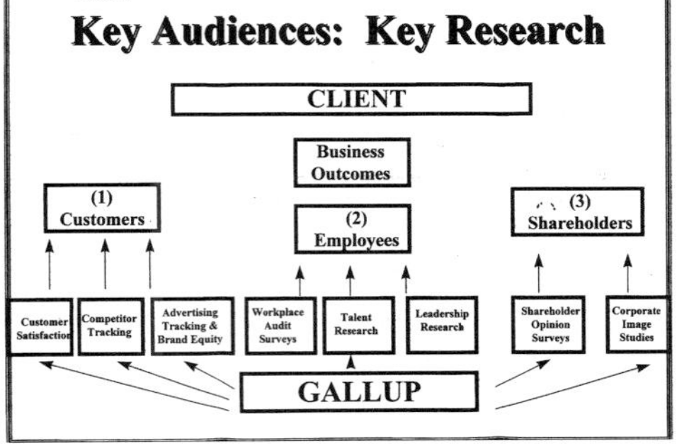

key drivers of overall satisfaction and the propensity to engage in repeat purchase or usage can be determined from statistical analysis. This helps companies to focus on the most effective levers of business growth.

For example, the most recent wave of an ongoing survey by Gallup for a financial services company found that speed of service was the strongest driver of their customers' satisfaction. At the same time, when comparisons were made with this companies main competitors, it was found that our client was receiving below average ratings on the measure of speed of service in the survey. This allowed the company to pinpoint initiatives to improve their service delivery on that issue and hence improve their overall ratings as time progressed, feeding through into customer retention.

Customer tracking surveys are often complemented by advertising and brand equity tracking. These allow companies to assess the impact of their marketing and communications efforts customers on their drive for growth.

FIGURE 2:

The Gallup Quality Service Audit Model

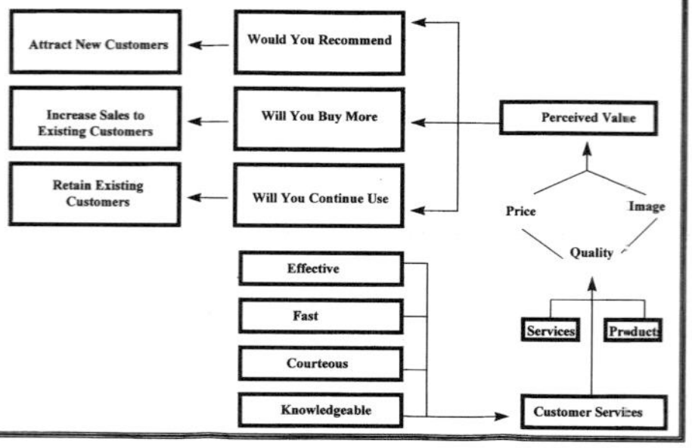

2 Employees

While customers have long been seen as a core focus of the research efforts of companies trying to expand, the spotlight has only fallen on employees in more recent years. There is some irony here since many companies are now realising (and stating very publicly, in annual reports etc.) that their people are their greatest asset.

Gallup has conducted a large number of employee surveys in the UK, Europe and globally, often during a time of great change for our clients. For instance, clients are often keen to gauge employee opinion after a merger, acquisition or management buy-out since the dynamics of a new business environment can have a strong impact on employee morale and motivation.

Such employee surveys focus on explaining two sets of outcomes (see Figure 3). Firstly opinion outcomes such as employee satisfaction and employee loyalty: both equally important as shorter-term and long-term measures of the overall mood of employees at a workplace. Secondly, Gallup also links these opinion outcomes onto business outcomes, including data on profitability, productivity, employee retention and customer satisfaction. Our work in integrating employee and customer opinion data has shown very strong links between the two and stresses the importance of employee satisfaction measures to business growth.

For example, one of Gallup's largest recent surveys for telecommunications client stressed the impact which higher levels of employee satisfaction (in key areas such as communications, teamwork and concept development) was having on outcomes such as customer satisfaction and retention. This allowed action plans to be developed in the units within the company where employee satisfaction was lowest and Gallup was able to priorities those key drivers where action would best be concentrated to achieve corporate growth.

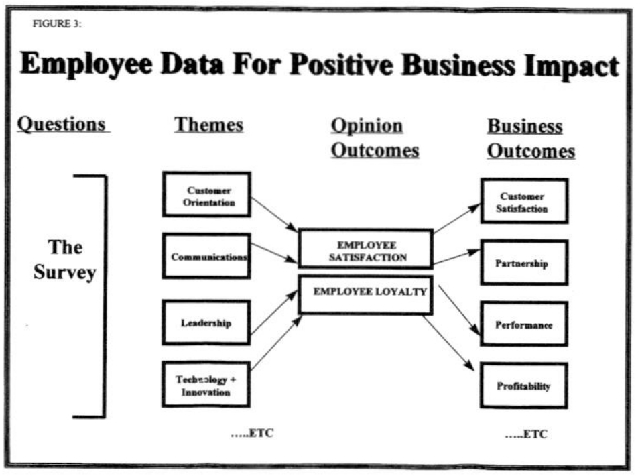

3. Shareholders

As with the views of customers and employees, shareholder opinion can be equally critical to corporate success, particularly at a time of growth. At both an institutional and an individual shareholder level, research can be conducted top ascertain levels of overall satisfaction with investment made in a company. The satisfaction rating is likely to have an important impact in terms of (see Figure 4):

- shareholder retention (ie: long-term commitment to investing in the company)
- shareholder advocacy (ie: will shareholders recommend the company to other likely investors)
- increase purchase (eg: would shareholders be likely to subscribe to any rights issues if offered)

Overall satisfaction with investment made can be determined by measure distinct perceptions held by investors. Firstly, how do they perceive the overall performance of the company, including the Board's performance? Secondly, how well do investors feel they understand the company, its strategic outlook and its policy decisions? And, finally, how well do they feel the company is communication about its performance through vehciles such as the Annual Report?

With measures of all these opinions in hand, companies can have a better understanding of where there future growth is likely to come from.

Conclusion:

Many of the most fast-growing companies are looking to integrate their research programmes. Using the same supplier for customer, employee and shareholder surveys allows insights into the interactions of the opinions of any company's three key audiences. In turn, it allows a complete assessment of the opportunities for and barriers to growth being faced during a stage of expansion.

Gallup is helping some of the world's fastest growing organisations to capitalise on these opportuntities and overcome those barriers. Effective, integrated research is the tool which is the key to optimising that growth.

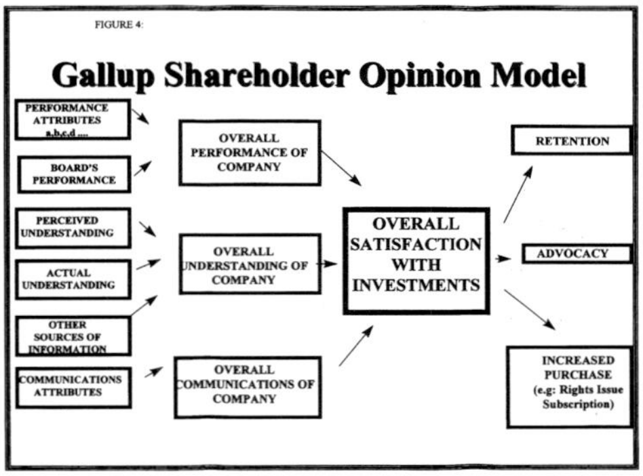

The Gallup Organisation (UK) Ltd
Apex Tower, 7 High Street, New Malden,
Surrey KT3 4DG Tel: 0181 336 6400

Pricing research

There are a number of techniques available here, but in general all set out to identify an optimum price, ie the highest price that will sustain the largest proportion of the market. These range from straightforward questioning techniques through to sophisticated trade-off methods which have the ability, not only to examine price elasticity, but also to identify the optimum product make-up.

Pre-testing advertising, point-of-sale materials, promotions and other marketing vehicles

Research can pre-test potential advertisements or promotional material (assessing elements such as message conveyed, appeal, stand-out, execution, medium etc) or track ongoing advertising campaigns (assessing awareness, message conveyed and success in reaching the desired target audience etc).

Trade research

Consumers or end users of the product or service are often not the only voices that need to be heard. Trade respondents (eg distributors, retailers, agents) can often be equally important to the successful provision of the product to the market.

Staff research

Staff often constitute the other 'forgotten' audience. However, in service industries where employees have become one of a company's key assets, assessing employee response to growth or extension into new markets can be crucial. Monitoring staff satisfaction, morale and needs in times of change and pressure often provides insights into how to increase motivation.

Customer satisfaction

In the last 10 years customers have become increasingly demanding and sophisticated in their requirements of customer service. Many companies have used this to their advantage by offering superior service as a way of differentiating themselves from the competition, particularly when there is little room for manipulation of the product.

Corporate or brand image and development

At the genesis of a product or service, brand or corporate image research aids the selection of the most appropriate brand positioning and communication. What are our brand values, and how do we demonstrate and strengthen our market position? These are all questions which research can answer.

Monitoring growing share of the market and nature of customer profile
Once a product or service is established, it is in the provider's interest to be aware of exactly who its customers are, for example:

- basic demographics (age, sex, socio-economic group, lifestage etc);
- behavioural and attitudinal make-up;
- linked product usage;
- shopping habits;
- media exposure etc.

Customer segmentation (either based on needs, attitudes or demographics) is a core market research analysis tool in targeting marketing and distribution strategy.

Market Research Agencies

Market research is generally conducted on behalf of companies by specialist agencies; nothing can replace an informed but objective approach from these external organisations. There are currently more than 600 market research organisations in the UK, many of them with extensive international capabilities and particular areas of expertise. Below are professional bodies which are able to at least give preliminary direction:

The Market Research Society (MRS)
15 Northburgh Street
London EC1V 0AH
Tel: 0171 490 4911
Fax: 0171 490 0608
e-mail: 101634.3461@compuserve.com

Association of Market Survey Organisations (AMSO)
16 Creighton Avenue
London N10 1NU
Tel: 0181 444 3692
Fax: 0181 883 9953

Association of Users of Market Research Agencies
c/o ISBA
44 Hertford Street
London W1Y 8AE
Tel: 0171 499 7502
Fax: 0171 629 5355

When considering which agency to approach it is worth taking the following into account:

- areas of expertise (eg NPD, pricing, customer satisfaction etc.);
- degree of experience;
- reputation;
- resources for the research project (staff and technical support);
- affiliation to professional bodies;
- level of senior contact/advice you require;
- international coverage, if appropriate;
- quality standards, eg ISO9000.

It is common practice to obtain quotes from up to three different agencies for any project. The more relevant information you are able to provide to an agency at this time, the more suited the research design will be to your needs.

Conclusion

In summary, no matter how much we think we know about the consumer, we must all admit that, by the nature of our professional function, we are in fact far removed from our customers and, in addition, biased in our outlook. It would be (and has been for many companies) very dangerous to make too many assumptions on their behalf.

Research International is a full-service, custom research agency with offices in over 50 countries around the world. Its UK operation offers a broad range of both standard and innovative research techniques, using both quantitative and qualitative methodologies. A wealth of corporate experience and resource makes it possible to offer some of the highest-quality research and consultancy available anywhere in the world.

3.2

Branding to Build Loyalty and Ensure Long-term Growth

Fiona Gilmore

Partner, Springpoint

For companies in the fast-moving consumer goods (FMCG) markets, such as Unilever and Procter & Gamble, brands are an important driver of volume growth. In purely financial terms, the importance of brands is clearly shown by the price that companies have been prepared to pay to win control of various brands. Nestlé, for example, paid £2.5bn — more than five times Rowntree's book value — to win control of the latter group in 1988. Other acquisitions have been similarly expensive and further illustrate the importance of brands to the relevant companies.

Examples of goodwill payments are shown in Table 3.2.1

Table 3.2.1 Goodwill payments

Acquirer	**Target**	**Goodwill (% of price paid)**
Nestlé	Rowntree	83
GrandMet	Pillsbury	88
Cadbury Schweppes	Dr Pepper	67
United Biscuits	Verkade	66

Source: Grieg Middleton

Branding is also important for companies in industrial and service sectors. With increased competition consistently being one of the key issues for CEOs in mature markets, developing and maintaining a distinctive brand is imperative.

Branding is ultimately about building loyalties, through emotional as well as rational values. A brand is inclusive. It is the tangible and intangible benefits provided by a product or service: the entire customer experience. It, therefore, includes all the assets critical to delivering and communicating that experience — the name, the logo, the advertising and literature, the products or services, the distribution channel, the reputation.

Branding is effective when all the elements which make up the customer experience work together. Overall control is, therefore, vital (as has been clearly demonstrated in this year's UK General Election). An organisation's branding strategy must matter to everyone within it, and be owned throughout.

How one creates or maintains the 'effective brand' is the million dollar question. In practical terms, there are some fundamental rules which it makes sense to follow.

Know your Customer and Focus on Core Competencies

Effective branding is *not* attempting to be 'all things to all people'. It is tempting, when one hits on a winning formula, to milk it. However, by doing so, you risk losing your core customer. A classic example of a company which lost sight of its core target group to its peril is Levi's in the 1980s with its 'polyester action slacks'. In everything you do, you need to keep your core loyalists, and their need and mood states, at the top of your mind.

You need to get and remain under your customers' skin – to know them so well that you can evolve your offer before they've realised they need what you're offering. And so that all your developments are totally in line with their expectations and competitively differentiated.

To be able to know, and to capitalise on knowing, your customer so well, it pays to have strong local management. Global or central teams can provide effective frameworks, facilitate speed-learning and be visionaries, but local teams often need to finetune ideas, in strategic and executional terms, to make the most of local opportunities.

The Imagination to Spot the Gaps

One of the master strokes of any successful brand developer is the ability to spot a market gap, and seize the opportunity with boldness and vision. A

HAVE YOU ASSESSED YOUR CORPORATE IDENTITY RECENTLY?

IS YOUR IMAGE SYMBOLLIC? COHERENT? APPROPRIATE?

It plays an important role in how you are perceived.

A well designed, well planned corporate identity should be all these and more.

TRUE DESIGN

Your company image should be working for you. If you are not convinced that it is, give us a call - we sincerely want to help. We are a graphic design consultancy with an excellent track record and a diverse portfolio of work to prove that we can.

0113 250 4299
2 MOORFIELD CHAMBERS
YEADON, LEEDS LS19 7EA

student at Yale called Fred Smith received the following response from his professor to a paper proposing a reliable overnight delivery service: 'The concept is interesting and well-formed, but the ideas must be *feasible* if you're to get higher than a 'c' grade.' Smith went on to found FedEx.

Heritage Matters but Keep it Relevant

Brands, whether corporate or fast moving, need to engage and appeal. A brand mythology can be created in the case of new brands such as Häagen Dazs. However, in the case of established brands, take care not to throw away your cultural roots or jettison your equities.

In some instances, a brand's roots are country or region specific, such as Coca-Cola or Boston Consulting Group. In others, they also reflect the founders' moral or philosophical motivations, particularly in the case of visionary organisations such as FedEx or Hewlett-Packard. You, and everyone within the organisation, need to grasp the essence of what the brand is. Only then can you, and all your creative partners, create essential brand saliency.

When an organisation or brand is rich in heritage it is important to respect and preserve it. It is not, however, imperative to ram it down the customer's throat. We return again to knowing the customer. Heritage and uniqueness can be important differentiators. However, it is how you refer to and communicate them that matters.

Live the Brand

With the plethora of communication channels at one's fingertips, and numerous contact points with the customer to control, it is becoming increasingly important for everyone within the organisation to 'live the brand' or 'walk the talk'. Your brand attains a deeper resonance if its internal and external projections are coherent.

Even if the Web and the phone may prove to be the future mechanics for purchase, with FedEx or UPS as the distribution channel, the on-line experience will need to be as fulfilling as the best in-store experience is today, and the delivery of the product or service consistent with expectations generated by the Web site or telephone conversation.

Create the Right Brand Structure

Along with organisational structure, considered brand architecture is important in effective brand development. There are four possible brand architectures. The 'monolithic' approach, with a single dominant corporate brand, such as that deployed by Sony, is highly focused and cost effective. The 'fixed endorsed' approach, with a strong straightjacket endorsement, as deployed by Kellogg's or Virgin, allows clear product line differentiation but ensures that the 'master brand' remains all powerful. The 'flexible endorsed' approach, implemented by Cadbury, allows sub-brands to become heroes, where appropriate, with the Cadbury's signature acting as endorsement. With the 'discreet' approach, adopted by Procter & Gamble with

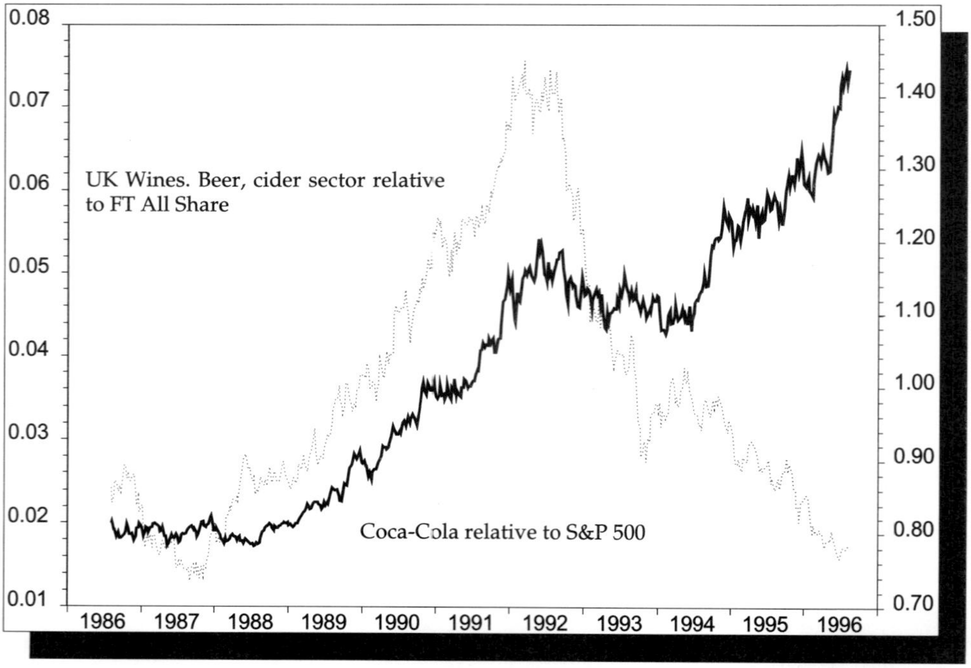

Source: Datastream

Figure 3.2.1 Advertising spend

brands such as Ariel, Pantene and Pampers, the corporate brand is not used overtly with consumers.

There are clearly pros and cons to each approach. Simplistically, the 'discreet' approach is costly — each brand needs clear differentiation and support — but the 'monolithic' approach can be limiting. With fragmentation and media inflation, the 'endorsed' and 'monolithic' approaches are becoming increasingly attractive.

Resist Pressures to Cut Back on Investing in the Brand

In this era of 'downsizing', it is all too easy to cut back on investment in marketing and branding. However, it is worth bearing in mind that those companies which maintain brand support even during a recession have demonstrated consistent earnings and volume growth. Coca-Cola, for instance, has consistently spent 8 per cent of total revenue on advertising, whereas the UK spirits companies spent on average just 3 per cent. Figure 3.2.1 highlights their respective performances.

Although advertising spend alone does not determine the out/underperformance of the share price, there is clear evidence that brands do respond positively to efforts to build value behind them. The way they are marketed

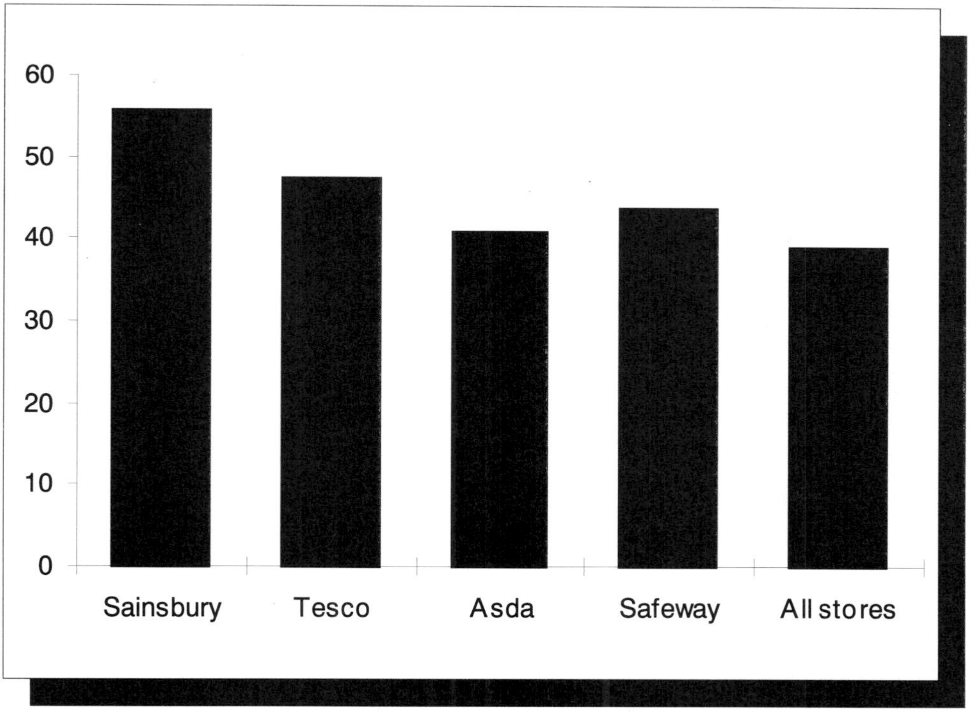

Source: Greig Middleton

Figure 3.2.2 UK food retailers, 1996, own-brand penetration (% sales)

is absolutely crucial both to grow their volume and to maintain their price premium.

It is true that, more and more, the customer is king, and is rightly reluctant to pay a premium if it is not clearly justified by product quality. The resulting growth in the penetration of own-label alternatives (see Figure 3.2.2) across a broad range of product categories from personal computers to personal care, and from food to cigarettes, has led to a host of companies revising their pricing policies to combat the threat to, and erosion of, their market share.

However, evidence suggests that neither the increased penetration of own-label products nor the notion that consumers have stopped shopping for superior value heralds the decline of premium brands. The decline can be attributed to those companies which have failed to support their premium brands, which have become too complacent or too short-sighted, factors which have helped contribute to their poor performance.

Fiona Gilmore is a founding partner of **Springpoint**, one of the leading brand positioning and corporate identity design consultancies in Europe. Over the last 15 years she has contributed to the development of corporate branding architecture, brand positioning and corporate identity programmes for some of the leading global organisations. Fiona has recently completed *Brand Warriors: Corporate Leaders Share Their Winning Strategies* (HarperCollins 1997) and has appeared on *The Money Programme* and *Question Time*.

3.3
The Electronic Commerce Revolution

Philip Vanhoutle
Managing Director, Dell

In the last few years we have witnessed a remarkable phenomenon: new information infrastructures —like the Internet — have exploded into popular, and business, consciousness.

This is nothing less than a new industrial revolution and it threatens to reshape our economic landscape.

The media hype around the Internet, with its emphasis on individual Web surfers and techno-enthusiasts, has obscured what will surely be its biggest impact — on business-to-business and mass consumer markets.

New business infrastructures, disintermediation of supply chains, new competitors, new opportunities, new markets, new industries, all flow necessarily from this electronic commerce revolution.

If that sounds all too apocalyptic, take a mundane example. Look at what Direct Line has done to the personal insurance industry in the UK. Now the whole banking establishment is talking about virtualisation of financial services, and when Bill Gates (CEO of Microsoft) says, 'Banks are dinosaurs. Give me a piece of the transaction business, and they are history', they take notice.

And the point is that, perhaps sooner rather than later, electronic commerce will affect everyone. All industries, all places, big and small corporations. The question is not if but when and how.

Already, thousands of companies have entered the electronic marketplace, via the World Wide Web, commercial on-line services and their own private networks. Initially this presence was experimental, tyre kicking, but ultimately it will let them do business electronically with the millions of small and medium-sized enterprises (SME) and tens of millions of individual consumers, in new ways and with radically different cost structures.

Consider a recent survey by KPMG Management Consulting of 100 top UK companies. This reveals that they expect almost one in five of their sales to come directly via the Internet in five years' time — that is sales worth £170bn.

The tyre kicking is surely over.

The Dell Experience

Dell Computer Corporation is the world's leading direct marketer of computer systems — and it has embraced the Internet as the ultimate direct sales channel.

At www.dell.com, Dell's customers can electronically design, price and purchase systems, and obtain on-line support.

In the US, Dell's Web sales are increasing by 20 per cent per month. The site is already generating revenues in excess of $1mn per day. We expect our UK site, which went live on 1 May, to be responsible for over 10 per cent of our direct sales by the end of the year.

The Internet was tailor-made for Dell, says chairman and CEO Michael Dell. Customers of all kinds prefer direct. They like the immediacy, convenience, savings and personal touches which the Internet direct customer experience provides.

The UK site aims to replicate the spectacular impact of Dell's US initiative and it has been received enthusiastically. In fact we had sold over $1mn worth of systems over the Internet within two months of its introduction.

The crucial point to understand about Dell's Internet initiative is that it is not a marketing exercise. The Web site is not just an electronic brochure — it is a complete on-line retail purchasing environment.

On the other hand, selling via the Internet is not a wholly new business channel either. It is a complementary direct sales channel, and an extension of our direct business model.

What are the Benefits?

We believe that there are clear benefits, for both Dell and its customers, in Internet-based trading. One of the most compelling is the speed of communications that the Internet provides. The computer industry is fast moving and frequently by the time our print advertising hits the streets, new products, new bundles — and new prices — are available. By accessing our Web page, customers can get the most up-to-date pricing within 24 hours of release.

For Dell, our Web site provides a controlled, reliable environment of the highest quality. Individual transactions are significantly cheaper. And the Internet extends opening hours — now we can do business round the clock at no extra cost

The bottom line is that, in our view, the Internet offers customers a better buying experience, and ultimately it will be Dell's preferred direct business channel.

Eventually we will offer incentives to customers who use the Internet route — but there will be no compulsion. And the beauty of the solution is that even those customers who do not want to complete their transaction over the Web come to us on the telephone far better informed — which is good for us and for them.

What have we Learnt?

- There is no doubt that the technology for full electronic commerce is now in place. Security fears have been the big drag, but now secure transaction systems, using military-style encryption techniques, have arrived. The real challenge now lies in educating and reassuring potential users. We feel that experience and confidence will lead them to accept new methods just as they took to credit cards and ATMs.
- The UK is ready. Historically, it has been slower to embrace new technology but it is taking to the Internet. In February 1997, an estimated 7 per cent of UK adults were Internet users, the equivalent of 3.4mn people. British use of the net is growing at 10–15 per cent a month, the highest sustained growth in Europe.
- Businesses contemplating introducing an electronic commerce channel should understand their business motives clearly at the outset. The Internet must be built into their overall strategic planning. For Dell, using the Internet is a business solution, not an advertising exercise. You need a disciplined business approach to designing your site and its content. You must ask what functions you really need and then devise a content plan.
- This is not a trivial exercise. It requires serious investment of money and time — and to succeed, it needs board-level buy-in.

Dell's UK Web site will be customised for continental European customers and rolled out aggressively throughout 1997. Deploying this solution across Europe represents an investment for Dell of around $3mn.

Clicking www.dell.com/uk

At www.dell.com/uk Dell customers can configure, price and purchase computer systems electronically.

By clicking on the Buy a Dell icon customers can select various options, including Intel Pentium II processors with MMX technology, memory and operating systems, and then generate instant price quotes. This level of customisation is not readily available to customers shopping in conventional PC stores.

They then select a purchase button to submit electronically a secure order with a choice of on-line payment options, including creditor debit card, purchase order or corporate lease. People who prefer not to make an on-line payment can speak to Dell's sales staff to complete the transaction.

For customers who still prefer to enquire by phone, the Internet provides a valuable introduction to Dell and the idea of buying direct. In the US customers calling Dell are nearly twice as likely to buy a system if they have previously visited the Web site.

Future plans for the UK Web site include on-line order status checking and technical support services.

Dell Computer Corporation, founded by Michael Dell in 1983, is now one of the biggest computer systems manufacturers in the world. In its last financial year its net income increased 91 per cent to $518mn on revenues up 47 per cent to $7.8bn. In Europe, sales for the year topped $2bn for the first time. Dell attributes its success to the direct-relationship business model it has pioneered. This is based on the principle that delivering PCs custom built to specific customer orders provides the most relevant solutions to end user needs.

3.4
Size Doesn't Matter with Direct Marketing

Martin Bartle
PR & Communications Manager,
Direct Marketing Association

It doesn't take an expert to work out that direct marketing (DM) is big business. In 1995 direct marketing expenditure passed the £5.5bn mark. DM activities represent 4 per cent of UK GDP, generating sales worth in excess of £23bn, and the annual growth rate for DM expenditure is around 12 per cent.

The definition of direct marketing is quite a contentious issue. The Direct Marketing Association takes the broadest view possible defining DM as, 'Communications where data are used systematically to achieve quantifiable marketing objectives where direct contact is invited or made between and company and its customers (and prospective customers).'

The business gurus of the 1990s have all focused on the 'glocal', with individuals like Rosabeth Moss Kanter preaching the dictum 'think globally act locally'. DM allows companies, large or small, to do exactly this.

Advances in information technology mean that small companies are able to compete with larger enterprises on a global scale. The use of direct marketing systems and techniques such as database marketing, the Internet and direct response advertising mean that 'one-to-one' relationships can be built with existing and potential client bases without large-scale sales and marketing teams.

The principle of one-to-one marketing, championed by Peppers and Rogers, is based on the idea that we are in the throes of a paradigm shift in marketing away from mass media, mass production and mass marketing to a system based much more on developing individual relationships with clients.

The salient point for marketers, in both Moss Kanter's theories and those of Peppers and Rogers, is that the size of an organisation no longer matters. In fact, in some ways the information-processing systems necessary to start marketing on a one-to-one basis are far easier to implement and operate if you are running a small business.

The principles of mass-media marketing are increasingly being obscured by the need to 'shout the loudest'. The information overload facing most consumers means that even the largest of companies is having to spend more to reach a smaller audience. One-to-one marketing means communicating more efficiently and effectively however large or small your customer base is. It concentrates on building relationships with individuals as opposed to scattergun relationships with demographic groupings.

The central elements of developing relationships with individual customers are dialogue and feedback. The mantra in business-to-business marketing throughout the 1990s has become 'get closer to the customer'; the same is becoming true of consumer marketing. It is now possible to compile a complete profile and history of an individual and develop a relationship with an individual as opposed to groups of individuals. In fact, there are now very affordable systems available for managing millions of individualised relationships.

Enough preaching: what does this all mean and how do you do it?

The basic principles of one-to-one and direct marketing are the same as any marketing campaign: define your products, identify your target market(s), select the media for reaching that market and think about how you are going to keep any customers you gain.

The real innovation revolves around the final point, customer retention. The systems necessary for developing relationships with customers are only limited by your own imagination and to describe all of the possibilities would be a thankless task. However, the basic principles of relationship marketing, database marketing, customer satisfaction and information-processing technology are key to developing a one-to-one marketing strategy.

An example of an integrated direct marketing system might consist of the following technologies and techniques. For a company selling consumer goods the idea would be to move from a retail to a direct selling model. Integrating the systems for contacting that company would be the first step. So whether a potential customer contacts the company by phone, mail or the Internet the information collected is consistent. This information is entered into a central relational database.

The next time that customer contacts the company, say by phone using call line identification (CLI) integrated with the consumer database, the person handling that incoming call can have the customer's details and history on screen before the call has even been answered.

Similarly, using an automated call-handling system, customers calling in to a company can select exactly what service they require, sales, customer care or product information etc, before they have actually got through to a member of staff. It is even possible for some transactions to be handled completely by an automated system, with credit card details being entered and validated on-line.

In summary, the technology available from telephone systems to databases should really be used as a corporate memory, helping sales and customer care staff know their individual clients. Whatever the size of an organisation, as long as the correct information is collected and collated on existing and potential clients, the process of delivering relevant products and maintaining brand loyalty should become second nature and far less time consuming.

Martin Bartle is PR & Communications Manager at the **Direct Marketing Association**. The Direct Marketing Association is a membership organisation which represents companies involved in direct marketing which sell their goods and services by direct marketing methods and companies which provide services to the direct marketing industry. Martin was previously the marketing director of a multimedia company and business & PR manager of the highly acclaimed political thinktank Demos.

3.5
Franchising your Business

Mike Spence
General Manager, Prontaprint Ltd

Founded in 1971, Prontaprint was the first franchised print operation in the UK and one of the earliest franchises to be established in the country. It was also one of the founder members of the British Franchise Association (BFA).

The concept was to provide high-speed print, copy and design services under one roof. Prontaprint's early success was based on new technology, which brought to the high street the irresistible appeal of speed, short-run quality print and value for money.

The opening of a pilot centre in Newcastle allowed the business format to be refined to a point where franchising plans could be developed. Once the business format was established, the first franchise agreement was signed in March 1973. Since then the franchise network has steadily expanded. By the end of 1974 there were 11 centres, with 150 in the UK by the end of 1980.

Today, Prontaprint is the largest quick print franchise with over 250 centres throughout the UK and Ireland, and a combined turnover of over £50mn.

Franchising can provide an attractive strategy by which to develop or expand a business. There are 541 known businesses in Britain which use franchising, with 26,800 outlets among them. The sector employs around 264,000 people with a turnover of £6.4bn.

In Prontaprint's experience, a decision to franchise should only be taken following careful consideration covering financial, operational and cultural aspects of the business.

There are a number of criteria which a business will need to meet prior to franchising. The most basic of these is that there must be a proven business format. A franchisor must be able to provide its franchisees with a complete system for operating a business. The business format for running the franchise must be well proven both operationally and in terms of financial viability.

One of the great attractions of buying a franchise from a successful franchisor is that it provides a route to starting a business, but one with significantly lower risks in comparison to starting up independently.

The 1997 NatWest/BFA survey showed that franchises are five times more likely to succeed than other business start-ups, with a commercial failure rate of 7 per cent. This is because the business concept has been proven at a number of different locations and, where necessary, the format and systems required to run the business have been refined.

Another attraction to a potential franchisee of buying a franchise is the strength of the franchisor's brand. The company needs to have a clear identity, including a distinctive name and image, which must convey appropriate messages regarding the company's business activity and stability in the marketplace, both to end consumers and to prospective franchisees. Prontaprint has retained a consistent and bold corporate identity, while strong marketing and public relations campaigns have achieved a high level of brand awareness.

It is essential that the franchised operation can stand alone as a business entity and that the systems of operation can be transferred to a franchisee in an effective and consistent manner.

The management and culture of the business must be suitable to the effective management of a network of independent franchisees. The relationship between franchisor and franchisee will be different to the conventional employer–employee situation and should be recognised as a partnership with people who are running their own businesses as opposed to branches of a larger retail chain. Managing the network and channelling the input of the franchisees can be two of the most demanding elements of developing a successful franchise operation.

As a franchisor, Prontaprint observes the marketplace, researches technological change, identifies business opportunities, devises marketing plans and creates training programmes on behalf of its network of franchisees. While Prontaprint takes responsibility for these strategic issues and offers on-going support and guidance, the franchisees are free to concentrate their efforts on the key aspect of meeting the needs of customers locally, and making decisions using the information and advice from Prontaprint Ltd, and ultimately developing a profitable business. Prontaprint aims to recruit franchisees of the highest calibre, often with a sales and marketing background and a hands-on approach.

Most franchisees buy a franchise for the challenge and satisfaction of running their own business as well as for the potential financial rewards to be gained from doing so. The franchise business format must, however, be sufficiently successful to enable the franchisee to generate good profits and a satisfactory cash flow. Prontaprint helps each prospective franchisee to prepare a business plan which can demonstrate the financial viability of the Prontaprint centre, taking into account the losses which are sometimes incurred during the start-up period.

The franchisor must be capable of providing adequate on-going support to franchisees, maintaining the brand's image and standards, and earning a reasonable financial return — franchising should only be adopted if it is an attractive strategy for the business in the long term.

Prontaprint is the largest quick print franchise with over 250 centres throughout the UK and Ireland. Dublin-based Adare Printing Group plc acquired Prontaprint in June 1996 and is committed to Prontaprint's continued development as a franchise. The two companies will be working together to develop the Prontaprint brand further.

3.6
Success in Selling into International Markets

Dr Allan Groden
Managing Director, Sanmex International plc

Sanmex International plc has achieved remarkable success in selling into international markets. Based in Rutherglen, Glasgow, the firm is a family-owned business and one of Scotland's fastest growing manufacturing companies specialising in the production of high-quality liquid and aerosol, household and personal care products.

Currently Sanmex exports to 36 countries throughout Europe, Asia and the Pacific Rim. Exports form 25 per cent of our business and this figure is expected to rise to about 30 per cent in 1997.

Since the appointment of an export director we have successfully penetrated new markets in such economically developing countries as Poland, Croatia and Russia. Sixty-five per cent of our exports are now to central and eastern Europe, compared to 5 per cent in 1994.

To understand how exports became such a valuable part of our business, it is vital to look at our progress since 1990.

From Reactive to Proactive

In the late 1980s, following a long period of steady but unspectacular growth, I decided that it was time for the company to change. We were a typical family company and not ideally equipped for the 1990s. After taking advice from consultants, I opted for radical change to ensure continued and increased success. As a result of good professional advice we committed ourselves to millions of pounds of investment in equipment, introduced a professional management team and targeted own-label products within the large discount supermarkets which were entering the UK.

By 1994, although we were supplying overseas markets, our export policy was rather eccentric and reactive and we tended to gain new overseas customers as a result of approaches made to the company rather than from a clear export strategy. In that year we secured an initial order from China for fly-spray worth £300,000. We were supplying air freshener to seven islands in the Caribbean; a de-static product for kaftans to the Middle East and shaving foam to Russia. We had just started to supply a whole range of aerosol household products and toiletries to almost all the central and eastern European countries.

Two awards which we received in 1995 recognised our export achievements and gave us an incentive to take a more proactive approach.

Sanmex received the 1995 TrailBlazer award, partly sponsored by *The Herald* newspaper, for the actions we took between 1990 and 1993 to develop new markets as our traditional markets were in decline. Steven Groden, our business development director, recently attended the specialist management training course at INSEAD, France, the biggest business school in Europe, which was the prize.

We also won the International Executive Scheme, a competition run by the Glasgow Development Agency (GDA), designed to boost export potential. The winners were judged on their commitment to growth and overseas development. The prize was £20,000 of financial support over two years, towards the cost of recruiting and employing an additional export executive; assistance was also offered in finding the right person to fill the post whose purpose is to develop the winner's export strategies. Subsequently we adopted a more focused export drive, targeted largely on eastern Europe which we identified as having great potential, and moved systematically into European markets on the back of existing strong relationships.

The Present — Growing Overseas Success

In August 1996 we appointed a new export director, with the relevant business and language skills and cultural knowledge, to take a more targeted and strategic approach to developing export markets. The export director decides which markets to target, visits each one to interview distributors and agents, sets up trading channels and monitors progress. Using this approach we have made breakthroughs in our targeted markets, mainly in former eastern Europe.

We also export to the Middle East and Australia and have just begun exporting insecticides to Hong Kong, following my visit to that area.

Exhibiting at the annual trade show — the Private Label Manufacturers Association Exhibition in Amsterdam — has helped us increase export sales. Following the 1996 exhibition we gained substantial new business and many new customers.

As a reflection of our progressive attitude to exports, almost all Sanmex aerosol products, which form the bulk of our exporting, are now in a number of languages. We also respond promptly to requests from individual countries; for example customers in Australia wanted weights on packaging to be in grams, which we were able to do.

We are committed to investment in plant and technology to allow for efficient and rapid management of export orders, thereby enabling a larger volume of business to be serviced. This includes the installation and utilisation of new bottle blowers, ultraviolet printers and computerised warehousing to move production and delivery on to a just-in-time basis.

The Way Ahead

A recent initiative in which we became involved was the University of Strathclyde's MSc in International Marketing group project. Companies, all small to medium-sized, were chosen to participate based on their manifest commitment to exporting. A group of six international marketing students — from Switzerland, Canada, Jamaica, Malaysia, Japan and Indonesia — worked closely with us to devise a detailed export marketing plan. The report presented to us a practical export marketing plan, recommending key potential new markets. We are now looking to implement the recommendations and will possibly be recruiting someone with the necessary language skills to do so.

Our Advice

Like Sanmex, any company aiming for growth through exporting should consider the following pointers:

- Take professional advice about the best way for the company to develop.
- Employ people with knowledge of countries to which you are looking to export, who understand the culture and speak the language.
- Invest in training and management. We have a shadow board made up of young managers whose role it is to take the company forward.

- Exhibit at relevant international trade shows to build up relationships with existing customers and meet potential new customers.
- Be far sighted in taking a proactive and planned approach to exporting.
- Do not become complacent about success in export markets and continue to seek new opportunities.
- Be aware of relevant public and private sector sponsored competitions and award schemes.

Sanmex International plc in Rutherglen, Glasgow, is an independent family company formed in the 1930s. One of Scotland's fastest-growing manufacturing companies, it produces high-quality liquid and aerosol household and personal care products for retailers in the UK and overseas. Sanmex exports to over 35 countries worldwide.

3.7
Pricing Methods[1]

John Winkler
Winkler Marketing International Ltd

Different pricing strategies can be associated with different periods in the product lifecycle. During the early growth phase of the market, customers are more concerned about product quality and performance. While demand is growing there will be easy pressure on prices. Later, when total demand is saturated, pricing pressure really starts.

Gaining or holding market share becomes important in a saturated market. New products are introduced and prices in some markets begin to collapse. As the market matures, the positions of leading companies become entrenched. Consolidated market positions, mergers and takeovers of minor suppliers characterise ageing markets. Margins are thin, but prices are often fairly stable.

The problem, of course, is that it is very difficult to determine the length of the lifecycle or even exactly where you are on the curve. Some cycles last only a few months (fashion products, some electronics, toys etc), while others may last for decades (heavy industrial equipment).

Some basic markets (for materials, finance or construction) continue with recurring cycles of booming conditions. But this is not guaranteed. Some very ugly price fights can break out in mature markets, even when demand is increasing. However, you will always come under pricing pressure when demand is faltering.

1 This material previously appeared in *Marketing Magazine*

Learning the Psychology of Pricing

Research into behavioural aspects of pricing shows that trade buyers and consumers have certain common attitudes. Prices are judged by comparison to reference points, including exposure to previous prices, exposure to competitive prices, expected price changes and belief in a 'fair' price to pay.

In general, the research shows that consumer and trade buyers are more sensitive to perceived price decreases, particularly around the average market price. A price increase of 10p on a £1 product will have far more effect in driving potential buyers away than a similar decrease of 10p will have in attracting them. Therefore a price decrease must be much stronger to move a market towards a product.

The further away from the market average price, either high or low, then the less sensitive to price changes the demand becomes.

Major brands are usually price leaders within their market segments and there is perceived to be a price difference between major brands, small brands, regional and generic brands. However, if all these prices move up by the same amount, then the perceived relative gap between these prices tends to close.

According to a major study of most categories of UK industry carried out by Dr Brian Farringdon, the most likely reaction of trade buyers to a price increase is to demand a cost breakdown and cost justification. Over two-thirds do this. But just as many say that they would also seek quotations from other suppliers — probably most of them would do this while continuing to squeeze their existing supplier, having no real intention of taking the business away.

There is a good deal of threat at times like this. Sometimes buyers mean their threats and they do take away their business.

Planning Discounts for Promotion

Often companies' promotional discounting and price offers are a rather static, regular affair without much excitement. Discounts and offers need to be mixed up to make an exciting package:

- Decide your total ad and promotion budget: allocate your basic expenses, literature etc. Allocate a proportion to theme advertising and promotional support.
- Divide your promotional budget into sales journey cycles: tie in with product support, advertising support and sales aims.

- In each period run one major and two minor promotions: these could include discounts to new customers or discounts to existing volume and settlement discounts.
- Negotiate special deals.

The Most Important Pricing Techniques

The four central pricing techniques are as follows.

Higher price strategies

- *Skimming* — pricing so high as to take off the top layer of the market.
- *Umbrella pricing* — pricing high in order deliberately to invite competitors to shelter under higher prices. This can be done by a quality and volume leader in the market to influence competitors into raising their prices.
- *Prestige pricing* — pricing at an artificially high level in order to sustain an extreme image of quality and to separate the product from the general market.

Competitive pricing strategies

- *Price matching* — copying the competition close to their prices.
- *Flexible pricing* — changing prices to meet varying competitive or market situations.
- *Trading down prices* — moving prices downwards to open up new layers of demand.
- *Pricing points* — use of psychological pricing positions to make prices seem cheaper, for example, or second-hand trade-in prices.
- *Phase-out pricing* — holding prices firm in a declining situation, or raising prices in order to maximise profits when in the process of phasing out products or services.
- *Discount pricing* — the offer of special prices for particular orders.
- *Promotional pricing* — mixing special prices, which are usually advertised with a limiting date to secure extra sales volume. The price can be mixed with the offer of free or extra product, or free credit for example.

Low prices

- *Pre-emptive pricing* — low prices in order to discourage others from entering the market.

- *Penetration pricing* — to win a large slice of the market, to open up a new low-price segment of the market or to gain market entry by very low prices against the average.
- *Predatory pricing* — really low prices for a limited period to secure other business at full price and to attract custom to other products.

Negotiating prices

- *Bundling or bunching prices* — putting a complete deal together with many extras in order to produce a single packaged price.
- *Unbundling or breaking prices* — the reverse to the previous technique, where a complete package is broken up and negotiated piece by piece.
- *Packaging and adding on pricing* — constructing deals where parts of the deal vary in price depending on the prices for the rest of the deal. A main product may be sold at a low price only if extras are included in the deal, for instance.
- *'Buy it and cook it' pricing* — a deal taken at very low cost indeed, probably at quite a loss initially, because it is known that later variations to contract or agreed later price increases or inflationary factors will make the deal highly profitable in the long run.

Making Price Increases — A Seven-Point Guide

1. *Put up your price when everyone else does.* Don't hold back, hide in the forest.
2. *Not too much at any one time.* Consumers relate to competitors' prices, just like industrial buyers; but retail buyers relate increases to 'norms' such as inflation.
3. *Not too often, either.* Consumers are less sensitive to this, but retail trade and industrial buyers become upset at the administrative work involved.
4. *Not too seldom.* Some people and trades only move prices once a year. This plays into buyers' hands. Not often enough, this.
5. *Move something down when you move something up.* Save up your product's improvements to explain away price increases. This means less irritation for buyers if they see that you are trying.
6. *Look after your key accounts.* Give them advance warning, possibly a moratorium.
7. *Provide sound, true explanations.* Your sales executives must say something. Give them something to say.

Winkler Marketing International Ltd is based in Brighton. John Winkler has written for a number of publications including the *Sunday Times, Marketing Magazine, Management Accounting Magazine*, the *Independent* and *Financial Times*. He is also the author of a number of books including *Pricing for Results* (Butterworth Heinemann).

Part 4

World-Beating Products and Services

FINANCE & LEASING ASSOCIATION-AN OVERVIEW

The **Finance & Leasing Association** is the major UK representative body of the finance and leasing industry. Members are drawn from high street bank subsidiaries, leading finance houses, merchant banks, leasing companies and the finance arms of leading retailers and manufacturers. Members provide over one third of all UK fixed investment, 30% of all consumer credit and finance over 50% of all motor vehicles. Total outstandings for 1996 were over £80 billion. The Association operates a comprehensive code of practice which is binding on all full members.

For further information please write to
Finance & Leasing Association, 18 Upper Grosvenor Street, London W1X 9PB

NATIONAL PAINTBALL GAMES

Team Training, Building, Awareness or fun. From a Day of Paintball getting to know each other to a "Get outa That" Lateral thinking exercise. Over 30 Centres Nationally. One central contact.

NATIONAL PAINTBALL GAMES

95a Nutwick Road, Havant, Hampshire PO9 2UQ

E Mail: NOGUK@aol.com

BVQi

BVQI Ltd is accredited by UKAS to audit large and small companies to the ISO 9000 Series of Quality Management System

Contact: Rodger Newell, Business Development Manager.
Bureau Veritas Quality International Ltd (BVQI), Suite 12 - 14, Challenge House, Sherwood Drive, Bletchley, Milton Keynes MK3 6DP.
Tel: 01908 366724. Fax: 01908 366725. E Mail 106163.311@compuserve.com

BVQi BS EN ISO 9001: 1994 APPROVED BY BVQI

NATIONAL ACCREDITATION OF CERTIFICATION BODIES

KIDSONS IMPEY Chartered Accountants

Kidsons Impey Chartered Accountant

Providing business advice that counts to the SME sector

Contact: Nigel Bell, National Marketing Manager
Kidsons Impey Chartered Accountants, Spectrum House,
20-26 Cursitor Street, London EC4A 1HY
Tel: 0171 405 2088 Fax: 0171 334 4734

PEC Communications

0800 458 4500

Which telecomms company - confused ?
Let us maximise your savings ......

- ☎ Independent experts representing 8 leading carriers
- ☎ Reduced national, international, mobile and 0800 call charges
- ☎ Specialist software to analyse your telephone traffic
- ☎ Free impartial advice with no obligation

4.1
Exploiting Technology

Patrick Sheehan
Director, 3i's Emerging Business Team

In a recent article on British inventiveness, the *Sunday Times* said: 'it took the Japanese government to point out that 40% of all important discoveries in the last 50 years have come from Britain'.

The article, sadly, was featuring the difficulty that lone inventors have in securing finance for their ideas. One particular statistic, of only 0.5 per cent of all 4000 UK patents granted annually being commercially exploited, sounds lamentable. To me, however, the story was as interesting for what it left unsaid as for what it explained; for what it displayed about our national psyche as for what it revealed about the birth pangs of new products.

Britain is a country where inventive talent seems to flourish. At 3i we are constantly impressed by the world-class skill we see in British technologists. It is not our inventiveness that is at issue but our national ability to exploit it, sometimes even our national *desire* to exploit it. The very word 'exploitation' has unsavoury connotations in our language. For some it can feel easier to avoid altogether the difficulty, and the inevitable compromises, of commercialisation. The need for our industry to have real competitive advantage is growing. Increasingly, if we can get it, this advantage will be based on technology. Our need as a nation for effective exploitation of technology has therefore become more than just an interesting debating point. We need to build more world-class businesses on the back of our existing excellent technological innovations. It is clearly difficult to do this, particularly in new markets that are often volatile, and requires excellence in marketing, financial management and sheer entrepreneurial flair. The usual requirement of such a business to thrive is for a rare combination of single-minded determination, depth of experience in a management team, and drive.

If it is so difficult to raise funds to exploit ideas, as the *Sunday Times* article suggests, what is the magic ingredient? Our experience has shown that the catalyst that makes innovative companies successful, and therefore financially backable, is the quality and strength of the management team. Real success for a business comes from a healthy combination of high-calibre ideas or technology, excellent management and good-quality long-term finance. With the first two ingredients firmly in place, the funds, in my belief, are usually available. 3i is an active investor of risk capital in young companies and we are investing five times as much in technology-based businesses as we were at the start of the 1990s.

Investors such as ourselves do, however, inevitably find such companies relatively difficult to appraise. Often there is either no financial track record or the limited record that does exist gives no reliability guide to the future financial performance. In any event, the future value of the business is less likely to be determined by its profits than by more elusive characteristics such as its market share, the worth of its technology, or the willingness of larger companies to compete to acquire it at some stage in the future.

Few small companies have the necessary combination of requirements for large-scale success. Those that do — or in 3i terms 'emerging businesses', are often lucky enough to be operating in a market which itself has dramatic growth potential. Typically this new potential is based on technological development. However, companies in more mature markets, which can 'rewrite the rules' thereby giving themselves a clear competitive advantage within their niche, are also termed emerging businesses due to their dramatic growth potential. Although it is difficult to value emerging businesses, at 3i we have made this an area of both particular effort and expertise. We do not profess to get it right every time, but through our knowledge and financial stability we are able to make investing in emerging businesses a speciality.

Select Software Tools is a good example of the type of emerging business we are keen to back. It has helped revolutionise the market for computer-aided software engineering (CASE) products by offering affordable, accessible tools for the design, development and maintenance of computer programs. 3i backed Select Software Tools as a start-up company in 1990, then provided further funds on a number of occasions to fuel its growth before it listed on NASDAQ in October last year.

Stuart Frost, Select's managing director, has an in-depth knowledge of his market and a realistic vision of leading his company into the future. His vision has worked very well to date. From Cheltenham where the company is based, Select has built up an impressive list of customers including the Inland Revenue, British Aerospace and the Ministry of Defence and it now operates in the US and through distributors in Europe.

Select was aware that the market for its product was expanding rapidly and that to keep its leading position it would have to keep pace with market demand, both by filling potential orders promptly but also by continuing its research and development into new products. Until a company has reached critical mass it is difficult radically to increase the supply of its products or to invest in R & D. As Virginia Bray, Select's marketing manager, said in 1995 at the time of 3i's last investment, 'as a young business in a competitive market, it has been important to us to have the continued support of 3i. Their investments have given us the well structured financial support we needed and enabled us to respond to rapid and dramatic changes in the IT market swiftly and decisively.'

So, in short, what does it take to exploit technology effectively? First, it takes a realistic appraisal of its market potential and an understanding of how it will give a business some lasting competitive advantage. This potential value then becomes exploitable when the technology is combined with similarly excellent management and fuelled with appropriate long-term finance.

Patrick Sheehan is director of 3i's Emerging Business Team. The team was formed in 1995 following increased demand for finance from technology businesses. It funds companies at all stages of their life, providing both start-up and growth funding. 3i and the Emerging Business Team have specialised in financing technology businesses.

4.2

Growing through Innovation and Design

Paul Crake

Communication Director, Design Council

Dyson Appliances was a new business start-up just three years ago. Today it employs over 500 staff in its factory headquarters in Chippenham, and in 1997 will achieve a turnover in excess of £100 million. Dyson has breathed new life into what was a rather stale world of domestic appliances and now produces the UK's top-selling domestic cleaners. These cleaners retail at a price premium of between 35 and 50 per cent over their competitors, and outsell them by a considerable margin.

Dyson Appliances is a stunning success story: why have so few other British companies achieved this level of success? Perhaps the reason lies in the philosophy which underpins Dyson, a philosophy which is dramatically different from the 'cheapest cost' route pursued by so many British companies. Dyson strives to be design led and to use innovation to differentiate itself from its competitors. It is also obsessive about customer service and has built a comprehensive service system into its product offering.

Time and again management gurus lecture us on the need to differentiate ourselves from our competitors by adding more value; but this lesson applies to companies working at the inexpensive end of a market as well as those producing high-tech products. Tom Peters is keen on the example of Rubbermaid, a US company which specialises in making small hardware gadgets each worth just a handful of dollars. Rubbermaid works in what many others would think of as a commodity business: pile 'em high and sell 'em cheap. However, it applies design thinking to its products so that they perform a function which surprises and delights their customers.

The lesson is that running a commodity business is like being on a treadmill to nowhere. If your company is a commodity business you will see a slow and certain erosion of your profitability and a steady leakage of your customers to the new product offerings from your competitors, which offer greater profit margins than you can ever dream about. As your competitors innovate and increase their prices, the only response you can make is to offer your existing, rather tired product range ever cheaper, to squeeze out costs and to slash further your already pressured profit margins. In this climate design is seen as a cost rather than an investment, an expenditure of money to be minimised rather than an investment in future prosperity.

The sad results of such strategies are to be seen all around us: the last 50 years of British corporate history are littered with the corpses of manufacturing industry. It is a deeply depressing fact that since the Second World War Britain has failed to grow from scratch even one world-class manufacturing multinational. And yet the evidence mounts up to discredit the lowest-cost philosophy.

Let's start by looking at labour costs. Many UK companies are concerned that a minimum wage will affect their competitiveness. It's certainly true that the UK has one of the lowest hourly manufacturing labour costs in the developed world (around US$12). But compared to manufacturing labour costs in countries like India, Vietnam or China — where the hourly cost is measured in cents — we cannot compete on the basis of being a lowest-cost producer. To remain competitive we need to shift the basis of much of our manufacturing. Lowest cost is yesterday's solution; higher added value, through design and innovation, is today's.

Luckily, Britain is one of the world's most prolific inventors. According to Japan's Ministry of Trade and Industry, since the Second World War Britain has been responsible for over 40 per cent of the inventions which have been significant to Japanese industry. However, it is also true that our record of converting these inventions into commercially successful innovations is dismal. We seem to have a cultural problem.

Some startling figures appear in a report for the Design Council by London Business School's Centre for Economic Forecasting, and these illustrate how more companies can achieve competitive success. Devoting an additional 1 per cent of turnover to product development and design raises both turnover and profits by around 3 or 4 per cent over five years. The increase in turnover is strongest in consumer-oriented industries, and in profits in the engineering-related industries. These figures tie in with the lessons from existing research which show that 85 per cent of future production costs are determined by the end of the concept design stage. According to the Ford Motor Company design decisions are 10 times more effective than production planning decisions — and 100 times more effective than production changes — in reducing costs and improving quality.

One of the UK's biggest problems is persuading British companies to invest. On average, just 3 per cent of British companies have produced a new product in the last five years; and yet of the top 10 per cent of British companies nearly two-thirds have produced new products in the same period. This lesson is so obvious that it's astonishing that more companies don't heed it: but while British companies' profits rose by 18 per cent in 1995 their investment in R&D rose by just 4.2 per cent.

This chapter started with Dyson Appliances, but there are a large number of UK businesses which are succeeding by innovating: from Psion palm-top computers to JCB mechanical equipment, from Leckey support equipment for children with disabilities to Linn hi-fi systems, from NCR automatic transaction machines to British Airways and its first-class seats. Britain's most successful companies compete through innovation and design. This is a route which many more companies could follow, and would involve the added benefit of giving up the lowest-cost treadmill.

In managing corporate affairs and internal communications, **Paul Crake** has pioneered a series of systems that use new media to striking effect and has led the development of the Design Council's Internet site.

The Design Council is the UK's national authority on the effective use of design. It works to inspire the best use of design by the UK in the world context, to improve prosperity and well-being.

4.3

Continuous Improvement of Products: Value Management in the Next Millennium

Nicholas Dalton

Business Development Manager, XR Associates Ltd

The past decade has seen significant changes in the nature of markets and in the expectations which customers have of the products and services they consume.

Customers, especially in the industrialised West, are becoming increasingly sophisticated, demanding and discerning, and now expect top quality as a matter of course. They are also demanding more features and benefits in the products they are purchasing, yet are reluctant to pay extra for those benefits, often because they can get similar features as standard from other manufacturers or providers.

What does this mean to growing businesses which already have a position in the marketplace and which wish to sustain that growth well into the next millennium? It means continually improving products in line with customer requirements; it means using innovation and creativity so that products 'excite' the customer; and, most importantly, it means achieving all of this at minimum cost so that products can be offered to the consumer at a competitive price.

This market-driven change is one of the reasons that we have seen the reemergence of a technique first employed in the 1940s by Lawrence Miles of General Electric, called value analysis/value engineering (VA/VE).

Value analysis/value engineering is now in increasing use in British manufacturing, construction and service sectors. The approach, although it has undergone much refinement since its introduction, seems to have 'come of age' and is in tune with the challenges facing business today.

VA/VE in the 1990s has, at its core, many of the accepted characteristics of progressive management today, including empowerment, teamwork, innovation and creativity, process ownership and improvement, and the building of cooperative relationships with stakeholders in the business.

Value management studies are most effective when structured in a workshop-based programme. So successful has been the introduction of value management in both Europe and the USA that teams formed to study products and processes have achieved savings of 20–40 per cent on the cost of bought-in parts to the major end user. In most cases, this has been achieved with the added bonus to both customer and supplier of enhancements to the original purpose and function of the product.

The teams are comprised of members from key disciplines — those with the expertise to implement change — and usually includes representation from quality; purchasing; design; production and finance. The inclusion of representatives of similar disciplines from key suppliers opens up the entire supply chain to cost reduction and value improvement.

The VA/VE approach is a structured, disciplined process focused on identifying and analysing products and processes from a functional perspective, with the objectives of saving cost, reducing the amount spent on less valued functions and creating alternative ways of carrying out the same function, all of which contribute to more value to the customer. The cornerstone of VA/VE is the equation:

$$\text{Value} = \text{Function}/\text{Cost}$$

where *value* is defined as the reliable performance of that which a product or process must do to make it work or sell at the least possible cost; *function* is that which a product must do to satisfy the customer, measured by performance, reliability, durability, serviceability and quality; and *cost* is the expenditure of a resource, time, money, people, energy and material.

Under the mentorship of a skilled VA facilitator, the team is taken through a one-day preparatory meeting at which team members accumulate data relevant to the study, such as cost information, details of the supply chain and customer feedback.

At the actual workshop, some two to three weeks later, the team reviews the gathered data during the information phase (see Figure 4.3.1) which focuses them on the main cost drivers, defined as those processes, functions or design features which increase cost but do not in themselves add value to the customer. In the subsequent function phase, the teams are encouraged to look at what the product *does*, rather than what it *is*. This is a powerful input to brainstorming, which takes place in the creative phase. The workshops harness the innate creativity of people and focuses them both on improving existing products and services (value analysis) and on products at an early design stage (value engineering). The programmes also create breakthrough thinking and innovation, especially useful for future product development.

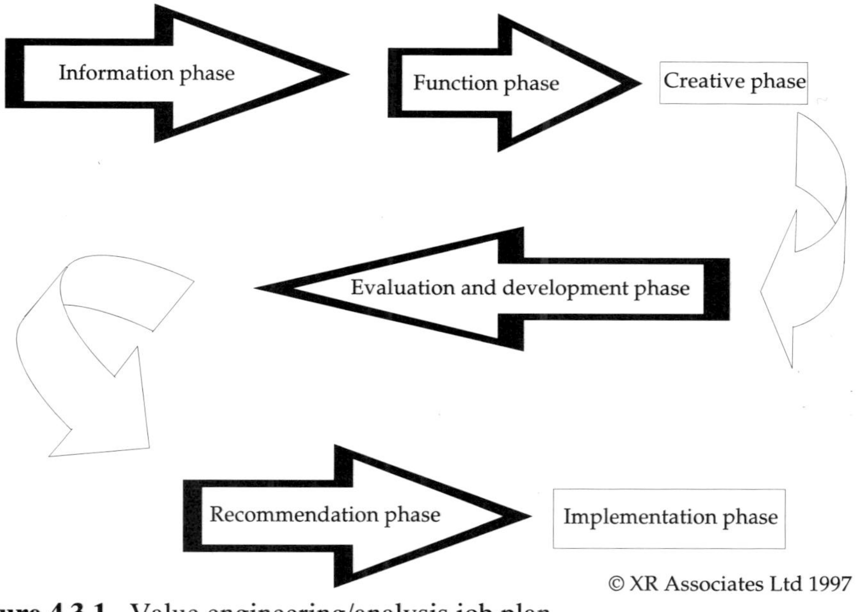

Figure 4.3.1 Value engineering/analysis job plan

The large number of ideas generated are then sorted, filtered and analysed in the evaluation and development phase until the team ends up with a number of key proposals which are fully defined in terms of cost savings, value improvements, investment needed to implement, payback periods and an action plan for implementation. The team will present proposals to management in the recommendation phase with a view to gaining immediate approval.

There is evidence that value management will be increasingly relevant to businesses providing either products or services. Progressive, best-in-class companies regularly apply value engineering at the early design stage to optimise design and reduce costs. As approximately 70 per cent of product lifecycle costs are built in at this stage, this presents an enormous opportunity for change. It does not end there. As the product goes into production, it is regularly subjected to value analysis study to remove unnecessary costs as changes in circumstances occur such as new technology, new materials and different processes.

Any organisation contemplating the use of value management as an effective business tool should be keenly aware of the following:

- Management commitment is of paramount importance, not just towards the genuine empowerment of your people, but to the enormous energy and enthusiasm required for the implementation of generated proposals.
- Understand what it is that customers require and truly value in your products and services, whether you are the producer of the end product or a supplier of a part of that product.
- Be prepared to be much more involved with suppliers in areas such as sharing of information, design decisions, communication and processes which affect both parties.
- Be ready to challenge the current working practices, habits and attitudes within your company, for it is those areas which often keep unnecessary cost in the system.

Opportunities exist not only in manufacturing, where VA/VE has its roots, but also in construction, distribution, leisure, healthcare and education — in fact anywhere there exists a propensity for unnecessary cost and waste to occur. We are now, some would argue, well and truly in the value era.

Nicholas Dalton BSc (Hons) has a background in the oil industry, in manufacturing and in training. He has performed VA/VE consultancy work for key clients in various business sectors in Europe and the USA. He is business development manager with XR Associates Ltd. **XR Associates Ltd** is a leading practitioner in the highly focused area of value management, dedicated to the elimination of waste and the attainment of higher added value and increased profitability. XR operates from offices in Britain, Germany, Spain and the USA.

4.4

Benchmarking as an Aid to Growth

Nicolas Prime
Policy Adviser, CBI

Whether you are the manager of a small firm or a giant multinational, the likelihood is that you will have a similar goal, be it the desire to be the most profitable or the fastest growing company within your particular sector. But how do you know if or when you have reached your target? Was that target challenging enough to make you 'best in class'? Or is someone else already surpassing your performance? The first you will know of this will be your competitive disadvantage in the marketplace, as was the case for Xerox in the late 1970s.

What is Benchmarking?

In 1983, Xerox found that the retail price of Canon photocopiers was less than its own manufacturing costs.[1] Xerox sent a team to Japan to compare the performance of its competitors to its own. The result of this exercise was a benchmarking programme to raise the performance of Xerox in the US.

Of course, it could be argued that an organisation the size of Xerox could draw on huge resources in the implementation of such a programme. At

1 *Survey of Benchmarking in the UK — Executive summary* (1993) CBI's National Manufacturing Council/Coopers & Lybrand.

such a late stage, many smaller companies would have struggled. However, by taking a more proactive approach to the management process, benchmarking should not be beyond any enterprise, regardless of size.

Xerox describes benchmarking as a continuous, systematic process of evaluating companies recognised as industry leaders, to determine business and work processes that represent 'best practices' and establish rational performance goals.

The Benefits

Managers have a duty to maximise the growth potential of their company. Knowing where you stand in the competitiveness league will show you how much more is available to your company. Benchmarking allows you to measure the gap between yourselves and the competition and signposts you in the right direction for closing this gap. Without such a measurement, any targets set are more likely to be subjective assessments based on past performance or hearsay. Benchmarking eliminates this uncertainty and provides an objective assessment of the relative positioning of your company, whether within a specific industry sector or a broader selection criteria.

In a CBI National Manufacturing Council/Coopers & Lybrand Survey of benchmarking in the UK in 1993, respondents recorded the following when asked for the benefits of benchmarking:

- Enables meaningful and realistic targets to be set.
- Helps companies gain new insights.
- Motivates staff by showing what is possible.
- Provides early warning of competitive disadvantage.
- Fosters step change and 'quantum leap' improvements.
- Promotes teamwork and cross-functional learning.

What to Benchmark?

Almost any measurable procedure or attribute can be benchmarked. However, when considering undertaking a programme of benchmarking, in order to obtain the most from the exercise, it is important to start by looking at those areas which are most critical to the success of your business. This is even more important for companies with limited resources. If these areas are not already known, then ask yourself the following questions:[2]

- What would make the most significant improvements in our relationship with our customers?
- What would make the most significant improvements in our bottom line?

Typical areas to include in a benchmarking survey might be:

- total quality;
- cycle times;
- cost of sales;
- sales per employee.

By selecting an area critical to your business, any improvements made will have the greatest impact on the performance of your company and ultimately on the bottom line. It is, however, important to note that this issue may change with time, for today's best practice will become tomorrow's norm. The advantage of benchmarking is that it keeps pace with best practice and allows companies who use this tool to do the same.

With ever-increasing competitive pressures, benchmarking could mean the difference between just surviving in the short term and realising your company's long-term growth potential. By continuously asking the right questions, it allows companies to leapfrog the normal evolutionary improvement process.

The Competitive Challenge Ahead

Benchmarking can be used in a number of different ways, depending on the needs of the individual company or site. Along with benchmarking your company internally or externally, it can also be used as a diagnostic aid. It can help you indicate if current programmes are delivering what they promised, act as a driver for a programme of change, make others in the organisation aware of the changes, or even function as a way of opening communications.

However, benchmarking is only as good as the actions it provokes. It merely provides a signpost for companies. But with a committed management and workforce, benchmarking can be an extremely powerful tool for

2 *Best Practice Benchmarking — An Executive Guide* (1995) Department of Trade and Industry.

instigating change in an organisation, ultimately leading to a more competitive company.

As the CBI National Manufacturing Council/Coopers & Lybrand Survey of benchmarking in the UK discovered, 82 per cent of companies who claimed to be benchmarking reported the exercise as being successful. No one felt it was unsuccessful.

The CBI is Britain's principal employers' federation, and its mission statement is: 'to help create and sustain the conditions in which businesses in the UK can compete and prosper'. The CBI has an important role to play in the development of the UK economy, in which the SME sector is vitally important.

The CBI's National Manufacturing Council (NMC) recognises the importance of benchmarking in improving the competitiveness of both individual companies and the economy as a whole. In 1995 the NMC, in conjunction with IBM and London Business School, launched its own benchmarking initiative — PROBE (Promoting Business Excellence) — and now has over 1000 international manufacturing companies/sites on its database.

Nicolas Prime was employed as an Engineer by British Aerospace Plc, working on a number of their commercial projects in both design and development. Following a degree in Economics and Marketing and a period at Coopers & Lybrand, he now works as a policy adviser for the CBI.

4.5

Protecting Innovation through Patents, Copyright and Registered Trade Marks[1]

Roland Whaite
Assistant Director, Marketing,
UK Patent Office

Getting the most out of a new idea must be the aim of every innovative company, but many try to sell or exploit their inventions without understanding the part that the intellectual property system — not only patents, but also registered designs, copyright and registered trade marks — can play. Thus, the business plan for producing any new product or service must include realistic costs for making clearance searches (to check that the product and its branding do not fall foul of existing patent or trade-mark rights) and for obtaining appropriate types of protection in the likely market zones.

Patents are granted for industrial processes or products that are new because they produce a new technical or functional effect. With over 250,000 patents actually in force in the UK today, it should be realised that most patents are granted not for major breakthroughs but mainly for incremental

1 This material is crown copyright

improvements to existing technologies. Patents cover every area of technology; for example, there are several hundred patents for childproof medicine bottle caps.

Basically, a patent gives the inventor the right to stop anyone else from making, using or selling the invention, although many innovative companies make their money from licensing others to use their inventions. Worldwide, there is about £200bn of activity every year in this so-called technology transfer with companies licensing to and from each other.

Most forms of intellectual property are territorial, and the normal advice is to get patent protection where your markets are. For Europe, a system called the European Patent Convention (which covers both EU and some non-EU members) enables an application to be made in English and processed through to grant, at which stage the final decisions about country selection (with translations) have to be made. Wider afield, the Patent Co-operation Treaty allows access to the patent systems of some 90 countries, via a UN agency called WIPO (World Intellectual Property Organisation). With product lifetimes coming down in many industries, you need to be sure of an eventual return, since you are likely to have to commit over £10,000 to secure a patent under the EPC (taking those professional fees into account) and a figure of £5000 per country is not uncommon in the global context.

Emphasising that the business plans and market surveys should inform the decisions on the type and level of protection to be sought, a different type of protection is available where the originality in a product can be said to lie in its shape. Although registered designs traditionally involve textile patterns, pottery, furniture, toys etc, they can be just as relevant for new technological items where the casing which perhaps surrounds a mechanism, such as a camera case, has some eye appeal. Then, design registration becomes available independently of any protection for the inward workings.

Although fees for design registration are fairly cheap, you do have to apply separately in every country where you need protection, and there is less harmonisation of law around the world than in the patent system.

It may be felt that copyright has no particular relevance in the industrial world, but practically any original creative work can be covered, whether artistic or in the form of engineering drawings, as a textual report or as a photograph, and whether in paper form or in electronic format. Ownership lies with the creator in the first instance not with the commissioner (unless the contract specifies the contrary) and it is the responsibility of the creator to assert authorship and identify a date of origination. Since there is no government body to which application can be made, many groups band together to act as collecting societies, such as the Copyright Licensing Agency or the Publishers' Association.

Computer software is very much an area where copyright is relevant and companies have to be careful not to allow the unlicensed copying of programs on their premises, since both the Business Software Alliance and the Federation Against Software Theft are very active in gaining injunctions against those companies where they can gather evidence of illicit copying. The basic rule is simple — if you are going to copy anyone else's work in whatever form, seek permission first.

All the rights so far referred to are directed to protecting your innovation or creative works. Registered trade marks, however, are promotional and a trade mark or brand name is likely to be the most valuable marketing tool a company will have.

Trade marks indicate the origin of goods or services, with the Bass Red Triangle being the first UK registered mark, still in force 120 years later. Under the 1994 Trade Marks Act, previously unregistrable marks, such as distinctive 3-D shapes and slogans, can now be registered. In this sense, 'distinctive' means distinctive of one trader as opposed to other traders in the specified area of goods and services. Although it is early days, the first applications under the Community Trade Mark (OHIM) system are now being processed. There is little doubt that UK companies should be actively talking to their trade-mark agents about registering any marks currently not registered, while at the same time keeping an eye on what is going through the Community Trade Mark system, since there may be the need to oppose any mark which could clash even with an existing UK registration.

Although there is nothing to say that you have to register your brand names or logos, those which are unregistered are going to be increasingly on the defensive against those who have registrations in the UK and in Europe generally, even if you were trading that way before they registered.

There is a growing band of company executives who believe that intellectual property really matters in a competitive world, and they are prepared to retain the services of professional advisers such as patent and trade-mark agents, solicitors with intellectual property experience and licensing executives. Even if protection is not at the forefront of your thoughts, then the dangers of infringing someone else's intellectual property should concentrate the mind, especially as ignorance is not going to be a defence at law.

The Patent Office is the statutory authority in the UK for the granting of patents, and for the registration of designs and trade marks. Its Policy Directorates provide advice to government on the domestic and international issues affecting intellectual property legislation. Roland Whaite had 25 years' experience as a patent examiner, before in 1990 becoming part of the publicity and marketing team which is tasked with increasing the awareness of British industry and commerce of the opportunities and benefits provided by the system of IP protection.

4.6

Optimising the Use of Intellectual Property

Tessa Bucks
Partner, Boult Wade Tennant

Industrial research and development in industry is invariably directed at meeting the particular needs identified in manufacturing or in the marketplace. There may be no better marketing slogan than 'new', but resources may not always be best used in the quest to provide something new in the marketplace. What is new depends on what is already available, and existing intellectual property and in particular patents provide one of the most useful and accessible bodies of material which can show what is available. A careful assessment of what is already known through published patent specifications at an early stage in a project can reveal existing solutions to the problem at hand. There are solutions which could be adopted where there are no existing monopoly rights and those which need to be avoided because of others' rights. An appraisal of existing intellectual property rights at the outset is a must to avoid waste of time and resources later on.

Some significant areas of waste of resources can easily be identified:

- developing products or processes that are already available for a profitable market;
- developing products or processes which cannot be made or sold or trade marks which cannot be used because of existing intellectual property rights;
- developing products or processes or trade marks which cannot be protected by enforceable intellectual property rights *and could therefore be copied by third parties.*

These areas of waste can be prevented or reduced by creating a high level of awareness of what others are doing or have already done and using your own and others' intellectual property to plan an appropriate strategy.

The immediate need is to identify the most appropriate sources of information for a particular technical field. The most obvious sources include competitors' product information, trade journals and published research papers. However, others' intellectual property, and especially patent specifications, provide a wealth of both technical and commercial data. They are, by their very nature, detailed descriptions of the latest innovations in all areas of technology. Patent specifications publicly set out technical developments often long before trade literature is published. Decisions are frequently made by companies on the basis that there is nothing on the market which solves this problem. This is dangerous, as the solution may infringe another's patent if it discloses a similar solution *which has not yet been commercialised*. Commercial databases of patents and trade marks from all around the world and other technical literature exist which can be searched in a number of ways on-line.

The information that your company actually needs should be clearly identified before any research commences and will depend on your company's position in the market for the product to be developed and the maturity of the market itself. For new fields of interests, businesses and markets, subject matter searches are most likely to be useful; for established markets and businesses, searches for literature associated with a certain company may be more useful.

The strategy adopted for handling the resulting information is vital. The information must be directed to technical personnel, so that they know what ideas to pursue and what to abandon, and to the decision makers who are concerned with planning the organisation's intellectual property portfolio or determining whether existing technology should be bought in rather than developing it in-house with appropriate feedback loops.

The rationale for the intellectual property system is that it offers an incentive for innovation by protecting investment in intellectual activity through limited monopolies. A sound strategy for your own intellectual property will further help to reduce the wastage of resources, especially if attention is paid to:

- in-house practice to ensure that the best protection can be achieved for the products/processes which have been developed; and
- appropriate intellectual property filing programmes.

Good in-house practice requires thorough documentation of the project and the development of all ideas resulting from the project right from the outset. Drawings, inventor's notes and assignments from designers/contractors/employees may be needed both to prove ownership of rights and to prove non-infringement. Significant amounts of time and money are wasted on legal fees in trying to sort out issues where insufficient evidence is available.

A central library of information and project coordination will help to avoid in-house duplication of research and development.

In setting up a cost-effective filing programme for intellectual property rights, it should first be established why protection is being sought. If it will bring real commercial benefits to your company or prevent the competition from entering a certain field of interest, these are sound reasons. Generally those products constituting a real breakthrough in technology should command a higher budget, and those of more marginal benefit a lower one. A further consideration is the life of the product. A product with a short lifecycle may not justify a broad filing of patent applications. Utility models in certain key areas would be cheaper and perhaps more appropriate. Trade marks may in some cases provide the most effective protection.

If you are considering worldwide protection, do you occupy the worldwide market? If not, there may not be any commercial point in obtaining patents or other intellectual property rights that you cannot monitor or enforce.

You should also take into consideration how you intend to make money from your intellectual property, whether through your own endeavours or through licences. The latter route may, depending on the size of your company, justify a broader geographical coverage, but only if you can find licences.

Tailoring your intellectual property programme to give priority to your key markets will help to avoid wasting money. While full-scale worldwide protection is ideal and sounds good, it is expensive and will be beyond most budgets; accept that you will have to allow some areas to remain unprotected and try to ensure that they are the least important to you commercially.

Thus, unnecessary wastage of your resources can be significantly reduced by optimising the use of intellectual property, and by adopting a good intellectual property strategy which ensures that appropriate information is sought and used to its best advantage, that decisions on your intellectual property rights are made as early as possible and that they are properly protected so as to enable income to be generated from then.

Boult Wade Tennant advises on all aspects of intellectual property protection worldwide including the filing and prosecution of patent, trade mark and design applications before the UK and European Patent and Trade Mark offices; the evaluation of existing rights; and infringement matters relating to patents, designs, trade marks, copyright and confidentiality. Our attorneys can also advise on strategy in relation to short- and long-term commercial aims.

4.7
Technology Transfer

Tim Cook
Managing Director
and
Jim Shedden
Life Sciences Sector Manager,
Isis Innovation Ltd

Challenges and Opportunities to Growing Businesses

All over the world there are researchers and developers in academic, government-funded and privately funded establishments, inventing new products and processes (generically know as intellectual property or IP), some of which will be applicable to your growing business. The costs of using third-party IP are the sum of three components:

- the cost of identifying and contacting sources of relevant IP;
- the time spent developing a relationship with them and doing a deal which is usually management intensive and may well include some lawyers' bills; and
- the cost of the deal itself which may include a downpayment, picking up patent maintenance costs and/or a royalty.

Depending on the style of management in your company, there may also be a cost in demotivating your brightest technologists, who may see some of the fun work going elsewhere or even see third-party IP as a threat.

The benefits of transferring IP to your company are that you can access technology which you may not have time or resources to conceive or develop yourself and, in general, the technology is available on a shorter timescale. An additional benefit to the company, some would say the major sustainable business benefit, is the relationship that develops between the technical staff in the company and the researchers in the academic institution.

Stages in an Effective Technology-Transfer Operation

Decide to do it

The key stage, which is often performed too late or not at all, is for the strategic managers in the relevant part of the company to decide that they really do want to license in some technology. Sometimes it is a last resort when an internal development programme has failed to deliver, in which case internal management is crucial to avoid the 'not invented here' effect, whereby the company's technical staff are not committed to the acquired technology and so its chances of successful exploitation are reduced. The skills of those managing the operations are critical. If you do not have staff with both technical and commercial skills, experienced in technology-transfer methodology, you might consider contracting in, at least for the first time you try it.

Identify the IP required

It may be that one step in a process is proving difficult, or that the company needs a new manufacturing technique to make a new component, maintain a competitive position or perhaps a completely new product is needed to add to the range. Alternatively a research breakthough may allow a whole new area of products for the company to make and sell to diversify its offering.

Identify potential sources of this IP

From cold

Academic establishments all have an industrial point of contact (called variously industrial liaison, research support, contract office etc), so if you know an institute it is relatively easy to find the right person. Some universities, eg Oxford University which, through Isis Innovation Limited, manages the Oxford Innovation Society, are proactive in building networks and relationships. Similarly, commercial organisations will always have a contracts or commercial office to start you off. If you are not aware of the relevant research groups there are published directories of research which will point you in the right direction. Trade associations, professional associations and business libraries have also proved good sources of leads.

From an on-going relationship

Unless the particular piece of IP is to solve an isolated, once only problem, we suggest that an on-going relationship with relevant researchers may prove a valuable asset. Such relationships can be built up from trading or conference contacts, from employing graduates from the institution or from industrial-sponsored research students. We have found this latter very rewarding because, in addition to the work the student performs, the contact with senior research staff is very valuable.

Doing the deal

The stages in purchasing IP are the same as any other deal and negotiating skills are the key tools. First, ensure that you are negotiating with someone who can sign off on the deal. It is very frustrating to spend time negotiating prices with an academic and then find you have to do it all over again with the licensing officer. The more you know about your own and the researcher's negotiating position the better. For example, if there is a rule that some institute has a defined minimum deal below which the officers are not allowed to act, there is little point demanding that they do. If, on the other hand, you are negotiating on a patent that expires in a few months, you always have the option of waiting and saving the licensing costs. Similarly, you need to know the cost of the alternatives to your company so that you know when to get up and leave the negotiations. Do not expect these negotiations ever to be easy. Occasionally they are, but even then you are left with the feeling that you could have done a better deal!

After the deal

Having bought the licence, it is important that, where possible, you continue to cultivate your relationship with the inventor. A great deal of additional value can thus be extracted. This relationship can be nurtured through consultancy, formal meetings or even informal chats. However you do it we are sure, based on numerous experiences, that both your company and your academic partner will benefit.

Tim Cook, Managing Director, and **Jim Shedden**, Life Sciences Sector Manager, are both with **Isis Innovation Ltd**, a company owned by the University of Oxford specialising in the licensing of intellectual property developed in the university to existing and new companies.

4.8

Delivering Exceptional Service

Geoffrey Cole
Partner, Burton Sweet

Take a look at literature from a wide range of organisations and you would imagine that the delivery of exceptional service was standard throughout all industries.

So why do businesses often think that they give excellent service when to the customer it appears to be so average? This is a huge challenge for businesses, especially where product differentiation is difficult and service is the key.

Delivery of exceptional service starts with an understanding of who the customer is and what his or her needs are.

Customers are not only external to the business, we all have internal customers. Appreciating this and treating work colleagues as customers does focus the organisation on being totally customer oriented.

A request from accounts to sales for data to update records may be seen as trivial and not actioned promptly. But if it is overlooked any information sent out may be wrong and it is the customer who will be affected.

Training, empowerment and communication within the business are vital to ensure that all energies are aimed at delivering exceptional service.

Many assume that they know what the customer wants — 'low price' or 'good value for money' would be common suggestions. Very often, while these are important, the key issue may be delivery, quality or product/service guarantees. Asking the customer is so obvious. We should all be checking with our customer base to determine what the important issues are for them in using or buying our goods and services.

Interestingly, research into why customers do not come back to buy a second time indicates that it is not the price, delivery or quality of the product that has deterred them. In the majority of cases it is their perception of a company's indifference to them that persuades them to look elsewhere. It is not good for us to think we have a loyal customer base. We must continually work at it.

Do You:

- Know who your customers are?
- Know why customers buy from you?
- Thank customers for contacting you?
- Contact customers frequently to update them on products/services?
- Reward customers for frequent use of your products/services?
- Thank customers for paying you promptly?
- Welcome complaints and comments?
- Know what customers really want?

When we are customers, our first consideration is 'What is in this deal for me?' This is a vital perception and one which is important to understand and apply when dealing with our own customers.

The concept of TEAM — Together Everyone Achieves More — is widely appreciated and is vital to business success. Within smaller growing organisations all team members must be pulling together to deliver exceptional service for the customer.

For many, the receptionist is the first point of contact. For potential new customers this person provides their initial entry to your business. Very often this may be the person who receives the least amount of training and involvement in the business, when in fact they may know a lot more about the customers than the boss does.

Perception of indifference starts from the first telephone call or visit. The telephone ringing unanswered, a messy reception area, a disinterested, impersonal greeting, being left on hold or unattended in reception while someone is being found to deal with you. Why is the experience of contacting many businesses so disappointing?

Systems will provide the solution and avoid many customer frustrations. Answering the telephone in three rings is ok but not if you are then on hold for 30 seconds listening to Vivaldi before you actually talk to someone.

We must implement systems that empower our team, aid delegation and ensure everyone knows how your organisation deals with issues. Team members must take responsibility rather than passing the buck. It is really powerful if we welcome complaints and deal with them effectively. It is the customers who are unhappy and do not complain who are the problem —

they simply go elsewhere. A complainant wants us to get better — so we should amaze them with how we deal with the complaint.

A list of standard requirements for exceptional service can be drawn up by most managing directors. Meeting promises and delivery times with the right product/service at the quality and with the result that is expected for the agreed price . . . We are all striving for this. Differentiate by building a truly customer-focused team that actually delivers. By creating a vision and training team members, a business provides the basis for ensuring that the customer keeps coming back for more.

And finally, don't forget **FUN**. Our customers appreciate dealing with people who enjoy their work and our team will be stronger and more loyal in an environment that encourages them to excel. The benchmark is always moving: we must therefore keep our 'eye on the ball' at all times and stay focused on delivering exceptional service to our customers.

Burton Sweet provide business development advice to small and growing businesses in Bristol and the South West. As part of a total financial service, development specialists are focused on helping business and business people attain the corporate and personal objectives that have been set.

4.9

Importance of Managing Logistics to Growing Businesses

Paul Mainds
Managing Director, Cavewood

Although the term 'Logistics' can be applied to a broad range of activities this chapter concentrates on the link between supplier and customer. It is very important for any business to recognise that the physical links and controls which are needed to present the product to the customer deserve as much care and on-going attention as any of the upstream processes which have created the sale. Not only can repeat business be prejudiced by badly co-ordinated logistics, but costs can also soon leap out of control.

The classical areas to be considered under 'Distribution Logistics' certainly include order preparation, packaging, labelling and transport. Care must also be given to the contract issues of insurance and terms of sale, as well as the arrangements in place for the 'what ifs' when goods are refused, returned under warranty claims or even not paid for. All of these have a physical side which has to be properly planned for.

Logistics is much more than a question of cost control or planning for what might go wrong. It covers areas which can add real value to the sale and give real commercial potential. It can and should be made to be a part of the overall sales package as it represents the key physical link between the supplier's production line or warehouse and the customer's door.

Packaging

Packaging is a significant cost and insufficient packing may be even more costly. It is not only high-value goods that need looking after as they travel through various hands but even more care needs to be applied to lower value items. Handling time and money will be saved if goods can go straight into their point-of-sale packaging, even if they are then protected by an outer case for shipment.

Labelling

Labelling is obviously important in terms of identification of product, case contents, numbers and age. The use of bar codes and automatic readers can reduce errors and also lead to much tighter stock controls. Remember though that the labels may need to be read down the line by people without these technological aids and it is a good idea to see what can be done by the simple use of different coloured labels and clearer print sizes. The inclusion of pricing information or product codes may have to be agreed with your customer but is something that is easier to do within the UK where there is lower inflation, but harder to anticipate with varying exchange rates. Links to tracking systems, EDI and the Internet all have to refer back to package or consignment controls.

Transport

The choice of transport will be governed by the product characteristics and package sizes. Equally important though, will be the delivery time commitments given to customers. Throughout Europe (especially the UK) there has been a rapid growth in next-day parcel delivery services. The constraints of the sorting centres practically limit the maximum weight of a parcel to about 30 kilos. Living within the rules of these carriers can lead to highly competitive delivery costs. For larger shipments a range of options need to be reviewed, but generally a shared user, third-party system will always be more competitive than a dedicated vehicle whether bought in or owned.

The single market legislation and especially the abolition of customs clearance within Europe has revolutionised transport throughout the EU. It is not an exaggeration to say that a delivery to Berlin should pose no more difficulty than one to Beaconsfield or Blackburn. It is true that many exporters, both large and small, have not reacted as quickly as they should have done to this new potential.

The overseas possibilities by both air-freight and deep-sea containers have also opened up enormously to smaller companies. The global market is a reality and global logistics are already there, both as a challenge and a solution.

Other issues

Education in logistics is a developing area, but in the UK especially there has been a significant growth of professional staff linked to standards set by the Institute of Logistics, examinations and proper qualifications. Crime has become a growing challenge to all business and no more so than in the logistics field. Careful risk assessment should be undertaken and insurance companies, brokers, the police and security consultants are there to help.

Outsourcing in logistics has grown as much as it has in other areas. However, some companies have realised that this is not automatically a good thing and it is very important to make sure that both partners do have a common agenda and that the necessary controls and contracts exist before the plunge is taken.

Beyond the 'distribution logistics' issues there is a growing science of both pre-production and part-production logistics. Pre-production areas include:

- procurement;
- purchasing;
- pre-production manufacturing;
- inventory management.

The post-production phase will go beyond warehousing and inventory management to customisation, assembling the semi-finalised goods, testing, configuration and refurbishment.

This chapter has set out a number of topics within the logistics fields which most companies will need to address. Most of these considerations will be more applicable to larger and developing companies than smaller growing businesses that would typically regard these as part of their 'core services' However, the most important consideration is that these topics do not stand alone, but all link with one another and the overall commercial process.

For over 30 years **Cavewood** has grown and prospered, becoming one or the leading road distribution companies in Europe. It currently operates over 50 line services from UK to the major industrial centres of Europe, a comprehensive national distribution network and a specialised logistic service. The company is seen as a market leader and one with a major commitment to the latest IT systems.

Part 5

Funding

5.1
Funding a Growing Business

Nigel Beer
and
Jon Stratford
KPMG Corporate Finance,
MBO Services

The funding structure can make or break a growing business. It is essential to examine your existing structure and ensure that the business drives the structure and not the other way around.

It is important to recognise that every business is different and a structure that suits one company may not be appropriate for another. At the same time, you must be aware that the optimum structure for your business two or three years ago is unlikely to be optimal now.

How to Examine the Current Structure and Future Requirements

The three elements comprising most funding structures are term debt, equity and working capital. Each of these has individual characteristics which relate to their permanence and nature. Debt and working capital are loan instruments that require security, servicing and repayment. Equity is the permanent investment capital of the business. In parallel, there must be a clear understanding of the operating cash flows and the seasonal cyclicality of the business.

Taking the existing facilities, it should then be possible to overlay forecasts for additional working capital growth, capital expenditure or other investment areas (such as new product or market developments). This overall picture will highlight how the current funding structure matches the forecast funding needs. It is important to recognise that, while the total needs may be understood, the balance between different types of financing may not be optimal.

What is an Appropriate Structure?

An appropriate structure will match the funding to the use to which the funds are to be put.

Terms

The type of funding and hence its duration and repayment terms are key, and need to reflect the manner in which the business is forecast to grow.

For example, a business that will be incurring significant capital expenditure on establishing a new site with machines to last over a long period should look towards equity or long-term debt. Ideally a matching principle should be applied — a five-year loan for a machine with a five-year expected life.

Similarly, the need to cover cyclical changes in working capital is often achieved effectively via an overdraft facility or invoice-discounting facility.

It is also vital that the repayment profiles negotiated are consistent with the projected cash flows of the business.

Availability of funds

Having established the funds you need, the next step is to source them. The choice of funding institutions is as important as the type of funding itself. There are significant amounts of funds available to growing businesses, but you need to know where to look and how best to approach the funder.

Even in the current market it is easier to obtain funds if you are already established with a good track record. This is clearly a result of the higher risks involved in seed and start-up capital. However, there are a number of specialist, albeit smaller, funding sources for businesses at this higher-risk end of the market, where the returns to investors can be significant.

So which institution do you choose? There are a number of factors to consider, the most important of which are:

- *Type of organisation* — you need a funder which can understand the issues surrounding your business. For example, a high-tech company should approach funders with genuine high-tech experience.
- *Future suitability* — you need to establish if the funder will be able to meet your future funding requirements, and whether it offers a full range of funding instruments. Do not be tempted to approach a small funder which will not be able to grow with your business.
- *Personal chemistry* — developing a good relationship with your financier can have significant benefits in the future, in addition to making the fund-raising process less painful!

Approaching an institution

Perfect preparation prevents poor performance. It is essential that an approach to a funding institution is made at the right time and in a professional manner. While the cost of employing advisers may initially seem expensive, they can make the difference between success and failure in your fund raising. You must be able to demonstrate clearly where the business is going, how the funds will be invested, and why this is a good investment for the funder. Time taken in preparing for this is time well spent.

What are the Implications of an Inappropriate Structure?

If you have a structure that does not match your business, the company may find itself with cash-flow difficulties and results underperforming against expectations. In addition, management's eye might be taken off the ball. Management time that would best be focused on other areas is diverted to day-to-day cash-flow management to meet repayment schedules and general concerns about the funding structure.

The financing is driving the business instead of the business driving the finance, and in the extreme this can result in the business becoming insolvent. It is important to address the issue early and, if necessary, obtain advice on how to resolve the problem and thus prevent the unthinkable from occurring.

Funding a Growing Business

In summary, the most important points relating to the funding structure of a growing business are:

- Match the funding to the application of those funds.
- Understand the cash flows and cycles of the business.

- Manage the working capital to match the growth of the business.
- Ensure that you have a source of funds which fits with your business.

The overriding point is that each business is different and there are no standard prescriptions. A suitable structure for one may be wholly inappropriate for another. Taking the time to step back and look at your situation often gets pushed to the bottom of the list by day-to-day issues. It is worth remembering that, although there may be costs involved in refinancing existing facilities, due to the competition between funders providing wide choices of products and terms, these costs can be outweighed by the benefits of a new financing package.

A small investment of time now could make a significant difference to the future of your business.

KPMG Corporate Finance is a leading corporate finance house providing advisory services for a wide range of public and private transactions including mergers and acquisitions, flotations and management buyouts.

Nigel Beer has been a partner since 1989, following a two-year secondment to 3i. Nigel has wide-ranging experience in public and private transactions and specialises in software companies.

Jon Stratford is an executive in the MBO Services team, where he specialises in management buyouts and private equity transactions.

5.2
An Introduction to Public Equity Markets

Neil Austin
KPMG Corporate Finance

What do they Offer?

Public equity markets provide companies with:

- access to funds at the time of the initial public offering and subsequently through secondary issues such as rights issues and placings;
- a widened shareholder base;
- a trading facility and market value for the company's shares;
- an ability to use listed securities as consideration for acquisitions and for incentivising employees;
- raised corporate status and profile;
- a possible mechanism for achieving an exit for their owners (it should be noted, however, that it may not be acceptable to incoming investors for founders to sell a significant proportion of their holdings concurrently with a listing; exits, if desired, must be phased over a period).

Which Market?

The main factors to consider when comparing alternative markets are the following.

Trading record

Some markets may not be available in the short term where a company does not have the required trading record.

Capitalisation of company

Is the expected capitalisation of the company sufficient to satisfy the requirements of a particular market? While this constrains the choice of market, these requirements are also in vendors' interests since a company which is too small compared with the market 'norm' will attract little attention from market makers and analysts and will therefore not receive the full benefits of a public quotation.

Proportion of company which has to be brought to the market

Is the choice of market consistent with plans regarding retention of control?

Flotation expenses

Are the likely flotation expenses appropriate in relation to the size of the company and the funds to be raised?

Ongoing compliance/reporting requirements and costs

Are these reasonable compared to the scale of the company's operations, or will the burden of compliance outweigh the benefits to be derived from obtaining a quotation?

The Main Markets

Set out below are overviews of the main public equity market alternatives which UK companies seeking a quotation would probably consider.

London Official List

The London Official List — the main UK stock market — provides one of the largest, most liquid and most highly regarded markets on which companies can trade their securities. At April 1997 London Stock Exchange figures show that there were over 2700 companies quoted on the Official List with a total market capitalisation of nearly £3,600bn. The market's impressive fundraising abilities are available to companies from the time of flotation.

Companies looking to obtain a stock market quotation and which either do not have the desire, or may not satisfy the requirements, for admission to the Official List are now spoilt for choice. Their options, at least in theory, include AIM, NASDAQ, EASDAQ, Ofex (trading facility rather than formal market – see below) and a number of European markets including Le Nouveau Marché, Der Neuer Markt and the Dutch and Belgian exchanges.

Alternative Investment Market

The Alternative Investment Market (AIM) was set up by the London Stock Exchange as a market designed for smaller, growing companies. It offers an alternative to a full listing with rules more appropriate to the smaller or relatively new company.

In the two years since it was established, AIM has unquestionably proved itself a resounding success. It has confirmed the attraction of a junior market to the corporate sector, appeals to a range of investors and offers fund-raising capability, with more than £1bn having already been raised by companies on the market.

NASDAQ/EASDAQ

NASDAQ is the US market which has attracted high-growth companies, frequently from the high-technology sector. In line with other US markets where companies register with the Securities and Exchange Commission, the regulatory environment is onerous and the costs of compliance are correspondingly high.

EASDAQ opened in September 1996 and is the European equivalent of NASDAQ. Like NASDAQ, EASDAQ is aimed at high-growth companies and targets businesses with a potential market capitalisation at admission of at least £30mn. Admission and disclosure rules are similar to those of NASDAQ.

Ofex

Ofex is not a formal market, but a trading facility on a matched bargain basis managed by JP Jenkins to allow trading in the shares of unquoted companies. Companies looking to raise small amounts of equity, typically between £0.25mn and £1.5mn, may do so through a broker who typically places shares with private clients. An Ofex facility is obtained to allow shareholders to trade their shares more easily. Trades are performed off-market and Stock Exchange regulations do not apply.

EURO.NM

EURO.NM is a partnership of junior European stock exchanges which was formed in March 1996. EURO.NM is aimed at innovative companies which have high growth potential. The current members are the exchanges of Paris, Brussels, Frankfurt and Amsterdam and membership is open to participation by other European stock exchanges. EURO.NM offers a European network of regulated markets with common standards of listing, market and membership rules. The intention is for EURO.NM to operate as a single 'virtual' market, providing companies with easy access to a much larger, pan-European pool of investment funds. How AIM will interact with EURO.NM is still under consideration by the London Stock Exchange. However, given the successful development of AIM and the overall strength of the London market, London's participation would greatly enhance EURO.NM's prospects of achieving its objectives.

Table 5.2.1 Stock market admission requirements

	London — Official List	**London — AIM**	**EASDAQ**
Admission requirements			
Minimum total assets	None	None	ECU3.5mn
Minimum capital and reserves	None	None	ECU2mn
Minimum market capitalisation	£0.7mn	None	None
Minimum shares in public hands	25%	None	20%
Restrictions for directors on realising shareholders	None	12 months*	18 months
Trading history	3 years	None	None
Ongoing requirements			
Interim reports	6-monthly	6-monthly	3-monthly
Minimum capital and reserves	None	None	ECU1mn

*If no two-year trading history

Comparing Stock Market Admission Requirements

There are demonstrable benefits for companies in having a significant domestic shareholder base even if they have international operations or aspirations. Thus, the principal stock market options for UK companies seeking a listing are the Official List, AIM and, to a much lesser extent, EASDAQ. The admission requirements of these markets are summarised in Table 5.2.1.

Neil Austin heads the **KPMG Corporate Finance** new issues practice. He was a member of the Stock Exchange's Working Party which devised AIM, following which he was appointed to its AIM Advisory Panel. He is also a member of the Exchange's Primary Markets Committee. Neil also chairs CISCO, which represents the interests of quoted companies outside the FTSE350, their institutional investors and advisers.

A Management Buy in to Revitalise a Family Business

The origins of Maiden Outdoor Advertising lie in Liverpool in the 1920's when Arthur Maiden founded the outdoor advertising business. Over the next 70 years the business developed under family ownership to be one of the three leading outdoor advertising owners in the United Kingdom. Until 1991 the business grew steadily but consistently through organic growth and acquisition. In 1991 for the first time in 70 years the business lost money. Faced with the severity of the UK advertising recession and no clear management succession from within the family, the owners decided to sell.

Maiden enjoyed a strong brand in the outdoor advertising industry and a good reputation amongst its customers. Its green poster sites with the traditional Maiden logos are a familiar sight on Britain's roads and urban areas. The outdoor advertising industry as a whole however, suffered from its reputation as the "poor relation" of the advertising industry, its association with tobacco advertising and the "seedy" image of some hoardings in the inner city context. Outdoor advertising was seen to lack innovation and marketing focus.

Ron Zeghibe, a former corporate financier at Salomons, the US Investment Bank and Francis Goodwin, a former marketing director at one of Maiden's main competitors, More O'Ferral, identified an opportunity to buy the business from its family owners. Zeghibe, who had recently restored the fortunes of a Dutch street advertising business, after leaving the city, saw potential in the UK industry and in Maiden in particular.

After lengthy discussions with a number of venture capitalists against the background of uncertain prospects for the UK advertising industry, Zeghibe and Goodwin struck a deal with Morgan Grenfell Development Capital (MGDC) to acquire and refinance Maiden. Intensive negotiations with the owners followed and finance from MGDC raised over a four month period. In April 1993 Maiden was acquired with £20 million of financing. Zeghibe was installed as chief executive, Goodwin as marketing director and Ian Powell (formerly commercial director at More O'Ferrall) as finance director, supported by the long established incumbent management team.

Immediately the team set about the task to revitalise the business, develop a strategy to raise the profile of the outdoor advertising industry and seek growth through marketing and innovation. The task was broad ranging and covered all aspects of the business including sales, marketing, site development, systems and organisation.

The strategy proved to be immensely successful. Over the next two years the company consistently out performed its forecasts. As the market for outdoor advertising grew through economic recovery Maiden increased its market share. The management team who initially between them held 20% of the business saw profit and cash grow such that by June 1995 they were able to restructure the finances of the business, buy out MGDC at a valuation of £60 million and fund the acquisition of British Transport Advertising, (BTA), British Rail's principal track side advertising concessionaire and a significant competitor.

Using an aggressive financial structure involving senior debt and mezzanine finance, Zeghibe and his team were able to negotiate 100% control of the business just two years after investing a few hundred thousand pounds.

Having successfully integrated the acquisition of BTA, Maiden floated on the London stock market just one year later in May 1996 at a capitalisation of £80 million. The management's impressive track record over the previous three years, their unswerving commitment to the future growth of business (none of the management team sold any shares in the issue) and their demonstrable ability to grow the business both by organic growth over acquisition, proved to be an attractive story to the institutional investors. The company's market capitalisation post-flotation rose from £80 million to £130 million within a short period.

The Maiden success story is no doubt far from over. In analysing this success to date there are several themes that stand out. The opportunity arose because an outside management team saw potential in the business that the incumbent owners did not and were able to persuade MGDC that they had means to achieve it.

The venture capitalists for their turn, notwithstanding the poor outlook for the industry and the risks facing it from a possible ban on tobacco advertising, had faith in the incoming management's proposals.

Shortly after the management buy-in the business was described by one member of the management team as a "Rolls Royce that had been left lying unattended in the garage too long and needed a restoration and a polish". There is no doubt that the new management team very effectively polished and restored the business, they also saw that the medium term growth of the business would have to come from the market and invested in the business, its marketing resources, its poster sites, image and industry profile. Without that investment in growth Maiden would not have become the successful quoted company it is today.

This announcement appears as a matter of record only. Morgan Grenfell Development Capital Limited is regulated by IMRO.

Morgan Grenfell Development Capital Limited

Leading Management Buy-Outs

British Aluminium

£265 Million
Management Buy-In

Co-led by
Morgan Grenfell Development Capital Limited

NI Intressenter AB

SEK436 Million
Management Buy-Out

Arranged and led by
Morgan Grenfell Development Capital Limited

AB Cerbo

SEK238 Million
Management Buy-Out

Arranged and led by
Morgan Grenfell Development Capital Limited

The British School of Motoring Limited

£42 Million
Management Buy-Out

Arranged and led by
Morgan Grenfell Development Capital Limited

Maiden Outdoor Advertising

£21 Million
Management Buy-In

Arranged and led by
Morgan Grenfell Development Capital Limited

Calder Group Limited

£84.5 Million
Management Buy-In

Arranged and led by
Morgan Grenfell Development Capital Limited

Offices in London, Edinburgh, Paris, Milan, Hong Kong, Singapore

Morgan Grenfell Development Capital Limited
23 Great Winchester Street, London EC2P 2AX
Tel: +44 171 545 8000 Fax: +44 171 545 5282

Morgan Grenfell Development Capital Limited
35 St Andrew Square, Edinburgh EH2 2AD
Tel: +44 131 557 8600 Fax: +44 131 557 8306

For further information, please contact Susan Deacon
E-Mail: susan.deacon@uk.dmg.deuba.com

Deutsche Morgan Grenfell

5.3

Business Angels – High-risk Investors for Entrepreneurs

Danny Tomeh
Venture Capital Report

An Introduction to Business Angels

To reduce their risks and administrative overheads, as well as increase their returns, venture capital companies are increasingly focusing on larger size and shorter term investments with more established companies. The high-street banks continue to be reluctant to provide adequate loans for business start-ups and prefer to remain a source of low-risk, secured loan finance. This has perpetuated the so-called equity gap that entrepreneurs suffer, since their seed and start-up capital requirements are often for smaller amounts that carry higher and longer term risks. Fortunately for entrepreneurs, wealthy private investors or business angels as they are known, are beginning to address some of the problems created by the equity gap. The term 'business angels' refers to individuals who invest capital in small businesses and who will often be actively involved in helping the business to grow. The term became prominent in the 1990s and derives from the angels who invest in theatrical productions.

Entrepreneurs' expectations of 'venture capital' often fail to match the venture capital industry expectations of 'entrepreneurial ventures'. Venture capital, in its purest form, is capital invested in high-risk and early-stage ventures which offer the possibility of large capital gains to compensate for the high risks involved. However, the venture capital industry and the various venture capital associations use a much wider definition, which includes short-term investments in expansions or management buyouts for companies that are not listed on a major stock market, but may be listed on junior stock markets such as AIM.

This wider industry definition creates considerable confusion in the minds of entrepreneurs who seek 'genuine venture capital'. They set out on their search believing that there is a large pool of available capital, but quickly discover that this is not the case. In the UK, only 4 per cent of the total venture capital (including expansions and MBOs, etc) invested in 1995 went into 'genuine venture capital', – ie investments in pre start-ups and start-ups (1996 British Venture Capital Association statistics).

Business angels are likely to be actively involved in the businesses in which they invest, sometimes even working full time. Many have founded businesses themselves and have had successful business careers, so that they are able to bring management skills and industry contacts to the businesses in which they invest. In general, because business angels are individuals investing their own money, they are able to take risks, and to invest instinctively. They do not need to justify their actions to an investment committee and cannot be sacked if they make a bad decision. For this reason, a small, start-up, high-risk business is more likely to be able to attract investment from a business angel than from a venture capital company. A recent report has estimated that there are around 18,000 active and potential business angels in the UK (Mason & Harrison, 1997).

Types of Investment usually Associated with Business Angels

Business angels tend to make specific types of investment. Therefore, it would be helpful to consider briefly the most common types of venture capital that usually involve business angels acting individually or collectively as syndicates.

Seed capital

This is capital provided at a very early stage, perhaps to build a prototype, to conduct a market feasibility study, or to write a business plan and build a management team to a point at which the business can be funded as a start-up by a larger venture capital company. A typical seed investment will be £5,000–£100,000, will carry the highest risk of all investments, and will be unlikely to show a return for the investor for 7–12 years. For these reasons, the high risk and the long time scale, the returns on those investments which do succeed must be very large to pay for those which do not.

Start-up capital

This is capital to fund a start up. The sums invested will be larger, typically £100,000–£5mn. The products or services will usually already be developed, a management team in place as well as a detailed business plan that includes market research. The risks are still high and the investor is likely to have funds invested for 5–10 years.

Early stage development capital

This is capital to fund the development of an established business, but which needs capital to expand and is unable or unwilling to raise this as debt from a bank. There are fewer risks, although the business may still fail. A typical investment will be £300,000–£1mn, and the investor may seek an exit in 4–7 years.

What Business Angels Want from Entrepreneurs

Business angels tend to look at a number of factors when evaluating entrepreneurs and their proposals. The following factors are the most important:

- *Good impression of the founder/management* – Business plans need to give very detailed CVs of the key managers and what they have achieved. When potential angels first meet entrepreneurs, they will be looking for a good personal chemistry, as they will probably be working together through good and bad times for a number of years. They will want to feel confident that the management team understand their business and can achieve the targets stated.
- *Interesting projects with high returns* – Business angels risk their capital on the basis that the long-term returns are substantial. Angels generally expect a compound rate of return to exceed 30 per cent, and significantly higher returns for a higher risk investment. Angels also look for interesting investments that will give them personal satisfaction when helping the company to grow.
- *Use of funds* – An entrepreneur's proposal must include a statement about what funds are needed, what they are needed for and what percentage of equity is being offered. Angels usually expect to take minority equity stakes ranging from 20 to 40 per cent, often in redeemable preference shares. These ensure that the first profits of the company are used to repay the investment capital, before management bonuses or dividends, and often before any salary increases.
- *Current position details* – The proposal must include a current balance sheet, and a detailed breakdown of current liabilities. Entrepreneurs

How Venture Capital Report Links Entrepreneurs & Investors

Access the UK's largest private investor network

Venture Capital Report (VCR) is the UK's longest running agency for linking investors and entrepreneurial businesses seeking equity capital. Venture Capital Report, which is published monthly and is only available by subscription, features the business proposals of entrepreneurs seeking capital between £20,000 and £2m. VCR's 800 subscribers are predominantly private investors, popularly referred to as *business angels.*

Feature your new business opportunity in VCR

Business opportunities in the monthly Report are featured as detailed four to five page articles, prepared by VCR staff after reviewing business plans and conducting in depth interviews with the entrepreneurs concerned. The articles provide full details of the product or service being considered, relevant market and competition information, CVs of the entrepreneurs, financial data, suggested financial structure and complete contact information.

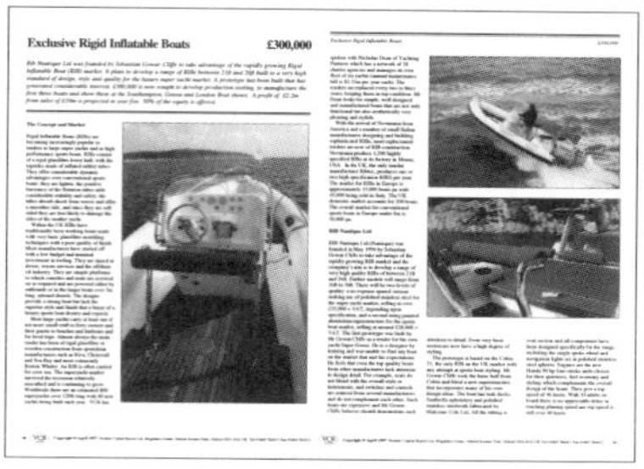

Attend VCR's Equity Investment Workshop

The unique workshop is designed to prepare entrepreneurs and potential investors for the practical issues associated with raising and making equity investments in seed and start up businesses. There is a seminar session, followed by a detailed case study led by Lucius Cary, VCR's chairman (who has himself made 44 investments of this type). The workshop covers deal structure, reconciling differing interests, legal agreements, post investment issues and exit routes.

Target venture capital companies more effectively

The VCR Guide to Venture Capital in the UK & Europe is often referred to as *'the bible of the venture capital industry'.* It helps entrepreneurs to effectively target venture capital companies and is the most comprehensive directory on *how* and *where* to raise risk capital from over 1,000 sources of capital. It includes essential details of major venture capital companies, actual investment portfolios, CVs of their key executives, investment preferences, etc (1,300 pages).

Tel 01865 784411 Fax 01865 784412 Venture Capital Report VCR - est 1978 -

need to set out what is unique about the business and to provide details of how and why forecasts will be met. They also need to demonstrate why they attract and retain their current customers, what their monthly revenues and costs are, what their margins are, and what they require to break even. Cashflow and profit and loss projections, and the key assumptions behind these forecasts, must be realistic and must be understood by entrepreneurs themselves and not just by their financial adviser.

- *Understanding of the risks* – Entrepreneurs' business plans must acknowledge the risks and show how they will be addressed. Entrepreneurs and angels also need to have a firm understanding of, and belief in, the company and its products, as well as a grasp of the critical success factors. They will need to demonstrate market demand by answering such questions as why customers will purchase their products in preference to other potential competitors (including customer testimonials) and the strengths and weaknesses of the competition.
- *Assessing an entrepreneur's proposal* – A Venture Capital Report and Oxford University survey of 500 business angels in 1994/95 found that the principal criteria for an angel's assessment of an entrepreneur's proposal were as shown in Table 5.3.1.

Table 5.3.1

Principal criteria for assessing a proposal (respondents could rank jointly)		
1st	59%	Impression of the founder/manager
2nd	29%	Experience and understanding of sector
3rd	9%	Projected profitability
4th	8%	Business plan content and presentation
5th	7%	Attractive margins
6th	5%	Venture location
	10%	Other

What Entrepreneurs Want from Business Angels

Entrepreneurs should bear in mind a number of important issues when considering a business angel investment. The following issues are the most important:

- *Long-term commitment and personal chemistry* – The entrepreneurs will need to find a business angel with whom they can work with on a professional and personal level. As equity investors, angels will have to have a shared belief in how to achieve the strategic vision of the company, and, in particular, they will need to be joint contributors in both good and hard times.
- *Contribute additional resources* – A good angel is a decisive one, and will follow up with hard cash after conducting the appropriate, due diligence and legal procedures. Angels can provide vital strategic input and may also contribute additional resources, such as manufacturing facilities or industry contacts. An angel's contribution also changes with the development of the business. At the earlier stages, they may wish to work full time in the business; at the later stages, they can advise when securing additional funding or exit routes.
- *Experience of founding and funding businesses* – Business angels who have founded their own business are more likely to empathise with entrepreneurs and be able to give relevant advice. Strong-minded entrepreneurs cannot work with angels who insist that their way is the only way of doing things. Also, just as angels need to know details about entrepreneurs' backgrounds, so too should entrepreneurs ask angels if they may talk to other people whom the angel has backed or founded a business with.
- *Similar expectations* – The entrepreneur and angel investor need to confirm their respective expectations and time scales before they begin to prepare legal agreements. These agreements must be seen by all parties as simple, fair and workable, and legally enforceable should the need arise. The agreement should state what actions will be taken if agreed targets are not met, as well as the angel's preferred exit route.
- *Trust and respect* – Trust can be difficult to create at the outset, but must be built upon. The partnership should be financially and personally rewarding for both parties. Although entrepreneurs are effectively in a position of control, a successful partnership requires a sense of joint ownership, otherwise both angel and entrepreneur can enforce their respective legal rights and make life unbearable for each other.

Targeting Business Angels

Entrepreneurs seeking an investment from a business angel, must begin with a strategy for finding the right one. Although various surveys estimate a large number of business angels exist, targeting and proceeding with the one(s) most suited to the business requirements is quite difficult.

Entrepreneurs should certainly try any friends and contacts they may have first. However, the choice may be limited. Mutual trust and respect is, of course, common, but other criteria for a long-term business relationship, such as relevant experience, strategic vision, sufficient cash and resources may not be apparent. If personal contacts are not appropriate, then it may be worthwhile to use one or more business angel introductory service to contact effectively a large number of active angels. These agencies link entrepreneurs seeking capital with a 'network' of investors interested in seed and start-up businesses.

To help decide which introductory service to use, it will probably be worth considering the following three points:

- *How many investors does the agency have and how much do the investors pay to belong to it?* In general, the higher the price paid by the angels, the more serious they are likely to be.
- *How long has the agency been established and is it prepared to give details of investments it has arranged?* The general rule would be to choose an agency which is prepared to give details of its track record.
- *What are the experience and business backgrounds of those running the agency, and the degree of help and support which you may expect?* If you are an experienced entrepreneur, you may not need any help in structuring your proposal to raise funds, but if not, then the personnel in a good agency will have had the appropriate experience and will be able to help.

Finally, if you decide to search for business angel capital, I wish you the best of luck with your venture. I would hope that in the future, when you look back at your own success, you decide to take the leap and help other entrepreneurs by becoming a much needed business angel.

Venture Capital Report (VCR) attempts to match investors with small firms in need of captial. Each month it features around 10–15 businesses, seeking venture capital of between £20,000 and £2mn. VCR has over 800 subscribers – the largest group of active business angels in the UK. They pay an annual subscription fee of £300 to receive the monthly Report. Entrepreneurs are charged £350 to have their projects published and a success fee of £1,000 plus 2.5 per cent of any risk capital raised through VCR.

VCR claims to be the most interventionist of the matchmaking bureaux, assessing projects at a depth not attempted by other services. Since it was established, VCR has been instrumental in achieving over 200 successful matches. Its clients have ranged from inventors and manufacturers to pubs and retailers. Five of them have attained a stock-market listing.

5.4
Grants and Incentives

Sarah Harris
Manager, Business Link West's Information Services

One of the most frequently asked questions to the Business Information line of Business Links and Euro Info Centres relates to the availability, or otherwise, of grants.

Business Links and Euro Info Centres in the UK are well equipped to handle these questions effectively, having access to full information on funding possibilities from UK and EU sources, and are able to advise on specific local opportunities.

While it is undoubtedly true that vast amounts of money from the UK government and from the European Commission are pumped into support for business activities, it is also generally true that this funding is not accessible by businesses directly from its source. In other words, the funds are put into schemes that are either nationally or regionally delivered.

Regional Funding

In some cases, funding is made available on a regional basis, directed at parts of the UK or parts of the EU that are lagging behind in economic development or have faced economic decline in a mainstay industry. This may either be long-term decline or relatively sudden, as with the decline of defence-related industries or the coal industry.

Alternatively, the money is made available 'horizontally', which means that the eligibility criteria do not include geographical parameters.

Funding streams are often directed towards support for employment initiatives, giving support to job creation, perhaps with the emphasis on youth employment, or to diversification of industry and either retraining or improving the skills of the workforce. In these instances, the funds are administered by government departments and the Training and Enterprise Councils (TECs).

The Department of Trade and Industry (DTI) supports businesses by allocating funds to the regional TECs, which are then able to respond to the support programmes offered by the Business Links. These cover:

- the provision of subsidised training geared towards the development of owners and managers of new and micro businesses as well as SMEs;
- subsidised consultancy for SMEs, marketing and quality issues topping the popularity bill;
- advisory services provided by Business Link advisers, including business development advice, technology and export advice.

Favoured Initiatives

EU funding policies also favour employment, education and training initiatives as well as heavily supporting environmental and energy-efficiency projects, research and technological development (R & TD) and innovation and technical-transfer projects.

However, should funding from these kinds of programmes properly be called grants? If the definition of a grant is the payment of a lump sum with no strings attached, then these schemes are not grants.

In cases where funding is made directly to a company, it is rarely for 100 per cent of a project and always with strict eligibility criteria.

If the project is viable, then it deserves time and effort put into it by the beneficiaries and a commitment to deliver some outcomes. The taxpayer should be secure in the knowledge that money is not being poured into a bottomless pit.

Creating Employment

If a subsidy for creating employment opportunities, or the chance to offer training to existing employees, is seen to be of advantage, there are many possibilities for the SME.

In the case of R & TD projects, funding may be to a level of 50–75 per cent. The UK funds two programmes — SMART and SPUR — which are both geared towards SMEs. In the case of EU R & TD funding, a partner in another member state and an academic partner, such as a university or research institute, are usually necessary.

It is not unreasonable from a business point of view that any bid or proposal for funding must be backed by a carefully thought-out application with defined objectives, projected outcomes and some key milestones so that progress and results can be measured.

Neither is it unreasonable to expect a company accessing the support of public money to be in a strong enough position to undertake some financial commitment in terms of matching the grant aid or meeting the repayment terms of a 'soft' loan.

Explore Possibilities

So what should an SME do to investigate the opportunities for grant funding? The answer is — explore all the possibilities.

- Ask the help of the local Business Link or Euro Info Centre, which will have access to all the information on possible schemes, their eligibility criteria and contact information.
- Expect to commit time and effort to accessing the funding opportunity successfully.
- Be realistic about assessing your chances of success on a cost/benefit basis.
- Above all, do not be beguiled by offers of untold millions of ECUs for fairy-tale projects in return for an up-front payment of several hundred pounds to cover the cost of a search. Instead, check with your local Business Link, Chamber of Commerce or Euro Info Centre.

These organisations can offer a full search service of a comprehensive database of grant information carried out in consultation with your company. In addition, through your local Business Link, you can access a range of supported services, including subsidised training programmes, consultancy and advisory services.

In addition, there are 22 official Euro Info Centres in the UK, linked to a network all over Europe, offering an enquiry and information service to local businesses. They can help you with potential business opportunities, to identify customers or suppliers or provide the latest news on European legislation and public sector tenders.

Sarah Harris is manager of Bristol-based Business Link West's Information Services department and Bristol Euro Info Centre, serving businesses in the West of England. For details of your local Business Link, call 0345 567765, and for the telephone number of your nearest Euro Info Centre, call 0117 973 7373.

5.5
Venture Capital

Norman Murray
Chairman, British Venture Capital Association (BVCA) and Chief Executive, Morgan Grenfell Development Capital Ltd

10 Things to Consider if you are Thinking of Raising Venture Capital

1 Venture capital is only suitable for ambitious, experienced managers of companies with a high growth potential.
2 Venture capital is invested in exchange for a stake in your company. However, the venture capital firm will *not* want to take day-to-day management control.
3 Venture capital is not just the provision of finance, it is a relationship which can span three to seven years or more and offers experience and contacts as required, which are rated highly by those who have raised venture capital and are not seen as intrusive.
4 With venture capital support, UK companies have demonstrated that they succeed and grow faster than companies using other forms of finance (see below).
5 Make sure venture capital is suitable for your needs.
   - Contact the BVCA and obtain *A Guide to Venture Capital*, which explains the venture capital process and has a chapter explaining what a venture capital firm would like to see covered in any business plans it receives.

- Find out more about the many other different sources of finance, such as grants, loans, invoice discounting etc. Contact your local Business Link, call the relevant trade associations, visit your library, read the national and local press, talk to your advisers (eg your accountant) and local businesses. While everyone will have their own view and many will have misconceptions, this combined with factual literature should help you to establish your own view.

6 How much finance do you require?
  - Venture capital firms and business angels are generally complementary sources of venture capital, as business angels tend to invest smaller amounts in earlier-stage businesses. For the purposes of sending out relevant publications, the BVCA draws a rough line at £100,000.
    - If you are looking to raise over £100,000 you will be sent a directory of members, which lists members' investment preferences (which vary considerably), their contact details and information on advisers' experience in the venture capital field.
    - If you are seeking less than £100,000, you will be sent *Sources of Business Angel Capital*, which lists 40 non-BVCA member networks which will aim to introduce you to individuals who may be interested in investing in your business. It also lists the investment preferences and contact details of 26 BVCA members who will consider smaller investments.

7 At what stage of development is your business?
  - Is it only a concept at the moment? This would be described as a 'seed' investment.
  - Has your company been established for less than three years and is it in the early stages of establishing its product or service? This is called a 'start-up' or 'early-stage' investment.
  - Are you requiring finance to expand your existing business? This would be 'expansion' finance or 'development capital'.
  - Are you needing capital to finance a 'management buyout' (MBO) or 'management buyin' (MBI)?

8 In what industry sector does your business operate and where are you located?

9 Only approach those sources of venture capital whose investment preferences match your situation regarding amount of capital required and the stage, location and industry sector of your company.

10 Details of every major UK venture capital firm which invest principally in the UK, UK business angel networks and other information can be obtained free of charge from the BVCA.

Venture Capital in the UK

In 1996 venture capital investment increased by 28 per cent to £3.2bn, a record amount. These funds were provided to more than 1000 new and developing businesses and MBO and MBI companies. As a result, the UK venture capital industry remains the largest and most developed in Europe, accounting for nearly 50 per cent of total annual European venture capital investment — and is second only to the US in world importance. Compared with the US, the UK venture capital industry, relative to GDP, invests more in early-stage and expanding companies. In 1995 in this sector of the market, the UK undertook three-quarters as many deals as the US, although the US economy is seven times the size of the UK's.

There has never been a better time for ambitious companies to raise venture capital than in 1997. Over £5.7bn has been committed by investors to venture capital funds over the past three years for future investment, and in addition to this are funds available from venture capital firms' own and parental resources.

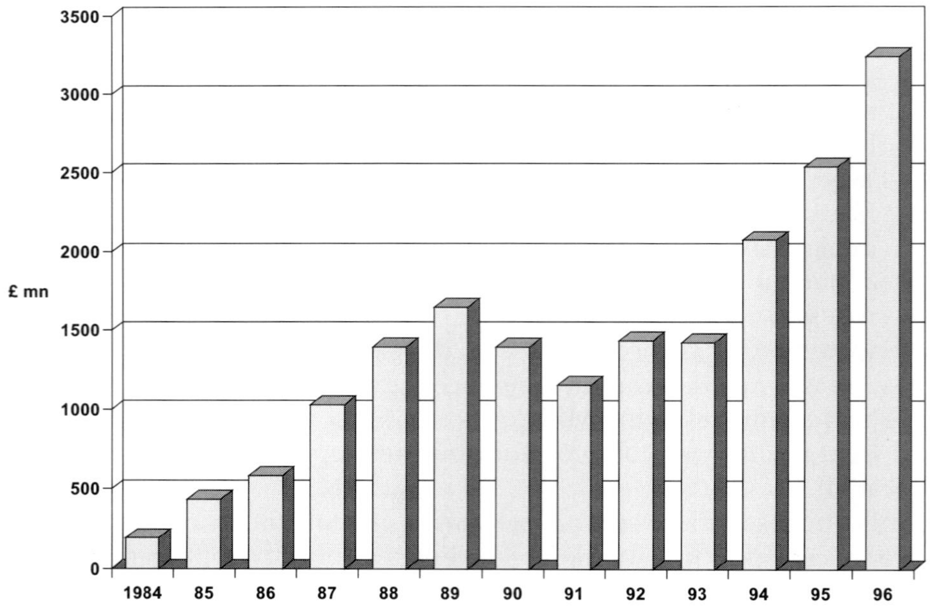

Source: BVCA Reports on Investment Activity

Figure 5.5.1 Funds invested by BVCA members

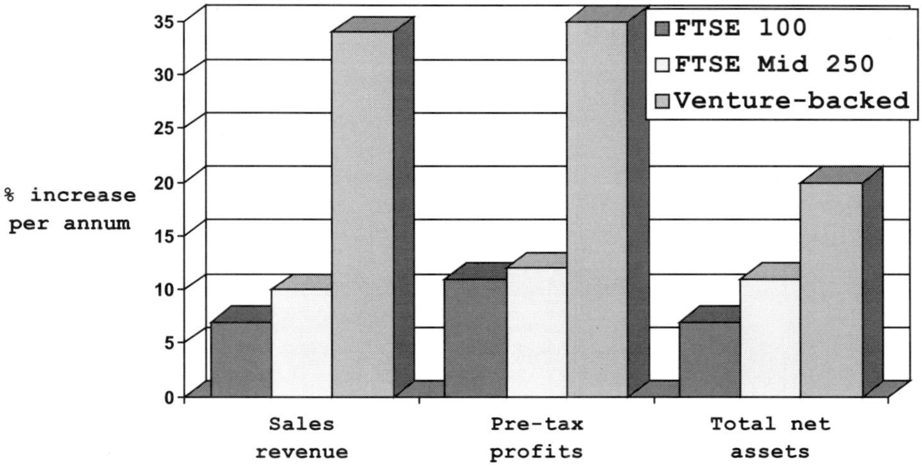

Figure 5.5.2 Venture capital helps companies outperform others

Venture Capital Helps Companies to Grow and Succeed Faster than Others

Almost 90 per cent of venture-backed companies in a recent BVCA/Coopers & Lybrand survey said that they would not have existed, or would have grown less rapidly, without venture capital. This contribution to growth was clearly quantified by the survey: on average venture-backed companies' sales rose by 34 per cent per annum (or five times faster than FTSE 100 companies), exports grew by 29 per cent per annum and investment increased by 28 per cent per annum.

The scope of venture capital's involvement in UK companies is significant. One million people in the UK are estimated to be employed by companies *currently* in receipt of venture capital. Over the four years to 1994/5, the number of people employed in venture-backed companies increased by 15 per cent per annum, against a national growth rate of less than 1 per cent per annum.

While the growth and success of these firms owes much to venture capital investment, the non-financial input by the venture capital firms is also a very important contributor. Of the venture-backed companies analysed in the survey, 88 per cent said that they had benefited from their venture capital backers providing more than just money. In particular, they rated highly venture capital firms' advice and guidance on strategic matters, financial

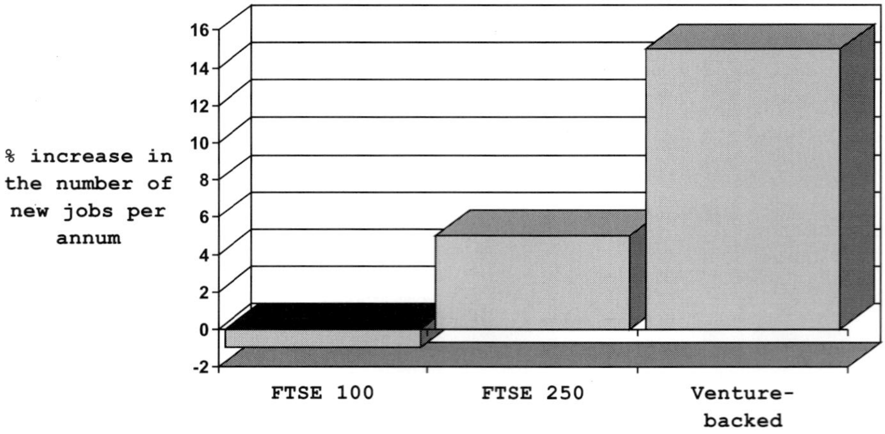

Figure 5.5.3 Venture-backed companies create more new jobs more rapidly than others

advice, their 'challenging the status quo', and acting as a 'sounding board for ideas'. This input was also seen as positive, rather than intrusive.

The **BVCA** represents every major source of UK venture capital, accounting for over 95 per cent of annual UK venture capital investment. It produces a range of publications to help companies find the right sources of venture capital, publishes regular research, runs training courses for its members and lobbies government on behalf of its members, entrepreneurs and unquoted UK companies.

Part 6

Building Competitive Organisations

Poor Basic Skills Cost Money

Every industry needs better-qualified and better skilled workers not just to increase productivity, but because the world of work is changing as technology advances and domestic and international competition intensifies. Basic skills are the essential building blocks for enhanced training and improved performance at work.

The Basic Skills Agency is the national development organisation for literacy, numeracy and related basic skills in England and Wales. The Agency's main aims are to raise the awareness of the importance of basic skills and to promote continuing improvement in basic skills.

Our research shows that almost 90% of jobs require good communication skills, including reading and writing and the majority of jobs require some basic maths. It is also clear that the level of demand for basic skills has increased substantially over the past five years.

We know effective basic skills training can play an important role in boosting company performance, making a quantifiable increase in production output and creating greater cohesion and flexibility within the workforce. As one training Project Director described;

> ***"...(we had not) anticipated such significant outcomes so quickly. It demonstrates that entire operations can be affected by key people, who have not been offered opportunities to develop the underpinning skills required for their jobs."***

However, despite these very positive outcomes, we also know the stark reality is that there are still too few opportunities for basic skills training. One of the most serious barriers to the development of basic skills training is the lack of awareness at senior management level of:

- the importance and relevance of basic skills competence amongst staff at all levels
- the extent of basic skills deficiencies in their current workforce
- the impact that changes in work organisation, quality systems and so on will have on skills requirements
- which agencies can offer support for the development of basic skills
- how basic skills can be delivered in non-traditional ways to suit shift patterns and production schedules and with minimum disruption.

There is an agenda here for all of us, whether employer, trainer, guidance worker or careers officer. Unless we ensure that every employee and every job applicant's basic skills are good enough, not just for the current job, but for employment in the next century, the UK will never compete successfully in the changing world market.

If you're interested in finding out more about how the Basic Skills Agency can help please call us on 0171 405 4017, fax us on 0171 440 6626, write to us at Commonwealth House, 1-19 New Oxford Street, London WC1A 1NU or send an e-mail to enquiries@basic-skills.co.uk.

6.1
Building Strength from the Top

Graham Alexander
Founder, Alexander

For emerging businesses wrestling with the challenges of growth, it is encouraging to know that, in one respect at least, they enjoy a fundamental advantage over their more established competitors. That advantage lies in the freedom they have to assemble — perhaps from scratch — a management board with the flexibility, leadership skills and vision to steer their development through the toughest conditions in business history.

The sheer speed and radical nature of change now transforming every facet of business life are making unprecedented demands on managers in general, and board members in particular. Responding effectively to the challenge of radical change demands a radical reassessment of the board's collective role and the qualities that its individual members must possess. Rewriting the rule-book on what makes an effective management board is now imperative. The problem is, no rule-book exists.

Without a clear definition of their roles, board members have traditionally focused — too often too closely — on the day-to-day operational detail of their business, frequently losing sight of the big picture and overriding strategic objectives. Today, however, the board's most important function is to instil their organisation with a clear sense of purpose and direction, bringing to bear the leadership skills required to make their vision a reality.

This is no small undertaking and demands a formidable degree of courage and commitment. To perform their role effectively, it is crucial that board members embrace the need for change collectively, unconditionally and wholeheartedly. They need to accept that constant change is a fact of business life that is here to stay. And in calling for change from the people they are leading, it is essential that board members act — and are seen to act — as role models and catalysts in equal measure.

Change is never easy, especially change that threatens the long-established roles and rituals typical of so many boards in the UK. Clearing away archaic practices to make way for a more flexible, agile corporate culture frequently demands a complete transformation of outlook and behaviours on an intensely personal level. Making those changes frequently requires the support and guidance of specialist consultancies with the expertise and experience to unlock the complexities of human behaviour and release the energy that comes from aligning people more effectively.

But having accepted the need for change, and having mapped out the steps required to achieve it, the board's next task is to define and impart the culture that it is now setting out to create. Increasingly, this process begins with a vision statement, a form of words that encapsulates the essence of an organisation's *raison d'être*. To produce results, a vision statement needs to be short, sharp and to the point. It needs to be directional rather than absolute, flexible and not prescriptive. Above all, it must inspire and convince employees that their individual success depends on pursuing a common goal.

At this point, precious momentum will be lost unless board members walk the talk, practise what they preach and align their own behaviour behind their vision. After all, if they are unable to demonstrate a personal commitment to the new order they are trying to create, how can they expect their staff to? Once again, putting theory into practice frequently means that board members have to change their behaviours and reset the habits of a working lifetime. That's tough, but not impossible. It may even mean accepting guidance, and sometimes criticism, from fellow board members.

This level of change is acutely demanding and calls for a rare mix of personal qualities that transcends professional skill and experience. A checklist of the essential qualities one would expect to find in a successful and effective board member would be headed by a single word: maturity. In other words, the ability to feel at ease with one's fellow board members, with one's employees — and with oneself.

From maturity flow other indispensable characteristics, among them:

- *Integrity* — a quaint term perhaps, but an indispensable quality. Integrity means giving your word, and meaning it; ensuring that you meet the standards that you have set for others.
- *Honesty and openness* — to admit problems and seek solutions. There is nothing more destructive than boards putting a brave face on a difficult situation to save its own members from embarrassment.
- *Flexibility* — to reappraise and reinvent the way you do business.
- *Confidence* — shot through with a dose of realism.

The personnel touch

Stephen Williams of Cedar International, the Human Resource consultants, sets out his views on the personnel issues that can be neglected when preparing for flotation.

AIM offers a very practical option for any company wishing to expand rapidly, but for whom listing on the main market may not be appropriate. Cedar International's experience has shown that these developing companies are usually highly entrepreneurial in their management style. They spend a great deal of time considering the financial, accounting and legal implications of seeking additional capital - including their admission to AIM - but often fail to take account for the other vital requirement for success: people.

This is where a properly developed human resources policy can help. Among the issues facing owners, directors and their advisers are succession, the need to strengthen operational management, the need to appoint proactive and relevant non-executive directors, and most importantly, the need to prepare a robust strategic plan.

Cash Injection

The potential for growth brought by an injection of capital raised on AIM has tremendous significance for the workforce as well as for the management and outside investor. It is often claimed that organisations succeed or fail largely as a result of their ability to manage resources. All too often the human resource is ignored.

Effective strategies for managing, motivating, training and retaining employees are always vital issues, never more so than when a fundamental change such as a move to public ownership is being undertaken. without the commitment, goodwill and enthusiasm of every member of an organisation, the future can be prejudiced.

The 'people' factor has for many years now been accepted as the single biggest reason for the failure of corporate change strategies, including many company mergers and acquisitions. Investigation has shown that failure is often based on the reactions and resistance of employees at all levels to a change being thrust upon them. The most frequently heard complaint is 'nobody talked to us about what was happening'. Any ambitious organisations with an eye to flotation on AIM must have a comprehensive human resource strategy integrated into the formal business plan.

Strategy

This strategy, which may take considerable time to devise and implement, must focus upon:

- Recruitment matters, defining business objectives and identifying the new skills required to achieve those objectives
- Development of existing staff through training and planned career management
- Communication and disclosure of all relevant information to key staff
- Renumeration geared to the new found status and profile of the company, acknowledging that the wider market will be only too pleased to obtain the services of your best performers if remuneration does not reflect contribution
- Retention of people by offering new challenges, and demonstrating a genuine interest in the aspiration of staff.

This strategy requires a commitment upon the part of management to the ideas of teamwork, openness and honesty. It also requires the creation of a cohesive culture often underpinned by external accreditation such as Investors in People and ISO9000.

All of these issues need to be clearly defined and expressed strategically to prepare the company for flotation on AIM. It would be a tragedy to fucus on the financial and legal aspects of AIM alone. By considering the people factor, the future viability of any new AIM company should be enhanced significantly.

For further information regarding the services of Cedar International, please contact Helen Pitcher or Leslie Newell on 0171 831 8383.

Cedar International is a full service HR consultancy offering support to corporate clients in executive recruitment, training and management development, career management and executive coaching Cedar is a member of IMSA, an international network of owner managed consultancies.

- *Toughness* — to cope with quite extraordinary levels of stress brought about by unprecedented change.
- *Energy and persistence* — to set the agenda and realise its objectives.

Other qualities are more complex, even paradoxical. The most effective board members are frequently *uncompromising compromisers*. In other words, they will argue their own case passionately and vehemently. But if the debate goes against them, they are then prepared to throw their full weight behind the board's collective decision.

At the same time, there is a great deal to be said for the *maverick* board member — an individual capable of posing the awkward question, thinking the unthinkable and slaughtering sacred cows.

Finally, no debate over the role of the board would be complete without briefly mentioning two vital points. First, the relationship between the chairman and chief executive. The bond between these two individuals has an immeasurable impact on the health and vitality of the body corporate. So clear, strictly defined job descriptions are essential to avoiding overlaps, misunderstandings and even conflict. It is equally important to define as precisely as possible the way the chairman and chief executive will work together in practice — their *modus operandi*.

Secondly, the question of non-executive directors requires careful consideration. They have one of the most delicate and complex tasks on the board. While non-executives have no direct control over the decision-making process, they have a crucial role to play in influencing it. Exercising that influence effectively depends to a great extent on the strength of their interpersonal skills. The importance of investing time and money in nurturing those skills — and the management skills of their fellow board members — should never be underestimated.

Graham Alexander is founder of **Alexander**, recognised leader in the field of organisational transformation. Alexander works with senior managers in major companies worldwide to bring about demonstrable and sustainable change. The company specialises in helping organisations to achieve lasting performance improvements by releasing their people's potential to meet strategic needs.

YOUR Next Career Move!

CONSIDER WHERE A MASTER OF ARTS IN BUSINESS MANAGEMENT COULD TAKE YOU

If you are a business owner

or

someone with managerial experience

or

have a suitable Degree

Now it's your opportunity to seriously consider our 28 month postgraduate MA in Business Management

It's good for you its good for your company...

- Modern distance learning techniques mean there will be minimum disruption to your company
- You will undertake and implement a project of strategic importance to your company and draw in the resources and expertise of the University's staff to complete it, helping you to utilise the raw skills you will acquire throughout the course.
- At the end of all you hard work you will receive a useful qualification from a well respected, traditional University

For further information contact: Wendy Wedmore, Programme Manager, InFinet, University of Wales, Bangor, Gwynedd LL57 2DG
Direct Tel: (01248) 382167 Fax: (01248) 383769
E-mail: abs035@bangor.ac.uk

inFinet

"University of Wales, Bangor, dedicated to academic excellence"

inFinet

BUSINESS GROWTH BY DISTANCE LEARNING

The Institute for Financial Education and Training (inFinET)

"I'm a widget maker not a manager. What's more I'm a successful widget maker. I had a brilliant Idea, a great product and I've sold millions of widgets". Does it sound familiar? The successful entrepreneur or middle manager who reaches a point in the growth of his/her business where suddenly he/she is expected to have all sorts of management skills and knowledge without ever having had a chance to acquire that knowledge or those skills through training. And how do you find the time away from work to attend lengthy courses when you know the work is just piling up back at the ranch?

The answer is a distance learning degree where you can study in your own home or office with minimal disruption to your working life. The University of Wales, Bangor, has developed the postgraduate, distance-learning Master of Arts in Business Management (MABM) which caters for the practising manager who may not have a first degree. The MaBM is generalist programme where the emphasis is on practical application in the workplace through the project which in turn is assisted by the knowledge gained from the academic modules. Project supervisors, chosen for their background in the appropriate sector, advise and guide you on the project. You organisation benefits from having a strategically importance piece of work completed by a knowledgeable owner/employee without the need to employ expensive external consultants but with added input from the Supervisors.

Some current projects include: Strategic maintenance issues in the process industry; business development options for a commercial construction operation; development opportunities in the private care sector; survival strategies for small charities. One current student, a manager of a small, commercial construction company put into effect marketing techniques acquires in the first semester of the degree and saw the benefits immediately. Another student, a Partner in a nursing Home chain, changed the basis of the organisation's staff appraisal system whilst studying Management and Organisational Behaviour - again with immediate perceptible benefits.

If you wish to find out how InFinET could help you and your business grow, please contact Wendy Wedmore, Programme Manager, InFinET, University of Wales Bangor, Gwynedd LL57 2DG. Direct Tel: 01248 382167, Fax: 01248 383769 e-mail abs035@bangor.ac.uk.

6.2

Flexible Work Arrangements in a Growing Business

Peter A Reilly
Senior Research Fellow,
Institute for Employment Studies

With all the talk about the benefits of flexible labour, it must be hard for businesses to resist the fashion. Yet the political rhetoric has lumped its different forms together, as if they provided a single solution to a single problem. Instead, managers surely want to know what will meet *their* business objectives. So in this chapter we aim to clarify the range of flexible options and the advantages and disadvantages of each.

Benefits

In general, the benefits you should derive from flexible work arrangements include:

- getting a better match between labour input and work demand;
- providing protection against changing staffing needs;
- acquiring specialist skills;
- reducing costs;
- improving productivity;

- meeting the preferences of employees/ or potential recruits;
- improving the quality of service or output.

What is Flexibility?

However, not all types of flexible work arrangement meet these benefits equally. A simple way of understanding is to group them into distinct, though overlapping, categories:

- functional flexibility;
- temporal flexibility;
- numerical flexibility;
- locational flexibility.

We will look at each in turn.

Functional Flexibility

This involves giving employers the freedom to move labour as required without the constraint of artificial demarcation lines, be they due to union rules or functional protectionism. Examples include making craftsmen and production workers in manufacturing industry multiskilled or, through one-stop-shop customer service arrangements, allowing agents to deal with the full range of client queries. Functional flexibility by achieving a more effective deployment of labour should improve productivity, lower costs and improve service.

On the downside, there are investment costs in training and often in new technology. Organising multiskilling can be time consuming, as job rotation is required to keep employees familiar with each aspect of their work, otherwise breadth leads to lost depth of skill.

Temporal Flexibility

This covers different ways of varying working hours. It should allow a better match between service or production schedules and employee input, thereby reducing costs and improving productivity. It also can be a selling point to employees seeking to meet domestic and work requirements. However, it can involve the complex administration of work rotas and time-off entitlements, and overtime can be expensive if it is inefficiently managed.

The choice of arrangement will reflect how structured the work patterns are (see Table 6.2.1).

Table 6.2.1 Temporal flexibility

Structured		Unstructured
Shift working	Flexitime	Overtime
Part-time working	Annual hours'contracts	Zero hours' contracts
Flexible working weeks		
Term-time contracts		

Definitions of the less common terms:

- *Flexitime* = variation in starting and finishing time within an overall accounting period of usually a month, but flexibility is often restricted to variation only outside core hours.
- *Flexible working weeks* = compression of normal hours into, for example, a nine-day fortnight or a four-and-a-half-day week to allow early closure, usually on Fridays.
- *Term-time contracts* = working only during school/college terms.
- *Annual hours contracts* = flexibility to vary actual working time within annual total contractual hours. This can be within a set pattern of work, but with seasonal or greater variation, and can allow extra staff to be called in if required.
- *Zero hours* = although there is a contract of employment no hours are specified, so the employee only works when asked to by the employer.

Numerical Flexibility

Flexibility in contractual arrangements (see below) allows the manager to vary the number of workers over both the short and long term to meet work requirements in an easier way than if they were all directly employed on 'regular' contracts which terminate only with retirement or through dismissal (see Table 6.2.2).

The cost paid for this flexibility may come from the fact that temporary workers are reputed to be less reliable and productive than 'permanent' employees, and have a higher turnover. This may lead to quality problems and a larger training bill. And when using agencies or consultants there is usually a premium to pay, although how big this is depends on relative wage rates.

Table 6.2.2 Numerical flexibility

Type	Status	Main use
Fixed-term contact	E	To complete a specific task or project or where future labour demand is uncertain
Temporary staff	E	To meet short-term work peaks, longer-term cover for maternity or illness or for seasonal work
Agency-supplied staff	O	To meet short-term cover, eg for holiday or sick leave or for seasonal work
Consultants/freelancers	S	To acquire specialist skills or expertise, or deal with one-off tasks

Key: E = employed by own organisation; O = employed by another organisation; S = self-employed

Numerical flexibility can go further through outsourcing an activity (catering, cleaning, maintenance etc) to a third party to supply the labour and manage the task on your behalf. There are a number of pros and cons to this (see Table 6.2.3).

Table 6.2.3 Outsourcing

Benefits	Risks
Cost savings	Unexpected costs
Better service	Service failures
Focus on core activities	Loss of control over activity
Better scheduling of service	Contractual inflexibility
Reduced exposure to regulations	Exploitation on cost/quality
Headcount cuts	Administrative burden

The balance between these opposites depends in part on what is being outsourced — how simple and easily packaged the operation is — but also on how well managed any contractual arrangements are.

Table 6.2.4 Determining the right flexible option

Drivers for flexibility	Possible solution		Benefits		Problems/risks
Reducing costs	Outsourcing	→	Efficiency of supplier	→	Contact monitoring
	Variable hours patterns	→	Aligned with work patterns	→	Complex administration
	Temps/agency labour	→	Lower wages	→	Questionable commitment
	Remote working	→	Reduced overheads	→	Problematic communication
Improving quality/ service	Outsourcing	→	Expertise of supplier	→	Loss of control
	Variable hours patterns	→	Better scheduling	→	Complex administration
	Cross-functional working	→	Seamless service	→	Expertise lacks depth
Increasing productivity	Multiskilling	→	End to demarcation	→	Loss of knowledge/skill
	Variable hours patterns	→	Aligned with work patterns	→	Complex administration
Hedging against change	Outsourcing	→	Termination of contract	→	Cost of early termination
	Temps/agency/contractors	→	Ease of manning up/down	→	Higher staff turnover
Meeting supply needs	Variable hours patterns	→	Fits employee domestic needs	→	Complex management
	Remote working	→	Fits employee lifestyle	→	Questionable productivity
	Temping	→	Gives variety of work	→	Questionable loyalty

Note: This is obviously simplified, especially with respect to the benefits and problems of the possible solutions.

Locational Flexibility

Locational flexibility describes the various ways of using employees outside the normal workplace, from mobile through partly home based, to full outworkers or teleworkers. The term is also often extended to cover those working in relocated back offices.

It has the advantage of using workers as needed and reducing overhead costs. However, investment, especially in computing equipment, is usually required and management costs may be higher. Some managers fear the loss of control over their workforce and the deterioration in communications if employees are not physically present at work. And, despite the benefits to employees of avoiding commuting, without the social interaction of work productivity and effectiveness may decline.

Conclusions

To get the most out of flexible work arrangements employers should:

- be clear about their objectives;
- do cost/benefit analysis of any proposals;
- guard against producing new rigidities;
- aim for win/win situations with employees;
- watch the legislative and labour market situations.

A broadbrush summary of some of the available options is set out in Table 6.2.4.

The Insititute for Employment Studies is an independent, not-for-profit organisation engaged in research and consultancy on a wide variety of humanresource issues.

Prior to joining IES, **Peter Reilly** worked for a number of years with Shell in a variety of human resource roles.

6.3
How to Create a High-Performance Team

Lynne Smitham
Teamwork

Building a team is serious stuff — it takes work, but the rewards can be tremendous. Teams can be mediocre or they can outperform your wildest expectations in terms of innovation, productivity and quality. Most managers recognise the enormous performance potential in a team. But they often mistakenly believe that once the team has been constructed it will miraculously perform by merely working together. Some do, but most don't! To create a high-performance team you need to take regular time out together to establish and agree the following basics.

A Crystal-Clear Team Vision or Purpose

Most teams don't have a vision. Many managers assume that if they have communicated the purpose to a team, then it must be known. Beware! Telling people something and them fully understanding or personally committing to it are two very different things. It's impossible to get everyone pulling in the same direction if there is no common view of what they are trying to achieve. Ask each person in your team to describe the purpose — you may be surprised!

A common purpose unifies people, it creates commitment and sharing of skills, knowledge and resources. To do this you must get team members together regularly to explore fully and agree what it means to achieve the goal in terms of required roles, skills, resources, implementation and obstacles.

The Basic Skills Agency

The Basic Skills Agency is the national development organisation for literacy, numeracy and related basic skills in England and Wales.

Our main aim is to promote continuing improvement in basic skills.

The Agency is committed to offering support for the development of effective basic skills programmes for children and adults by providing advice and materials for teachers of basic skills.

If you would like to find out more about the range of help that the Basic Skills Agency offers, then call us on 0171-405 4017 or write to us at the following address:

The Basic Skills Agency
Commonwealth House
1-19 New Oxford Street
London WC1A 1NU

Tel: 0171-405 4017
Fax: 0171-440 6626
www.basic-skills.co.uk

People must feel as if they have an intimate understanding of all the issues concerned. Be prepared to change the purpose radically — or even dump it when it no longer adds real value to your customer or your company. You can't ask people to apply their best to something that has no relevance.

Measurable Goals, Targets and Milestones

These are the specific, measurable targets, deliverables and milestones that the team will achieve to reach the ultimate purpose. Team members must decide how and when they will measure success in these goals or their commitment will be missing. It is important to define both qualitative and quantitative measures for each goal. In companies the achievement of a goal is often measured digitally — either the goal was achieved or it was not. Having qualitative measures helps the team get value from the process as well as the end point. This keeps their focus and motivation high.

Mutual Trust Created through an Agreed Approach

Trust is an essential ingredient in a high-performance team. Where trust is high communication is more open, conflict is handled in a constructive way and people recognise and respect each other's positive intentions. If something goes wrong it is not seen as a conspiracy — just a mistake! Trust is a characteristic that develops over time as people get to know each other and begin to understand how best to work together. In some teams it never develops.

When people have different standards and approaches, misunderstandings arise and frustration and cynicism can undermine efforts. The basis of trust is knowing what other people stand for, their values and working styles. It needs more than time together in the pub to nurture real trust. You must take the necessary time to agree a common approach to how the team will work together day to day. This can include whether meetings will start on time; whether deadlines will be met; how decisions will be made; who will do what; who is responsible for what; what will happen when conflict occurs; how confidentiality will be maintained. There are no right or wrong ways for the team to work — only ways that people agree and feel committed to uphold.

Best Use of Skills, Knowledge and Resources

This is about having the right skills available within the team and getting people to share their knowledge and resources in order to achieve the goal.

NOT ALL TRAINING IS ABOUT PUMPING IRON

The strength of Edexcel's qualifications is recognised throughout the business world. The weight behind the Edexcel name comes from the merger last year of BTEC and the University of London Examination and Assessment Council.

Our range of qualifications covers all sectors and all levels from tailor-made certificates and diplomas for individual organisations, to modern apprenticeships and national vocational qualifications.

EDEXCEL FOUNDATION

So whether you are recruiting new staff or need to train your own personnel, use Edexcel as the benchmark.

ED EXCEL

For more information, contact our Customer Enquiry Unit on 0171 393 4500 (tel) or 0171 393 4501 (fax) or write to them at Edexcel Foundation, Stewart House, Russell Square, London WC1B 5DN.

BTEC London EXAMINATIONS

EDEXCEL FOUNDATION INCORPORATES BTEC AND LONDON EXAMINATIONS

Edexcel Foundation is a registered charity. London Examinations is a trademark of the University of London.

It is unusual to be able to put a team together with all the required skills in place. When your team lacks skills, create a clear focus on learning. Do this by identifying the key skills needed to achieve the goal and assessing people's current skill levels. Then encourage them to plan their development step by step, with clear goals and milestones.

Make it easy for people to apply their new skills by changing work processes if necessary. Develop a culture within the team of 'no failure — only feedback' by regularly getting the team to review their performance with the emphasis on learning and improvement rather than blame.

To help the team to gain most from each other's expertise, everyone must fully understand their role and responsibilities in the process. Each person needs to bring a recognised distinctive competence to the party. When someone has no differentiating skills or expertise, it is almost impossible for them to carve out a meaningful role in the team. Be prepared to switch team members around to make more use of their skills or to remove them if their skills are superfluous to the purpose.

The work process must also enable people to learn from each other's experience and skills. So encourage people to discuss issues, speak up when things go wrong, work on things together, brainstorm problems in groups of two or three, have regular updates so that communication channels stay open.

Strong and Flexible Leadership

The biggest challenge for most managers in building the team is in changing their own working style. Traditional roles of managers have emphasised ordering change from above without sharing real power throughout the company. A team needs leadership, not management, and these are two very different roles.

All team members need to take an equal role in shaping the team's destiny. They must define the goals, evaluate their own performance, solve their own problems. They must identify areas where innovation, productivity and quality can be higher. As a result the leader becomes the enabler, communicator, coach, mentor, supporter, conflict mediator, visionary, influencer and negotiator. This takes highly developed interpersonal and influencing skills and a preparedness to devolve power and decision making — which sometimes feels risky.

In well-developed teams leadership will reside in the most appropriate person to deal with the current situation — usually the person with the greatest expertise in this phase of the task. This means that the formal leader will need to step aside and let a team member take over, albeit temporarily. For a leader with a tender ego this can be difficult!

WE'LL HELP YOU GET BETTER AT WHAT YOU DO

CULTURE CHANGE
TEAMWORK
STRESS SOLUTIONS
PEAK PERFORMANCE

Joyce Chandler Consulting
appreciating matters

We make change work for you, by reducing stress, boosting morale and addressing corporate culture issues. Our tailored approach fosters peak performance, greater productivity, enhance teamwork and helps create a culture supportive of new organisation directions.

Our executive coaching, leadership development programmes and expertise in performance consulting support you in dealing with the human side of mergers, acquisitions, restructuring and alliances.

Make Joyce Chandler Consulting a part of your team. Call us!

Joyce Chandler Consulting, Organisation & Personal Development Specialists
4 Latham Road, Middlesex TW1 1BN
Tel: 0181 891 5503 Fax: 0181 891 0844 Email: 101636.2607@compuserve.com

DOES *NLP* REALLY WORK IN ORGANISATIONS?

Clients come to us with unique complex high-risk problems. They want someone to work <u>with</u> them to develop and implement meaningful medium and long term results.

Mr. X, a client of ours, is the Marketing Director in a company that had recently gone through huge change. This change had left many of the people within the organisation very demotivated. A majority of these people formed the client-based of his department.

The main problem Mr X and his team experienced was HOW to stay in rapport with the despondency and gloom while showing themselves to be a lively go-ahead department?

By exploring the generalisations people elsewhere in the organisation were making and by challenging phrase, such as "this will never work" or "everyone's going to leave", we were able to help the marketing department find ways to free up thinking; theirs and those of their 'client' departments. We did this by introducing and applying the tried and tested tools of Neuro-linguistic Programming (NLP).

The Marketing Director with his team learned to maintain rapport and were able to challenge some assumptions and beliefs about the change.

A measure of our combined success? "Our company's doing well. "We (the marketing department) are often described as bringing a 'breath of fresh air' to those we work with" is a comment Mr. X beamed on the last occasion we met.

If you are curious to learn more about NLP, the autumn and spring *SYNERGY WITHIN...*
open public training and leadership seminars and our performance consultancy services.
*Call **Joyce Chandler**, Practice Director on 0181 891 5503.*

Excel in Business with NLP

Just ask yourself how valuable it would be to your business if you were to increase customer satisfaction by 20% in less than 3 months?
This is exactly what the export and distribution department of Glaxo Wellcome achieved working with Excel Communications (HRD) Ltd utilising the benefits of NLP.
Maybe you have admired someone else's skills or talents and wanted to be as accomplished?
Originating over 20 years ago, NLP gives us the techniques to be able to "model" or replicate excellence, it provides an exciting major breakthrough in understanding how we as humans function. Now we know more about how we make sense of the world, how language affects our experiences and how we are programmed or organised either for failure or success. We investigated NLP twelve years ago and immediately saw the positive commercial implications once we had made it user friendly for the business world. After all, for the first time we now have proven methodologies for change, something all businesses want. Nowadays, the majority of companies recognise that the growth of their business is totally dependant on the continual growth and the development of their people. As has been stated many times, "learning may be your only competitive advantage". Excel Communications are working with many blue chip, medium and small organisations both in the private and public sector generating growth using leading edge methods including NLP. These may be major change initiatives, bespoke projects or specifics such as negotiating, presenting, teamwork, selling, assertiveness or developing the developers workshops. We also run an internationally certified NLP Business Practitioner programme. In Glaxo Wellcome, the NLP approach we took to achieve the outstanding results was to model the behavioural competencies required for successful customer service and efficient distribution. This meant everyone could learn to perform in these given areas and, in fact, 98% of the staff achieved their performance targets on time.
Perhaps time for development is an issue?
To address this for the Glaxo Wellcome project, excel designed and delivered short training sessions on site, hence, limiting the amount of time away from the job and continually reinforcing the learning.
How would you like to increase your market share by 254%?
This is exactly how much a major credit card company in the states was able to increase a customers use of their card over alternative cards when they trained some of their telephone operatives in NLP skills in a closely evaluated pilot. They also rescued customer attrition rates by 67% and queries were dealt with in a single call rather than the several calls required by the non-NLP trained staff. Another Excel NLP success was with a medium sized company whose revenue doubled to £4 million in the 2 years we worked with their management team. They wanted to rapidly expand their market share, increase productivity and move from a very autocratic management style to an empowered workforce. All this was achieved and the average age of the workforce was 24. There just wasn't the time or experience available to support the growth of the business without the use of NLP. So the final question is, can you afford the time and business lost by not giving yourself, your people and your business the advantage of the most advanced, proven methodologies to increase performance and success? NLP is the fastest growing and most exciting contributor to human development. It can seriously improve your motivation, profits and success. To find out more, call Clive Garton on 01628 488854 or e-mail us at excel@excelcom.demon.co.uk.

Barclays, GlaxoWellcome, Dun & Bradstreet, Reuters, etc

The competitive advantage that keeps you ahead of the game

What helps these companies Excel.

One thing all these companies have in common is they all use Excel Communications as a supplier of choice in developing the performance of their people.

Your company may be smaller or in a completely different market. However, our common link is we all want to grow and be even more successful.

Whether your organisational strategy relies on individual and team performance, or maintaining competitive advantage through building business relationships, we should be talking about how, through the use of Applied Neuro-Linguistic Programming (ANLP) our two companies can work effectively towards your corporate goals.

With 13 years partnering our clients worldwide, taking advantage of Excel's ANLP experience could be the most significant move you make towards even greater business excellence.

Take the opportunity today, speak to one of our experienced trainers or consultants. It costs nothing to find out more.

EXCEL COMMUNICATIONS (HRD) LTD
45 West Street, Marlow, Bucks SL7 2LS
Tel: 01628 488854 Fax: 01628 488864
E-mail: excel@excelcom.demon.co.uk

Most teams will only make the time to establish the above factors when things start to go wrong. By then time, energy and commitment have been wasted. Make sure that your team hits the deck running, take time when you win the contract or open the department thoroughly to explore and agree the above involving the whole team. Then make sure that you review this together regularly. It is well worth the investment in time, unless of course you are satisfied with mediocrity.

Teamwork is a management development consultancy specialising in helping teams and individuals develop the skills and work practices to achieve exceptional business performance.

UNLOCK THE POTENTIAL . . .

WORLD CLASS

© INTERNATIONAL

World Class Training Programmes for companies with World Class objectives in mind

- ***Don't restrict your training to job skills***
- ***Give your company the edge***
- ***Release the power of the employee***
- ***Help to change the way you work in your company***

Empower the people, change the culture, drive bottom line and customer focused benefits *together!*

. . . do you really want to get there ?

Dramatic improvements in client operational performance is the goal of World Class International, one of Europe's leading Management Consultancies based in South Hampshire. Our Consultants and Trainers work from offices in the UK, Mainland Europe, USA and South Africa and serve clients from all business sectors including one third of the UK's Times Top 100 companies.

Our Consultancy services are firmly focused on delivering measurable and sustained improvements in both customer and shareholder value for our clients. Technical expertise includes:

- Performance Benchmarking;
- World Class Manufacturing;
- Supply Chain Management;
- Business Process Re-design;
- Information Systems Development;
- Activity Based Costing.

In all of these techniques we can provide change project management as well as client team facilitation and training.

Training forms an integral part of all our change management programmes. Without culture change and employee ownership of new ways of working it is unlikely that any improvements in the business will be sustained. Let us help you move from the current 'flavour of the month' initiative to a culture of ongoing continuous improvement.

For further details please contact Philip Lund, Business Development Director at:

World Class International Ltd.

Technology House, Parklands Business Park, Forest Road, Denmead, Hampshire PO7 6XP

Tel: +44(0)1705 268133 Fax: +44(0)1705 268160 CompuServe: 101540,1515

6.4

Hobsons Publishing plc: A Success Built around the Needs of Employees

Chris Letcher
Managing Director Education Group, Hobsons Publishing plc

In the last six years, Hobsons Publishing Education Group has grown dramatically in both revenue and profit terms. Staff numbers have increased from 25 to more than 125. What is the blueprint for our success?

The key to growth, we believe, is our attitude towards our employees. Our philosophy is to recruit bright, young, ambitious people and then provide them with an environment which allows them to advance, rewarding them accordingly. The company is fuelled by the energy and true dynamism of a large collection of very bright young people. The business challenge is to provide the support and infrastructure that make continuing development possible.

Our policy is to recruit new graduates with no previous publishing experience, and to promote from within. We operate a meritocracy. This means that we have no 'outsiders' coming in to senior positions at Hobsons — or other positions, for that matter. In fact, the only person in the division with experience at any other publishing company is me!

The ramifications of this policy are essentially twofold. All our managers have started in the same place and they have a proven commitment to the company and its culture. This means heavy investment in structured and ongoing training. Many companies these days pay only lip service to the idea of staff development. We pay, I believe, considerably more than lip service. Many, if not most, organisations, proclaim that they are 'customer driven'. However, in shaping the organisation to the needs of the customer, a successful company also responds to the needs of the *employees*, given that they are the most valuable resource a company is likely to have.

The needs of Hobsons employees are met in a variety of ways. The most valuable, I believe, is through consistent staff development. We do not have staff development 'programmes' — our approach is focused on the development of each individual, relating to his or her current position and future in the company. Although we have grown rapidly in the last 10 years, both financially and in staff numbers, we have paid considerable attention to ensuring that our existing employees develop, *in their eyes*, along with the success of the organisation as a whole.

What does this mean in real terms? Most significantly, it means a heavy and ongoing investment in training. We currently spend an average of £1500 a year per employee on training, which includes a minimum of 10 'formal' training days per year in an employee's first year with us (in addition to on-the-job training), and a minimum of six days per year thereafter.

Because we place such absolute importance on training, we had to spend considerable time finding a suitable company to work with us, understand our corporate culture, and tailor and develop their programmes to our business needs. Most training companies will say they do this. Few, in our experience, do. The company we use now is an outside contractor virtually on the payroll. Its staff spend an inordinate amount of time on our premises, monitoring and training individuals and groups. They have become an integral part of our business.

Of course, these tactics are relatively high risk. We introduce enthusiastic, relatively inexperienced yet intelligent people to dynamic and intense situations. Several young managers (aged 25 or 26) in the Education Group control budgets of over £2 million after only three years with the company. Why does our strategy work?

It works primarily because of our philosophy. We believe that the benefits overall far outweigh the risks. If you recruit clever and vigorous people, you have to let them use their brains. As an example, one of our publishers was recently tasked with launching a new title in Hong Kong, which involved securing a considerable amount of revenue in a new market. We have several successful publications covering graduate recruitment in other areas, but Hong Kong was virgin territory for us. The received wisdom was that we should employ an outsider who was an expatriate with substantial knowledge of the area. We ignored this and sent the *de facto* publisher, who had been with Hobsons for three years since leaving university. She obtained the necessary revenue during a one-week, first-off visit.

For such a strategy to be successful, management must be flexible in its attitude to employees, accepting that people develop in different ways and at different speeds. Our view is that the success of Hobsons depends on using the strengths of employees. If someone is not succeeding in one position, we will help them switch to another. We have just received our second Investors in People Award.

However, growth needs to be focused on a goal, otherwise you will have anarchy. Senior management provide support and guidelines. And around a pliable structure, which gives relatively inexperienced managers a high degree of very real power, we impose rigid, sometimes apparently petty disciplines. Staff are always encouraged to 'push the walls further away' — indeed, we believe that this is a prerequisite for personal and hence corporate growth. But the walls are still there to be expanded. So, for example, we have quite strict rules about smart dress at all times, timekeeping and human values — we won't employ people who 'dump' on support staff.

We also have a highly defined system of promotion. At each level, the objectives, job description, training and rewards are clearly set out. On a hierarchical ladder, the best climb faster and higher, driving company growth and success.

The organisation is structured essentially as discrete 'businesses', run by highly motivated, focused and well-trained young people. These businesses operate in associated areas and draw on central resources within a clearly defined, hierarchical structure.

The Education Division is divided into the school leaver and graduate market. Each team is headed by a Publishing Director, responsible for the bottom-line profitability of his or her group. Both Publishing Directors have accumulated ten years' experience of the market. The two large teams are sub-divided into ten smaller publishing groups, focusing on narrower areas such as UK Graduate Recruitment. These groups are managed by publishers and trainee publishers, responsible for around eight salespeople and six or seven editorial staff.

I suppose that it seems blindingly obvious that companies should have a strategy which focuses on people. But in my experience, many do not. Our business in future will become more complex, as will many other businesses. We will do more electronically, more overseas. Therefore we need teams of people who are able to deal with complexity. This will shape our recruitment requirements, our training and staff development programmes, and our remuneration structure.

We believe that structure, discipline and good management will produce products appropriate for the marketplace. Our goal is to maintain growth by continuing to concentrate on the development of our prize asset — our people. No matter how it is structured, no matter how many excellent systems are in place, no company will be successful without the right people.

Hobsons Publishing plc formed in 1974 as the publishing arm of the Careers Research and Advisory Centre, was floated on the Stock Exchange in 1987. It is now part of the Daily Mail and General Trust. Hobsons employs more than 200 people at its UK offices and publishes a range of directories, guides, magazines and multimedia products.

BRUNEL
UNIVERSITY

Brunel University exists to provide high quality education and research of use to the community

DEGREES IN BUSINESS ADMINISTRATION FOR WORKING MANAGERS

BSc (Hons) in Business Administration
by Distance Learning

A rare opportunity to remain in employment while studying for an Honours Degree specifically focused on contemporary management issues. This course provides a comprehensive exploration of the main management disciplines within a flexible, modular programme over a four year period.

- A number of optional modules in addition to core subjects
- Two three-day residential schools develop essential interpersonal and groupwork skills
- Culminates in a substantial business research project
- Start dates December and January
- Modules may be studied on an individual basis
- Exemptions from certain modules may be available to holders of approved business qualifications

For further information contact:
Jackie Strange, Distance Learning Course Manager, Division of Management Studies, Brunel University, Uxbridge, Middx UB8 3PH.
Tel: 01895 203159, Fax: 01895 203149,
Email: Jackie.Strange@brunel ac.uk

The Brunel MBA

Multi-modal: full-time, part-time and distance learning with the option of switching mode if personal circumstances alter. The Brunel MBA is a flexible modular programme designed to enhance your value as a manager in an increasingly competitive and uncertain job market. The course comprises:

- A core section on Foundations of Business Management, taken by all students
- Specialist pathways in Information Management or Managing for the Future, with further specialisms added progressively
- A significant research project related to your chosen option

Applicants will normally be graduates, with at least two years, post-qualification, work experience at middle to senior management level prior to starting the programme.

For further information contact:
Pauline Seston, MBA Administrator, The Brunel MBA, Brunel University, Uxbridge, Middx UB8 3PH.
Tel: 01895 203064, Fax: 01895 203149,
Email: Pauline.Seston@brunel ac.uk

BRUNEL UNIVERSITY

During its 30 years as a University, Brunel has become renowned for its combination of academic learning and practical application across its entire range of courses. With a strong tradition in technology and the sciences, the University has grown steadily in both size and reputation, and is now recognised as a major force in higher education. It has four campuses – at Uxbridge, Runnymede, Twickenham and Osterley. The School of Business and Management Studies is based at the main Uxbridge campus on the western edge of London, within easy reach of Heathrow airport, the M40, M4 and M25.

Brunel has always fostered extensive and rewarding links with industry and commerce, resulting in courses and research which are highly relevant to the needs of the business world. In the last decade the University has topped the *Financial Times* graduate employment league six times. Its active research programmes ensure continual updating and adaptation of teaching to match today's constantly changing technological and business environment. The Brunel MBA and the distance-learning BSc in Business Administration are designed to enable working managers to improve their business knowledge, skills and understanding in the context of programmes which aim to meet both career and personal development needs.

The School of Business and Management Studies incorporates the Graduate Business School responsible for the Brunel MBA, the Division of Management Studies which offers a range of undergraduate single and joint Honours degrees, including, since 1994, the unique distance-learning BSc in Business Administration, and the Division of Business Studies responsible for a variety of Diploma, Degree and Professional Development courses. The School also offers Masters and Doctoral programmes on a part- or full-time basis for graduates wishing to develop further their interest in particular management areas. Specialist pathways in the Brunel MBA programme are provided initially by the School of Business and Management Studies and the Department of Information Systems and Computing. New specialisms will be added progressively, drawing specialist teaching support from across the whole of the University's broad spectrum of expertise.

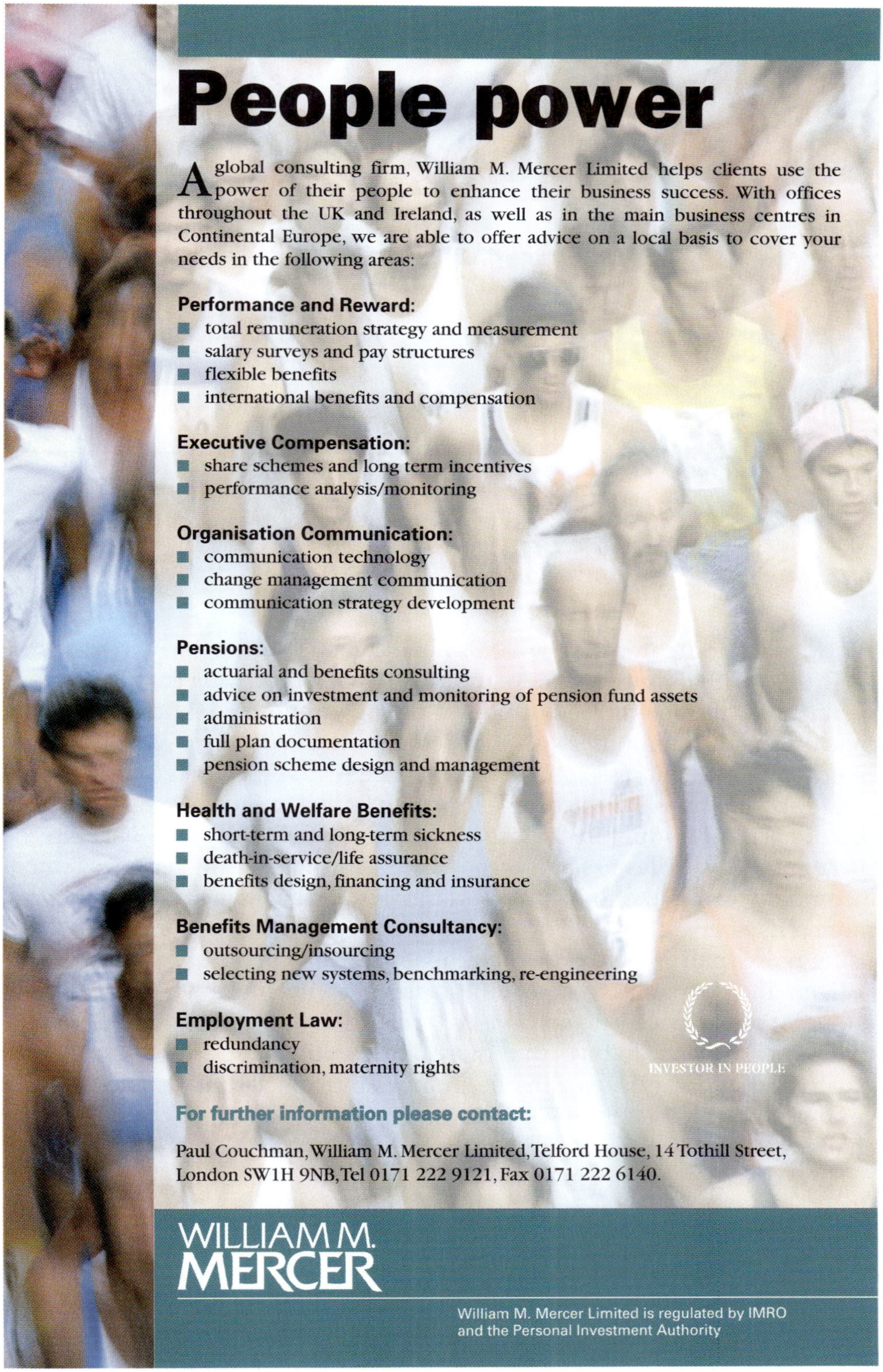
People power
A global consulting firm, William M. Mercer Limited helps clients use the power of their people to enhance their business success. With offices throughout the UK and Ireland, as well as in the main business centres in Continental Europe, we are able to offer advice on a local basis to cover your needs in the following areas:
Performance and Reward:
total remuneration strategy and measurement
salary surveys and pay structures
flexible benefits
international benefits and compensation
Executive Compensation:
share schemes and long term incentives
performance analysis/monitoring
Organisation Communication:
communication technology
change management communication
communication strategy development
Pensions:
actuarial and benefits consulting
advice on investment and monitoring of pension fund assets
administration
full plan documentation
pension scheme design and management
Health and Welfare Benefits:
short-term and long-term sickness
death-in-service/life assurance
benefits design, financing and insurance
Benefits Management Consultancy:
outsourcing/insourcing
selecting new systems, benchmarking, re-engineering
Employment Law:
redundancy
discrimination, maternity rights
INVESTOR IN PEOPLE
For further information please contact:
Paul Couchman, William M. Mercer Limited, Telford House, 14 Tothill Street, London SW1H 9NB, Tel 0171 222 9121, Fax 0171 222 6140.
WILLIAM M. MERCER
William M. Mercer Limited is regulated by IMRO and the Personal Investment Authority

6.5
Empowerment and Process Ownership

Bill Jarrett
Consultant, XR Associates Ltd

World-class companies in the 1990s have come to realise early in their maturity that with the emergence of the global market, seeking competitive advantage can no longer be supported only by innovations in technology, machinery and computers as their competitors will also have access to them. Business success comes from more effectively managing their only unique resource — their people — through unlocking the unrealised potential of each individual in the organisation. Sir John Harvey-Jones, in the prologue to his series *Troubleshooter*, said: 'The biggest single improvement a company can make to its business performance is to get people to work more effectively together. I do not know of a single British company who is using more than 50 per cent of the capability of its people.'

Even in companies where multiskilling is the norm, it is no longer enough to train people to achieve competency in job-related tasks. To customers who choose to buy from those companies, competency and quality of product and service will be the minimum expectation. Customers are continually seeking added value without added cost, which constitutes the challenge and the opportunity for those businesses.

How does a growing business which is already established in a marketplace anticipate the changes which are already on it and those that will affect it in the future?

The growing business must not only recognise that customer needs will be constantly changing but must also make all of its business processes more effective by devising a strategy to enable the development of a continuous improvement culture. It must be geared to the elimination of waste in all its forms so that price pressure can be met from reduced operating cost rather than through reduced margins. The world-class benchmark determines how that strategy might be defined and is documented through the emergence of Japanese companies in the world economy. The perception of Japanese products in the 1950s and 1960s was of bad design, poor quality, poor reliability, poor durability and old technology. Today that perception is almost the exact opposite. How did this spectacular change occur? The origins were in the theories of Professor W Edwards Deming, an American business improvement academic, who espoused the use of statistical quality control, and a structured 'plan, do, check, act' cycle (see Figure 6.5.1) to achieve improved standards of products through continuously improved design. Japanese companies took the concept to heart, and set about improving every aspect of their business process in a step-by-step approach, developing the skills of their workforce. Gradually the focus of management had changed from being directive (passing down rules and regulations to the workplace) to being supportive (customer focused, in a learning, no-blame environment) to create an empowered, highly skilled workforce, who had been trained in all of the tools and techniques which were developed from the original concepts of Professor Deming and with his assistance and support to form what the Japanese call *kaizen*, and what we in the West have come to know as continuous improvement.

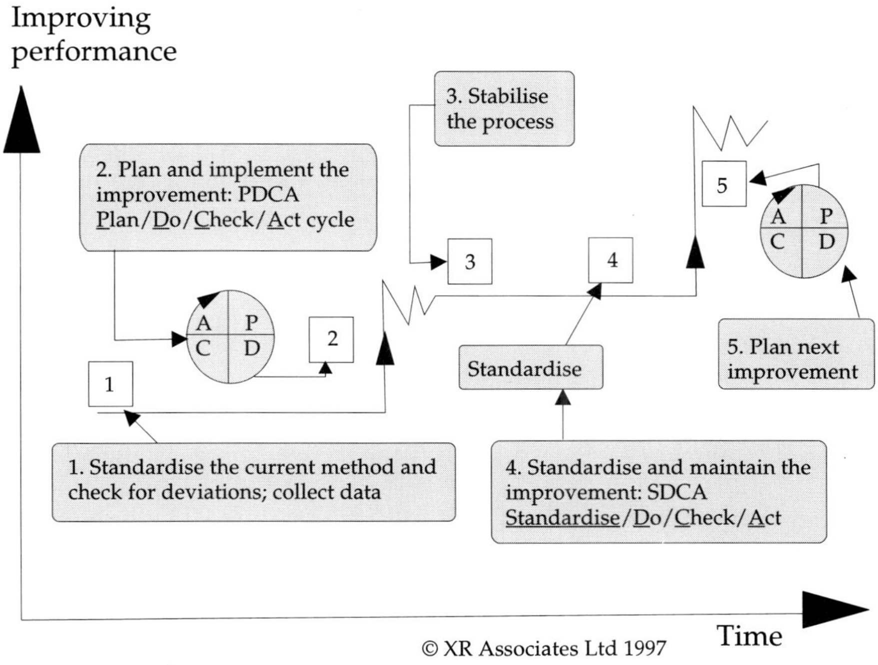

Figure 6.5.1 PDCA/SDCA concept

The acceptance of the need for a continuous improvement culture involves a radical change in the way that we think about the structure of an organisation.

Traditionally we think of a pyramid, with management at the top and the workforce at the bottom, leading to the wrong conclusion that management is more 'important' than the workplace and the workforce. In a continuous improvement culture, the importance of the workplace is given prime recognition, since it is where the work is done and where the value of the company's products is created. It is also where customer satisfaction (or dissatisfaction) will be achieved. Management and all non-workplace departments in this culture are supporting the workplace better to fulfil customer needs, and recognising the workforce as a unique group that knows most about its job and can contribute most to improving it. Our traditional pyramid has been turned upside down (see Figure 6.5.2).

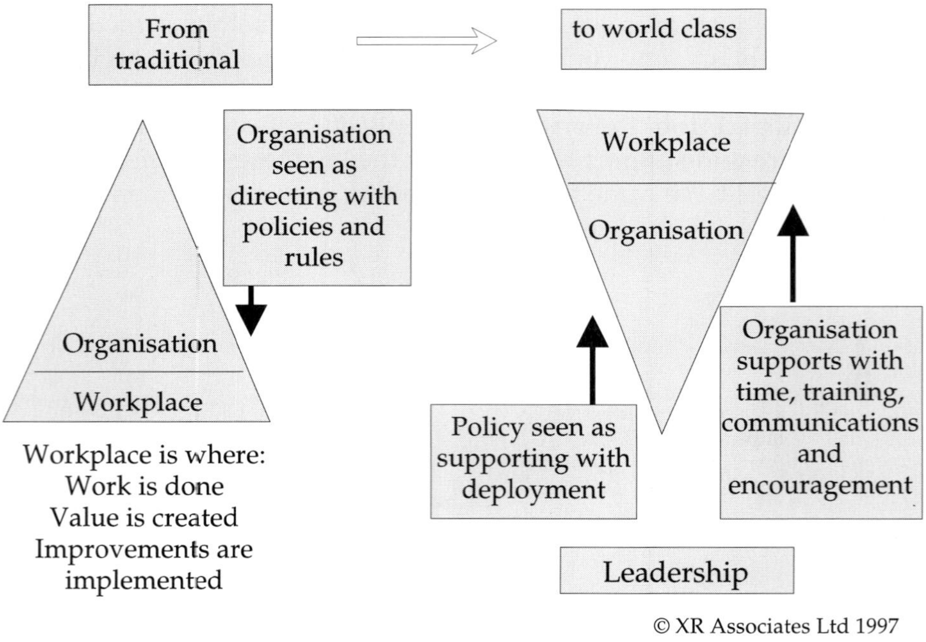

Figure 6.5.2 Support for the workplace from the whole organisation

In order that improvement at the workplace can be realised, the first step is the focused training of employees in teamwork, both cross-functionally and in natural work groups, brainstorming and the rules which apply, and use of the tools for data collection to facilitate a 'speak with data' norm. This can then be followed by learning the concepts, systems and tools of a continuous improvement culture.

The learning process is most effective when structured in a workshop-based programme, which addresses real problems in the workplace or office environment. This enables employees to use their existing knowledge of the process, combined with acquired new knowledge and experience in the use of the systems, tools and methodology of continuous improvement. These workshops enable them to effect immediate and permanent implementation of easy improvements to the process within the timeframe of the workshop, and helps them identify and plan for implementation of further opportunities on a continuing timeframe. Typically, the outcome of workshops involving three cross-functional teams assisted by a skilled facilitator has been the identification of measured opportunities for improvement which reduce set-up time by 50 per cent, improve productivity by 10 per cent, improve quality (measured in parts per million) by 40 per cent and result in space/inventory reductions of 60 per cent.

The format of the workshop allows participants to learn and practically apply:

- flow process analysis, which shows a process in its elements and establishes value-adding and non-value-adding activities;
- set-up time reduction (SMED) and multiple activity analysis which differentiate on-stream and off-stream activities;
- total productive maintenance which involves all functions in the achievement of total production through pursuit of improvements to overall equipment effectiveness (OEE);
- cost of quality which measures the effects and costs of detection versus prevention.

These are practised on the basis of identifying problems and waste, starting with problems which can be solved easily by implementing solutions which cost little or nothing or give best value, thinking of quality, cost and delivery, and *always* speaking with data.

The commencement of the journey toward a continuous improvement culture has been made by many British companies in the 1990s. Although this was spearheaded within the automotive industry, the concepts, strategies and tools are applicable to any organisation, large or small, which has a vision or plan for the future which is shared with all employees, and where the opportunities for development are used to make the vision a reality.

Bill Jarrett, a qualified chemist and metallurgist, has had extensive experience in manufacturing and general management. He is a consultant with **XR Associates** and a specialist in culture change, process improvement, cost reduction and training to maximise individuals and teams in pursuit of continuous improvement in business performance.

Part 7

Reward and Compensation

7.1
Strategy in Employee Benefits

Chris Welford
Principal Consultant, PA Consulting Group

Employee benefits should be provided in a carefully thought-out manner. All too often they are not! They exist in a piecemeal fashion and the resulting impact on employees is not as motivational as it should be. Organisations that are successful in providing employee benefits can teach growing businesses some important lessons. These lessons are essentially about strategy and flexibility.

Reward Strategy

The most important lesson is perhaps the most simple one. Employee benefits are an important part of the *overall reward strategy*. There should be nothing complicated nor mysterious about reward strategy — it is merely an expression of what an organisation values in its people and what it is prepared to pay for. The reward strategy in a thriving company will allow managers to attract, retain and motivate the appropriate quality of people. It will also clarify how employees will be recognised for increasing their worth to the organisation.

The Role of Employee Benefits

Because employee benefits are part of the reward strategy, their role should be clear. They may be an attractive addition to basic salary or they may compensate for a basic salary that is not, in itself, particularly competitive. It must be clear whether they are paid to focus attention on key business performance issues, whether they are paid to reflect status or whether they are paid to reward loyalty and long service.

The Distribution of Employee Benefits

In the successful organisation, staff will perceive the distribution of employee benefits as fair. This strengthens their motivational impact. There are a number of ways in which benefits can be awarded, but the key point to remember is that, whatever method is used, it must be robust:

- *Job size* — certain benefits may be associated with differences in job complexity or accountability. This presupposes that the organisation values this sort of measure and that a suitable method of evaluating job size has been implemented. It does not, necessarily, require a formal job evaluation scheme to be used, and many rapidly growing organisations prefer to describe a fairly broad series of roles rather than use a system of greater complexity.
- *Personal performance* — in other types of organisation, the accent is far more on the difference between people than the difference between positions. If this is the basis on which benefits are offered, then the method of discriminating between the performance of individuals must be highly reliable. Inevitably, this means that the organisation will have a clear set of values and may have developed a framework of desirable behaviours. It is also likely to have an established and respected appraisal system.
- *The market* — many organisations will be operating in several employment markets and it is vital to know the range of benefits which competitors are offering staff. This is particularly important at recruitment stage. Although staff rarely leave for the provision of benefits alone, not supplying a particularly valued benefit (or not providing it to the level desired) may be very demotivating for some people. Having stressed the importance of market comparisons, it is generally not wise to be entirely market led. Successful organisations do not slavishly follow survey norms!
- *A combination* — perhaps the best method is to acknowledge all three of the above and offer some flexibility.

Flexibility

Business advantages

Not only do people value choice, but there are sound business reasons for providing some element of flexibility in the benefit package. Organisations that offer flexibility discover which benefits are worthwhile giving by measuring their take-up. They acknowledge that their workforce is made up of different people, with different needs, and they are generally better at communicating the real value of benefits to employees. The general publicity is good as well — the organisation immediately has a competitive edge over those that offer no flexibility, in the eyes of employees and prospective employees alike.

Strategy

There are far fewer organisations in the UK than in the US that have been successful in implementing flexible benefit packages. Those that have been successful have at least one common denominator — they have taken a strategic approach.

This means deciding which benefits are core and which are non-core (core will often include pension, life insurance and sickness cover and non-core will often encompass additional pension contributions, car, preferential loans etc). They also balance the provision of flexibility with the cost of administration.

Conclusion

The important message is to stop and consider the options before doing anything. Think through what you value in your people, the way in which they *can* be rewarded, the way in which they *would* like to be rewarded and, if possible, offer them a little *choice*.

Chris Welford is an experienced HR consultant specialising in performance and reward. He has particular interest in reward strategy and the motivational impact of pay on individuals. Before joining PA, Chris held a consultancy position with KPMG and this followed a number of years spent in HR with ICI and the Woolwich Building Society. **PA Consulting Group** is a leading management, information and technology consultancy, operating worldwide from around 50 offices in over 20 countries.

7.2
Executive Pay in a Growing Business

Tony Vernon-Harcourt
Director, Monks Partnership Ltd

The ability of a growing business to attract and retain senior management capable of managing growth will be influenced by the company's reward policy. The company needs to consider:

- *base salary levels* — How should the salaries of the top management be set in relation to the base pay offered in similar companies requiring the same or similar skills?
- *incentives* — What package of annual and long-term rewards should be offered, which will attract top-quality management and align the interests of directors and shareholders?

Base Salary Market Position

Base salary policy will be influenced by the need to recruit. A high-growth business is likely to find it difficult to grow all its own management and may have to recruit from the marketplace to fill vacancies. It may, therefore, wish to set base salaries above the mid-market position for posts with similar skills.

However, by offering a competitive incentive package and by taking on individuals who see the new job as a significant promotion and who are attracted by the growth prospects of the company, salary levels may be kept around the median of the market. High rewards will come through high

Our clients really warm to our sense of commitment. Over 95% of them renew their Group Risk policies with Swiss Life each year.

But what do we mean by commitment?

For a start, we get especially fired up about service. A policy which has helped us win the coveted 'Investor in People' award.

Then there's our investment in the latest red-hot technology. Our new quotation and administration systems are fast and adaptable.

No wonder, we're number one in Group Critical Illness, number two in Group Life and number three in Group PHI.*

Contact your nearest Swiss Life office for more information. Assuming, of course, we've kindled your interest.

*Source: ERC Frankona 1997 Group Risk Surveys; measured by revenue premium.

Swiss Life
(United Kingdom)

Swiss Life (UK) plc is regulated by the Personal Investment Authority for Group Life Insurance.

Sevenoaks Tel: 01732 582000. **London** Tel: 0171 426 9400. **Birmingham** Tel: 01675 468700. **Reigate** Tel: 01737 227300. **Bristol** Tel: 0117 927 1400. **Liverpool** Tel: 0151 802 5000. **Edinburgh** Tel: 0131 220 7000. **Leeds** Tel: 0113 241 2400.

Swiss Life fully supports the principle that financial advice should be impartial and recommends the use of Independent Financial Advisers.

achievement, leading to good payouts from annual and long-term incentives. Keeping the fixed pay costs at a sensible level may be important in the growing company.

Factors Influencing Base Salary Levels

Having decided its base salary market position, the company will need to check pay against the market. Factors which influence pay include:

- the size of the business as measured by turnover or market capital and its status — parent or subsidiary company: a high-growth quoted business is likely to have a high market value and may consider that it is in the interests of shareholders to relate pay to market value;
- the nature of the business, including the sector or sectors in which the company operates and the extent to which the company needs individuals with the skills to manage business outside the UK;
- the level of responsibility of the job holder and the functional area in which the job holder works: some skills are more readily transferable than others and this will influence pay.

To illustrate the significance of various factors, we have reproduced data from Monks Partnership's *Remuneration of Directors and Managers — United Kingdom — April 1997*. The findings are based largely on survey returns from some 650 parent and subsidiary companies. Supplementary data for parent company directors is taken from annual reports.

Impact of size and company type

To illustrate the impact of size, as measured by turnover, we reproduce in Table 7.2.1 mid-market base salary levels for two categories of posts — chief executives of parent companies and managing directors of subsidiary companies. The figures also illustrate the significant differences in pay levels between parent and subsidiary company directors. These differences are influenced by the autonomy of the job holder and the freedom of the parent company director to act without reference to a more senior level of management.

Impact of sector and international involvement

Our research shows that directors of consumer goods companies tend to be better rewarded than directors of industrial companies of similar size. International management skills become increasingly important the larger the size of the company.

Table 7.2.1 Impact of size and company type — mid-market base salaries at April 1997

Approximate turnover £mn	Chief executive parent company £'000	Managing director subsidiary company £'000
10	85	62
25	105	79
80	132	101
150	148	124

Table 7.2.2 illustrates that a director of a consumer goods company is better paid in all size bands. The figures relate to a director of a subsidiary or business unit operating in a single country. The individual may be responsible for finance, sales, manufacturing or administration.

More precise sector breakdowns illustrate the impact of sector more effectively. All the figures in Table 7.2.3 relate to a functional director of a parent company. We provide figures for seven example sectors.

Table 7.2.2 Impact of sector I — mid-market base salaries at April 1997

	Director of single country subsidiary company	
Turnover £mn	Consumer companies £'000	Industrial companies £'000
20	47	46
50	56	53
100	63	59
200	71	66

Table 7.2.3 Impact of sector II — mid-market base salary at April 1997

	Director of £100mn parent company £'000
Buildings materials and construction	84
Electronics and computer	90
Engineering	85
Oil and chemicals	94
Pharmaceuticals	91
Household goods, clothing, toys	87
Retail and distribution	87

The extent to which the company operates outside the UK also has an impact. The figures in Table 7.2.4 compare mid-market base salaries of companies with more than 50 per cent of sales outside the UK with those with less than 50 per cent of sales outside the UK.

Table 7.2.4 Impact of sales outside UK — mid-market base salary at April 1997

	Director of parent company	
Turnover £mn	**50%+ outside UK £'000**	**Under 50% outside UK £'000**
100	90	87
200	105	101
500	130	124
1000	152	145

Additional research shows that the premium for directors of companies with the overwhelming majority of the business outside the UK and with most of their manufacturing outside the UK is of the order of 10–15 per cent.

Impact of function

If we assume that the overall accountabilities of the posts are similar, function has a limited impact on pay. The figures in Table 7.2.5 are for a director of a £50mn subsidiary company.

Table 7.2.5 Impact of function — mid-market base salary at April 1997

	Director of £50mn subsidiary company £'000
Finance	53.5
Sales and marketing	54.8
Manufacturing	55.0
Administration and legal	55.6
Information technology	57.9

The figures suggest that a company can plan its pay structure without close regard to function. The marketability of specialist skills and the perceived value of the job to the company can be given greater weight.

Base Salary Spread

We have shown above the mid-market base salary for each post or group of posts. About a quarter of the posts are likely to be paid 20 per cent or more above the mid-market figure and about a quarter 15 per cent less than the mid-market figure.

Setting the base salary at an appropriate level is critical to the value of the whole package, since most annual and long-term incentive plans and pensions will be related to base salary levels.

Incentives

Most board senior management posts in UK parent and subsidiary companies will be eligible for:

- an annual bonus;
- an allocation of share options or some other form of long-term plan.

Although many larger companies are developing alternative forms of long-term plan, share options remain the norm in medium to smaller companies. In a high-growth business, share options are likely to remain the more attractive long-term reward in a smaller quoted group, since the costs of options do not have an impact on the profit and loss account and have a positive impact on cash flow. Most alternative long-term plans have an adverse impact on the profit and loss account and have an impact on cash requirements.

Annual bonus

A typical annual bonus plan will take the following form:

- An entry level of achievement will be set below which no bonus is paid. In a growing business, the entry point will be set to represent a significant improvement over the prior year results.
- A target level of achievement will be set at which about half the maximum bonus is likely to be paid. Achieving target will be seen by shareholders as a 'good result'. Target may be defined as a stretching budget.
- An upper limit will be established at which the maximum bonus is paid. The level of achievement at which maximum bonus is paid may vary from about 105 to 125 per cent of target, depending on the growth prospects of the company.

To illustrate typical annual bonus practice, we show in Table 7.2.6 median target bonus levels and typical upper limits for selected posts. Larger companies will tend to have higher limits than those shown in the table.

In general terms, the bonus at target is likely to be about half the maximum bonus, but some plans may require above target performance before bonus is paid, particularly if the base salary is above the market median.

Share options

Most UK companies will make an annual grant of share options. Practice with regard to the annual grant varies widely and the figures in Table 7.2.7 are broad indicators only. The right to exercise options will normally now be dependent on the company achieving a real growth in earnings per share of 2 per cent per year in excess of inflation or some other appropriate performance target. Participants make nothing out of share options unless the share price increases.

Table 7.2.6 Bonus plan targets and limits as % salary

	Target bonus for good results % salary	**Maximum bonus for outstanding results % salary**
Chief executive — parent company	20	40
Director — parent company	20	40
Senior manager — parent company	15	30
Managing director — subsidiary company	20	40
Director — subsidiary company	15	30
Senior manager — subsidiary company	10	20

Table 7.2.7 Typical share option grants as % salary

	Annual value of share option grants as % salary
Chief executive — parent company	100
Director — parent company	75–100
Senior manager — parent company	50–75
Managing director — subsidiary company	75–100
Director — subsidiary company	50–75
Senior manager — subsidiary company	Not normally eligible

Conclusion

Setting a competitive base salary is critical to the total value of the package and the company needs to take account of a range of factors about the nature of the company and the responsibilities of the job to determine an appropriate salary level.

The balance between base salary, annual bonus and long-term rewards needs to reflect the circumstances of the business, the need to recruit, the vulnerability of the company to poaching of key staff and the need to align the interests of top management and shareholders.

Tony Vernon-Harcourt is a director of **Monks Partnership Ltd** and an adviser to both large and smaller companies on board and senior management pay, incentives and benefits.

7.3

Share Options

David Henry Cohen
Partner, Paisner & Co

Companies wishing to offer shares to their staff can take advantage of generous tax breaks but need to ensure that the 'scheme' they select is appropriate for their particular circumstances.

The key objective is that employees who buy shares should be taxed as lightly as possible. UK tax law starts from the assumption that free or cheap shares are a form of remuneration which should be subject to income tax. Fortunately, this does not apply to benefits received under the three types of 'approved' scheme. These schemes must comply with various statutory conditions and are then approved by the Inland Revenue.

The most popular of the three (see Table 7.3.1) is the company share option plan (CSOP). Participants, selected at the complete discretion of the directors, are granted an option to buy shares in the future, paying whatever the shares are worth at the grant date (for an unquoted company this value has to be agreed with the Revenue). The attraction is that if the share price increases the employee buys at a discount, whereas if the price falls he or she can abandon the option and will have lost nothing.

The rules of a CSOP impose two main restrictions. First, options cannot be exercised — ie converted into shares — for at least three years. Secondly, no individual can at any time hold options over shares which will cost more than £30,000.

The other two Revenue-approved arrangements are savings-related share option schemes (SAYE schemes) and profit-sharing schemes. In contrast to CSOPs, both must be open to all employees who have been with the company for a qualifying period of up to five years and benefits have to be shared out on a like-for-like basis (usually pro rata to salary).

Table 7.3.1 Approved scheme statistics

Period	No of schemes approved		
	Profit sharing	SAYE	CSOP
1995/1996	43	116	347
1996/1997	55	176	422
Cumulative total to 31 March 1997	1256	1693	6937

An SAYE scheme is a combination of a share option and a savings contract. To obtain an option an employee must sign up with a building society or bank for a three- or five-year contract, the proceeds of which — including a tax-free terminal bonus — must be enough to finance the exercise of the option. The monthly savings contribution can be anything from £5 to £250.

The profit-sharing scheme operates by means of a trust. The employer makes annual tax-deductible contributions which the trust uses to buy shares in the company. These shares are then earmarked for qualifying staff so that the shares remain registered in the name of the trust for three years, but belong to the relevant employees who are therefore entitled to any dividends. At the end of the three-year period the shares are transferred free of charge to the employees. In any tax year, no individual can receive shares worth more than 10 per cent of salary, with an upper limit of £8000.

Reference was made previously to the conditions which need to be satisfied to achieve approved status. The condition which tends to be the biggest obstacle for unquoted companies is that scheme shares must not be subject to any restrictions not applying to other shares of the same class. This is very broadly interpreted, so that it is often not feasible for a company with an approved scheme to compel departing employees to sell back their shares.

If a company is unable — or unwilling — to satisfy the Revenue's conditions, there is nothing to prevent it establishing a non-approved scheme. Employees will then be subject to income tax rather than capital gains tax.

Although the two taxes are currently charged at the same rate, approved options can exploit the CGT (capital gains tax) annual exemption — currently £6500 — and are also outside the scope of PAYE and national insurance contributions (imposed on non-approved schemes by the Conservative government's last Budget). Moreover, a non-approved option is taxed on the notional gain at exercise, whereas with an approved scheme

Table 7.3.2 At-a-glance guide to the three approved employee share schemes

Scheme type	Participation	Share price	Individual limit	Minimum holding period	Maximum holding period	Effect of employment termination	How is share purchase funded?
CSOP	Employer's discretion	Market price	£30,000	3 years	10 years	Employer's discretion	From employee's own resources
SAYE	All employees	80% of market price	£17,250 (5-year savings contracts)	3 years	7 years	Depends on reason for termination	From employee's savings contract with building society
Profit sharing	All employees	Shares are free	10% of annual salary (£8000 maximum)	3 years	5 years	Employee retains shares	By the employer

liability is generally deferred until the shares are sold — an important advantage if the company wants to encourage long-term share retention.

Increasingly, companies are choosing to link their employee share schemes to an employee share ownership plan (ESOP). An ESOP is a trust which buys shares in the company (with funding provided, directly or indirectly, by the company) and then distributes the shares to employees, usually via a share option scheme. This means that when an option is exercised the ESOP transfers the requisite number of shares to the exercising employee, which saves the company from having to issue new shares.

The fact that dilution of the other shareholdings will be avoided is just one of the advantages of using an ESOP. In private companies the main *raison d'être* of an ESOP will be to act as a marketmaker, a particularly valuable function if there are 'sleeping' shareholders whose shares can be bought in and then used to incentivise key staff.

There is a species of ESOP which, like the approved schemes, confers tax privileges in return for compliance with statutory requirements. All corporate contributions to a statutory ESOP are automatically tax deductible and shareholders selling to a statutory ESOP may qualify for a very flexible rollover of CGT liability on their share gains.

However, until very recently companies had been deterred by the very rigid statutory conditions — particularly that shares could only be distributed via an approved profit-sharing scheme. However, following the 1996 Finance Act, statutory ESOPs can now be linked to the more popular SAYE scheme, which has encouraged many companies to give them a second look. Table 7.3.2 summarises the options.

David Henry Cohen, a partner at City law firm **Paisner & Co**, is a specialist adviser on employee share schemes and ESOPs. He is the Chairman of the Share Scheme Lawyers Group and was voted 'Experts' Expert' in a survey of share scheme lawyers. He writes regularly for the *Financial Times*.

7.4
Company Cars

Roy Fewster
Managing Director, Lex Vehicle Leasing

The company car market is worth around £20bn to the British economy in new and used car purchases alone. This chapter looks at how the market is changing, why company car sales continue to rise and why more and more companies are looking to outsource their company car fleets.

In 1996 sales of new company cars exceeded those of private buyers, taking 54 per cent (1.1mn) of the UK new car market. In 1997 Lex believes that this figure will rise to 1.2mn.

Based on these figures, car manufacturers are becoming more reliant on this market sector to help keep their production plants busy.

For this reason, it is not just the traditional fleet manufacturers such as Ford and Vauxhall which are benefiting from this increase in sales. Other makers such as Volkswagen and Citroën, and even smaller car makers such as Mazda and Hyundai, are now wooing the corporate buyer.

The result is that company car choice lists are becoming more and more open. In June Lex released its fourth company car report, entitled *Driving for Safer Company Motoring*, on the state of the fleet industry and it reported that around half of all drivers receive a choice when getting their next company car.

That means that four-wheel-drive vehicles, multipurpose vehicles (MPVs) and sports cars are being driven by company drivers for the first time, in addition to the more traditional saloons and hatchbacks.

It is worth considering why these types of cars are now finding their way on to company car lists, when in the past the only choice has been whether you want a green Ford Escort hatchback or a blue Ford Escort hatchback.

KOGAN PAGE...
creating success

30 YEARS IN BUSINESS 120 Pentonville Road, London N1 9JN, Tel: 0171 278 0433, Fax: 0171 837 6348

The fleet strategy bible

No miracles. Just revelations.

In the beginning there was darkness. And confusion. Then it came to pass that Swan National became one of the largest car leasing companies in the land. Soon it was known that Swan National had more fleet funding solutions than anyone else. And Swan National commissioned a book on the subject and the people rejoiced.

Call Swan National on 0121 450 5760 for your FREE Henley Guide (Cover Price £25) - an indispensable guide to formulating fleet strategy independently prepared by the Henley Centre for Automotive Management. We'll also be happy to arrange a meeting to discuss your requirements.

Plus Now Available:
European Guide to Fleet Strategy.

Swan National

Member HSBC *Group*

Swan National Ltd, PO BOX 5693,
54 Hagley Road, Birmingham B16 8PL.

Managing Business Growth Through Better Fleet Management

By Phil Moorhouse
Finance Director of Northgate Motor Holdings

Commercial vehicles keep many businesses on the road and plays an important part in their growth.

Such vehicles are usually a function, and not its core business. Nevertheless, they are often a significant cost and influence on company performance, especially when delivery and distribution are key components to achieving customer satisfaction.

Given that, it is particularly surprising to realise that for many companies, their commercial vehicle fleet acquisition is often poorly planned, inefficient and costly.

An independent survey, carried out on behalf of Northgate Motor Holdings, clearly identified that not enough management time is set against vehicle acquisition policies. Almost half the respondents confessed they had no particular vehicle policy - all the more staggering given that most companies consider vehicles as one of their main operational priorities and costs.

Respondents all believe flexibility is crucial to business survival, let alone growth - a point often contradicted by their own fleet management policies. Too many companies automatically purchased or agree to long-term hire contacts and do not consider the alternative.

However, what is becoming increasingly apparent to companies is that to maintain a competitive advantage they need to focus on core activities, cost control and capital. Bussinesses have several options when it comes to commercial vehicle management - purchase, contact hire, fleet management and NORFLEX.

Purchase can be an attractive option, especially if the company wishes to acquire an asset base, has strong purchasing power and has no better use for the capital which will be tied up in the fleet. However, the purchaser does tip up valuable capital and takes on all the risks of ownership.

Fleet management is merely another form of outsourcing. A 'bolt-on' transport department offers certain advantages, but it must be remembered that the user still owns the vehicles and retains all risks involved in acquisition through purchase.

Contract hire may be a viable option for a business operating in a very stable market, but not many do. With contract hire, a company signs a binding agreement to take a specific number of vehicles for a pre-determined time (normally three or four years) with a mileage stipulation. Should any of the contact conditions be broken there are stiff penalties.

NORFLEX is a completely flexible, risk-free option for commercial vehicles. Unlike contract hire, Norflex gives the vehicle user total control, and freedom to alter the fleet to meet changing business needs. Unlike purchase and fleet management, it does not tie up capital or restrict the user to an ageing fleet.

Norflex also simplifies fleet administration and allows the user to improve cash-flow planning. In addition, Norflex is off balance sheet. Rentals are charged to the profit and loss account and because the company does not enter into a contractual agreement, no note need be made in the annual accounts.

What ever decision a company makes, it is important that more business people carefully consider all the options and build vehicle acquisition policies into their general business planning. To help come to decision read our 'Business Guide to Vehicle Acquisition', free to readers of the guide. Anybody interested in receiving a copy should send their business card to:

**NORFLEX CBI, Freepost DL650,
Darlington DL1 1BR**

ADAPTABILITY

In business, nothing seems to stay the same for long. Contracts are won and lost, new opportunities arise, needs change. That's why you need to ask yourself questions about adaptability – especially where your company's commercial fleet is concerned...

- Could you add or reduce the number of vehicles in your fleet easily and without penalty?
- Would you be able to avoid costly mileage restrictions if you suddenly needed to cover more ground?
- Can you change your vehicle mix without penalty?

WHEN YOU NORFLEX YOUR VANS THE ANSWER'S ALWAYS YES.

Run by Northgate Motor Holdings Ltd, Britain's premier commercial vehicle rental network, NORFLEX takes care of everything – but leaves you in control of your fleet.

Discover the RISK-FREE alternative to purchase, fleet management or contract hire.

SEND FOR YOUR FREE GUIDE TODAY!

The Unique Norflex Business Guide to Vehicle Acquisition compares your commercial vehicle acquisition options in the light of the overall success of your business.

Adaptability... tailored for your company's needs!

ENTER OUR FREE PRIZE DRAW

Win a day's driver awareness training with Britain's top driver training organisation. It's one day that could save your life – and an outing you'll never forget!

NORFLEX®

YES please send me my FREE NORFLEX Business Guide to Vehicle Acquisition

Name Mr/Mrs/Miss/Ms
Job Title
Company Name
Address

Postcode
Tel No.

Total number of vehicles in your fleet ☐

Made up of: ☐ cars ☐ light commercial

☐ HGVs vehicles

Your current arrangements (please tick the box):

Hire ☐ Contract Hire ☐
Purchase ☐ Fleet Management ☐

Any other relevant information:

POST FREE TO: NORFLEX, FREEPOST DL650, Darlington DL1 1BR
OR FAX this coupon back on: 01325 36 34 71
OR CALL 0800 52 52 36

NORFLEX®

CALL 0800 52 52 36 TODAY

The major answer seems to lie in staff retention and recruitment. More and more money is being spent by companies training their employees, and to make sure they stay with the company for a few years, better and better cars are being offered as part of the remuneration package.

The company car also plays a major part in the recruitment process. IT companies, for example, find that offering a BMW 3 Series, instead of a Ford Mondeo, makes the difference between attracting a potential employee to their company and losing them to the opposition.

This surge in interest in the company car by employers has meant companies such as Lex Vehicle Leasing, which purchase, manage and dispose of company cars on behalf of some of the UK's largest companies, has grown very quickly in the past two years. At the beginning of 1996 Lex's fleet size stood at 70,000 vehicles and since then the fleet has risen to over 85,000 vehicles.

The mainstay of this growth has been in contract hire, where a company hands the risk of buying, running and selling a company car on to Lex. Lex in turn charges the company a fixed monthly fee.

Companies find that contract hire is hassle free and for accounting purposes enables them to get the vehicles off their balance sheet. Alternatively, if a company wants to free up some capital, Lex can buy the fleet from the company and then lease it back to them.

Alongside this trend of outsourcing is a trend towards companies offering company car drivers the choice of an annual cash sum instead of providing them with a car. This move was fuelled by the government's move to tax an individual driver on the list price of his or her car.

This means that the higher the cost of the car, the larger the personal tax bill. But, research shows that employees regard the company car as an essential item in their benefits package, and they are prepared to pay the relevant tax bill. In fact, the latest Lex *Report on Motoring* estimates that just 10,000 drivers have taken cash instead of their car.

When examining the breakdown of company car sales, we can see that the move to a list-price-based personal tax system has not encouraged drivers to opt for cheaper, smaller cars. Instead, more drivers are opting for slightly bigger cars and the larger tax bills that go with them.

Looking at a profile of the company cars on the road in 1996, only 11 per cent had engines below 1.4 litres, while 63 per cent were between 1.4 and 2.0 litres and 25 per cent over 2.0 litres.

However, in the future, as smaller cars are fitted with larger, more efficient engines and items such as air conditioning, company car drivers may well be enticed back into a smaller company car. Whatever happens, we can be sure of one thing: the company car market is alive and well.

Roy Fewster is Managing Director of **Lex Vehicle Leasing**, the UK's largest contract hire and leasing company.

7.5
Pensions: A Double-edged Sword?

Dr Thomas Heron PhD MBA FCIS
Marketing Director, Jardine Reeves Brown Ltd

The Balancing Dilemma

Pension contributions can be a significant and long-term overhead for any organisation and employers must consider whether, and to what extent, they wish to provide income for their staff during retirement. Providing for a pension in retirement for your valued staff can be a double-edged sword. Reaching an economic but socially responsible solution, particularly for growing owner-managed firms, partnerships or management buyouts/ins, is no mean trick. Prime Minister Blair has already signalled his intention to bring about social change and New Labour will place greater emphasis on shifting pension provision away from the state and over to a partnership between employees and their employer.

Contributions by an employer to an occupational or personal pension plan are often the largest overhead after salaries and wages. Consequently great care must be taken to ensure that this overhead does not become an excessive drain on the resources of the company and that it ultimately provides the sort of pension envisaged by the sponsoring employer.

Getting the right balance between what you as a caring employer wish to provide for your valued employees and what they actually receive when they retire can be two different things. It is highly unlikely that even the most experienced directors from manufacturing, pharmaceuticals, chemicals, computers or other non-financial services sectors will be able to translate much of the actuarial, insurance and legislative gobbledegook which pervades the jargon of the pensions industry. Therefore getting *the best possible independent advice* in *plain and simple language* on how to set up and manage chosen pension arrangements is critically important.

Knowing what questions to ask of any pensions adviser will not of itself turn the employer into a pensions expert, but it should assist in the process of understanding for the layperson.

Questions about New Pension Arrangements

Before seeking this advice, there are some key questions that all prudent employers should ask before embarking on pension provision. For example:

- What can I afford to contribute? Do I wish to fix my contribution to a regular proportion of my overall salary bill, or am I prepared to accept that my contribution may vary if I opt to provide a pension based on my employees' salaries during their employment?
- What level of income do I wish my employees to receive in retirement? This may mean choosing between a defined benefit plan (ie the income in retirement will be principally based on their years of service and expressed as a percentage of their final/average salary), which effectively provides a projected income level, or a defined contribution plan (the amount of the employer's contribution is normally based on a percentage of the employee's salary), which provides a pot of money which can be used to purchase an annuity. The income from the annuity will vary according to annuity rates at the time of purchase.
- If I opt for a defined benefit plan, what will be the ongoing administration and actuarial costs and will I be liable for any deficiencies caused (say) by underperformance of the underlying investments of the pension plan? Alternatively, if the investments of the plan perform well, will I be able to take a contributions holiday?
- If I opt for a defined contribution plan, can I determine what level of income my staff will receive in retirement?
- Do I want to provide additional benefits such as a pension for the spouse (or partner) in the event of the former employee's death before or after retirement? Do I wish their pension payable in retirement to increase in line with inflation? If so, how much will this cost now and in the future?
- Do I wish to set up my firm's own occupational pension plan or should we purchase a plan from an insurance company (an insured plan)? What are the advantages and disadvantages of each course of action?

- Should I encourage my employees to set up their own personal pension plans to which I will make a regular contribution? If so, how much can I legally contribute on a regular basis?
- What are the ramifications for the company and the employees if the company falls on hard times and cannot continue to make regular pension contributions?

Questions about Existing Pension Arrangements

Many employers already contribute to a pension plan for their employees. Often the plan was initiated during the early days of the organisation's development and was consequently appropriate for the circumstances at that time. These pension provision arrangements may no longer fully meet the needs of the sponsoring employer or the demographic nature and needs of the present workforce. Additional questions need to be asked:

- Is the company's contribution expense still acceptable to the directors and shareholders?
- Are my existing pension arrangements still appropriate for my employees?
- Should the various levels of staff have their own pension arrangements which better reflect their unique circumstances?
- Should we remain 'contracted in' or 'contracted out'?
- Are we paying too much for the services of our scheme actuary?
- If we change from a defined benefit to a defined contribution scheme, how much expense could the company save?

There is no simple answer to these fundamental questions and the optimal solution for each employer will differ. That is why independent pensions advice is so important. Employers are increasingly likely to assume greater responsibility for pension provision, in conjunction with their employees, and so it makes sense to consider carefully how you want to structure your pension plans.

Communicate this Unseen Benefit

Finally, having considered all of the above and implemented a pension plan for your employees, don't fall foul of the error of many established companies: they fail to *promote this extremely valuable benefit to their staff*. Income in retirement is a valuable benefit, so make sure that all of the members of the pension plan/s to which you contribute are fully aware of your contribution to this unseen and longer-term benefit. Generally speaking, older employees are more concerned with their pension arrangements and tend to keep themselves abreast of their pension provisions. However, it makes sense, if you have a growing workforce, to provide regular bulletins or newsletters to all plan members reminding them that you care for their well-being even when they will no longer be members of staff. This can be a powerful tool in promoting the profile of the company, as well as informing all staff of their future income and statutory rights.

Dr Thomas Heron is Marketing Director of **Jardine Reeves Brown Ltd**, a highly innovative firm of actuarial, employee benefits and investment strategy consultants. Dr Heron has written extensively on financial services issues and is a renowned expert within the UK and the EU on the marketing of intangible services and business to business marketing strategies.

7.6

Taking Advantage of Workplace Health Solutions

Peter Fermoy
Public Relations Officer, BUPA

People are a company's primary asset. It follows that employers should be interested in the health of their employees, whether because of an altruistic motivation of genuine concern or a simple question of economics.

Absence from work is estimated to cost British business at least £13bn a year. It can totally disrupt a company's operation if a key member of staff becomes ill and, if the absenteeism becomes protracted, this may become a real problem for the company in terms of productivity and therefore profitability.

The significance of health promotion and prevention in healthcare is increasingly acknowledged, and BUPA believes that future healthcare strategies should focus on the valid role that can be played by prevention alongside cure.

The Health and Safety Executive estimates that 2.2mn people suffer ill health as a result of their work every year, with a loss of over five million working days. Despite this, it is BUPA's experience that employers require further persuasion and that wider arguments are needed to reinforce the basic financial argument. With this in mind, BUPA has sought to 'educate' the employer, increasing awareness of all the benefits associated with providing their employees with workplace health programmes.

For example, in considering the specific areas of stress, workplace health can make a vital contribution to risk management and avoidance. In essence, less stressed employees are far less likely to make mistakes. In particular, BUPA seeks to encourage companies to view the adoption of workplace good health as a standard to be sought and attained.

Whether voluntary or compulsory, it is clear that success is dependent on the adoption of a holistic approach. Good management and employment inherently involve the provision of good occupational health programmes, and similar arguments are needed to persuade employees of the merits and benefits of workplace health promotion.

BUPA's experience has illustrated that a crucial consideration is that of 'confidentiality'. What will the employer do with any health information about the workforce? Will 'sick' employees be replaced by 'healthier' applicants? In this regard, BUPA has the advantage of being a medical company which can therefore provide (and crucially is *perceived* to be in a position where it can provide) guarantees of confidentiality.

BUPA's approach has been to design a series of 'measurement tools'. These are based on the premise that the key to the successful implementation of any workplace programme must start with a complete understanding of the nature of the actual health implications and needs of the workplace. The analysis is necessary to reassure employers that subsequent health programmes can be sufficiently targeted to obtain tangible improvements.

Through 'health profile' and 'well-being' questionnaires, BUPA has sought to measure the current levels of employee health and general well-being. Aspects of the workplace which do not contribute to these can then be identified and advice given to both employers and employees.

The 'health profile' questionnaire aims to carry out a health risk appraisal of employees, providing them with an easy and accurate way of measuring their own current level of health; identifying aspects of their lifestyle that are placing their health at risk; and providing practical advice and guidance on how they could improve their general health and well-being.

Its employee appeal is that it provides a personal health profile, carried out on behalf of but distinct from the employer, within the workplace. This aspect provides the employee with the much needed reassurance of confidentiality.

The 'well-being' questionnaire places greater emphasis on the specific effect of the workplace on the employee and how much their work is a source of pressure in their lives. It is based on official figures which show that, at any one time, one in three people in the workplace show unhealthy stress levels, and is designed with employer follow-up in mind, for example through the likes of stress seminars. Given the effects of stress on employee health, work standards and satisfaction, employers are encouraged to consider what they can do to relieve workplace stress and to consider the benefits they themselves will accrue through a less stressed workforce. BUPA supports both employer and employee throughout.

BUPA pioneered health screening in the UK in the early 1970s and today has the most extensive screening network in Europe. As screening techniques and services have become more sophisticated, and in the wake of growing public demand for advice and information on how to live a healthier lifestyle, so BUPA has evolved.

BUPA Health Monitor, a recent addition to BUPA's health screening range, consists of a medical screen and consultation with a physician and at least 40 individual tests such as lung function, muscle strength, estimation of body fat and blood profile.

BUPA Health Monitor is not only designed to detect any health problems but clear emphasis has also been placed on the importance of a healthy lifestyle and how to achieve it. The client's on-going relationship with his or her personal health adviser will go a long way towards enabling people to make lifestyle changes which result in positive health and well-being.

Both employer and employee have much to gain from successfully developed and implemented workplace health programmes. In encouraging a more positive approach to employer–employee relations, both parties benefit from reduced absenteeism, increased productivity, reduced risk through reduced stress, increased work standards and satisfaction.

The potential certainly exists to educate both parties, gaining their support for an increased role for health promotion in the workplace. The next step involves focusing on taking the initiative forward in terms of how the programmes are delivered.

A key issue here will obviously be resources, particularly for growing enterprises. Such businesses will more than likely be unable to provide their own in-house systems and it may therefore be necessary to consider the nature of external provision.

Given its present programmes, BUPA is ideally placed to offer consultation on the possible role of the independent sector in the design and delivery of programmes of health promotion in the workplace.

BUPA is the UK's leading independent healthcare company and is both a purchaser and provider of services.

In the UK, BUPA is the largest health insurer; the largest independent provider of hospital beds, has a major health-screening operation and has developed businesses in occupational health and care of the elderly.

BUPA is Europe's only healthcare business to offer both finance and provision based in more than one member state. It has the largest and most comprehensive international business of any British group, owning Sanitas, Spain's second-largest healthcare company.

Part 8
Managing the Risks

Curriculum Vitae

Name:	National Britannia
Address:	Caerphilly Business Park Caerphilly CF83 3ED
Telephone:	0990 168 748
Facsimile:	0990 168 747
e mail:	enquiries@national-britannia.co.uk

Qualifications:	ISO 9002 National Training Award 1988 National Training Award 1992 BPCA Technician of the Year 1992/3 BPCA Technician of the Year 1996/7
Association Membership:	Royal Institute of Public Health and Hygiene (RIPHH) Institution of Occupational Safety and Health (IOSHH) Society of Food Hygiene Technology (SOFHT) Chartered Institute of Environmental Health (CIEH)
Occupation:	Environmental Hygiene and Safety Specialist
Main Responsibilities:	Implementing Health and Safety Management Systems Providing practical advice on any environmental hygiene and safety issue Responding to the needs of clients
Other Responsibilities:	Food Hygiene Surveys Legionella Surveys COSHH Assessments Accident Investigation Risk Assessments

Other Experience:	Environmental Hygiene - including pest prevention Environmental Building Services - including feral bird control Training - courses in Asbestos Awareness and Health & Safety
Hobbies:	Keen involvement with client Health and Safety Steering committees. Providing a 24 hour telephone hotline for any Hygiene or Health & Safety issues. Constantly reviewing quality procedures. Keeping up to date with legislation.
References:	Available on request.

Thank you for taking the time to consider National Britannia for this important position. We look forward to hearing from you soon.

8.1

Risky Business

Gary Stott
Sales and Marketing Director,
Sedgwick UK Risk Services

Any business entrepreneur knows that reward goes hand in hand with risk. It is an uneasy relationship, but the fact is that to succeed we must accept the possibility of failure. This chapter puts the case for a risk-managed approach.

Can you accurately forecast the worst financial net loss that your business could sustain? Do you know the initial risk position of your business or organisation? These are critical initial questions which must be answered in developing any strategy for the effective management of corporate risks.

For growing businesses in particular, risk is an essential factor that must be top of the agenda when it comes to forward planning. As companies grow and develop their customers, workforce and supplier base, so their exposure to risk increases.

However, it is also a fact that small and medium-sized businesses tend to place less emphasis on risk management than do their national and multinational counterparts. The implications can be severe. Without the back-up of group resources, where could that company relocate in the event that its premises become damaged through fire or flooding? In many cases, businesses are aware of those companies, or even competitors, who would be available to help, yet few take the trouble to make formal arrangements.

Growing businesses also tend to be more reliant on one or two senior executives and do not have layers of management to rely on. In the event of illness or death of senior personnel, the company must be prepared to meet the immediate and long-term challenges of running the business. The expectations of customers must also be considered. As businesses grow, customers become more demanding and expect much quicker recovery from an incident than many businesses currently plan for. For example, in business handling and processing information, minutes may be the maximum tolerance before the customer takes their business elsewhere.

So, having established the consequences of risk, how should it be managed? In the 1980s and early 1990s, the principles of risk management started to take hold in the UK, but the move was primarily driven by the need to control the cost of insurance. Organisations seized the opportunity to reduce premiums by investing in risk-control procedures.

However, since the publication of the Cadbury Report in 1992 — which endorsed a risk-managed approach — and the emphasis on issues such as environmental liability and occupational health and safety, risk management has taken on board-level significance.

One of the critical steps is the development of a business recovery plan which identifies the key risks to the business, evaluates each risk for magnitude and likelihood, assesses the financial implications and outlines preventive and recovery measures. In view of the importance of this information, it is alarming to find from our own research that one in four companies has little faith in its recovery plan and believes it would take no more than a single day of a loss of its systems to have a serious impact on its business.

Unfortunately, this stems from the problem that many plans are prepared as a form of intellectual guidance, rather than action oriented. The purpose of any continuity plan is to identify what people must do, when they must do it and with whom they must communicate. Companies which believe that management doesn't have time to devote to continuity planning need to ask themselves how they would cope following an incident causing critical business interruption.

Business owners must also consider the full financial cost of risk, which covers both the direct and indirect costs to business. Working on the 'iceberg principle', the direct costs of, for example, a fire, IT failure or product contamination represent only a small proportion of the potential overall costs. Hidden costs may include loss of key staff, fall in share price and loss of shareholder confidence, and the reinvestment required to repair reputation and return to profitable trading.

While certain costs are recoverable through insurance policies, companies lose out on the uninsurable elements. Sedgwick estimates that for every £1 recovered through insurance, a further £4 may be lost.

So that's the theory: what are the practicalities of risk management for organisations? Recognition is the key — prevention is always better than cure — but what are some of the areas of concern when applying risk management principles?

Absence Makes the Heart Grow Fonder ... or Does it?

A CBI survey in 1996 revealed that 175 million days are lost through absenteeism, with a direct cost to industry of £10bn. Indirect costs, such as lost productivity, could add a further £6bn to this figure giving an average cost to every employer of over £700 per employee.

Although the vast majority of sick days are genuine, employers can reduce losses by taking steps to control the work environment, thereby reducing the incidence of work-related disorders such as stress, and establishing good practices to encourage a speedy return to work.

In the US, for example, employee health is *the* biggest concern in risk management. In addition to the astronomical costs outlined above, it is the increase in regulations and the readiness of employees to sue over health matters that has led to this situation.

When Disaster Strikes

Disasters in varying degrees of magnitude can befall any company or organisation at any time. The prudent company will develop plans to ensure it will regain its feet and start operating again as soon as possible following a disaster.

Each hour is critical following a disaster. Whether it is the Kobe earthquake, the Manchester bombing or a localised fire within an office block, physical disaster requires contingency planning of the highest order.

Employer's Liability

Employer's liability is an ever-present risk for any firm. Maintaining health and safety standards, for example, is a huge area and one of the greatest areas of concern lies in the risks associated with homeworking. Between 3.3 and 10 million people are expected to work from home by the year 2000, significantly increasing employers' liability in areas such as damage to business equipment, claims from employees on damage to their own equipment, and damage to employee health from poor lighting levels, reflections, glare and noise.

Ultimately, any business investment decision must be based on the benefits which it will bring. While a risk-managed approach does not guarantee competitive advantage, it can help avoid competitive disadvantage and result in greater confidence among staff, suppliers, customers and shareholders. It should not therefore be viewed in isolation, but must be an integral part of the company's business plan.

Sedgwick UK Risk Services (part of the Sedgwick Group) provides risk management consultancy and insurance broking services to organisations throughout the UK. Its clients range from the industrial, commercial and public sectors, to financial services, local authorities and NHS trusts. With 17 regional offices, Sedgwick UK Risk Services combines personal service with the worldwide resources of the Sedgwick Group to inform clients on all aspects of business risk from contingency planning, MBOs to disaster management and business interruption.

HEALTH AND SAFETY
BE SEEN TO BE CLEAN

Should someone come to harm on your business premises today the cost could be very high indeed.

Fines as high as £12,000 plus costs, which have been imposed on small firms convicted following injury accidents, are merely the thin end of the wedge.

Damage to reputation, share price collapse, civil litigation or even the threat of imprisonment for culpable directors may all come into play.

Moreover evidence from Health and Safety Executive case studies shows that insurance provides little real protection. For every £1 recovered by a business following an accident, between £8 and £36 falls outside the scope of the policy and is never recovered.

The question of directors' liability is also becoming a critical one. Increasingly directors as well as managers and those who set policy for a business as well as those who implement it are being called to account when preventable accidents happen.

However, while there is certainly no justification for complacency on health and safety matters, neither is there cause for despair or fatalism.

If a serious accident occurs it does not follow automatically that punishment via the civil or criminal courts is inevitable. The law does nor require businesses to ensure that accidents never happen. It merely requires that all reasonable steps be taken to prevent them.

The issue therefore, is to provide a safe working environment and prove if necessary, to the satisfaction of an environmental health officer or a court, that all such steps were taken.

That is where the role of the formal health and safety management system becomes central to the wellbeing of a business. A well thought out and properly implemented system not only reduces the chances of accidents dramatically but provides the evidence that "due diligence," was observed even where someone has unfortunately come to grief.

By providing an easily followed paper trail it can demonstrate how the business sought to protect its staff and customers from harm and show this in such a way which should convince any reasonable EHO that a prosecution is unjustified.

National Britannia one of Britain's leading environmental hygiene and safety specialists developed **HAS***check* four years ago as the country's first comprehensive and fully integrated health and safety risk management system.

Its growing success since then underlines the fact that senior business people are now focusing on health and safety as a critical part of their business and are beginning to believe that this issue can be managed successfully in the same way as any other aspect of their enterprise.

So far 1,200 major properties nationwide have installed the system, including two out of five shopping centres, many large office blocks, hotels, large stores, manufacturers, distribution and leisure outlets.

HAS*check* includes a site specific hazard analysis and defects report, the drafting of a site specific safety manual, staff training, follow-up audits at regular intervals, a certificate of compliance, access to round the clock professional advice via the Reponseline service and, uniquely, an indemnity against the costs of a prosecution.

In four years the indemnity has never been invoked because no business using the **HAS***check* system has yet been prosecuted for a health and safety offence. In rare cases accidents have occurred but in each case the documented records of tough safety measures on site have persuaded the local EHO that further action is unwarranted.

A typical scenario in a shopping centre may involve a customer slipping on a discarded chip and breaking an arm. On the face of it the centre has failed in its duty to protect but an examination of **HAS***check* records reveals that:

- Large notices were present on all entrances forbidding the bringing of food into the centre;
- CCTV cameras were placed close to the entrances and were monitored constantly to enforce this rule;
- Security staff patrolled the area around the entrances every 20 minutes;
- Floor cleaning was carried out daily and inspections for litter every half an hour:
- All staff were briefed regularly on their responsibility to ensure the floor was safe at all times:
- The centre manager conducted regular weekly and irregular spot checks to ensure all procedures were being observed:

All these actions will have been documented and verified showing the business did what the law required. It took all reasonable steps.

Accidents may still occur but, with a formal health and safety risk management system in place, the frequency will be reduced and the consequences for all from the employee and manager up to the board of directors will be far less daunting.

With health and safety it is not just a question of being legally clean. It is a question of being seen to be clean.

For more information on the full range of services available from* NATIONAL BRITANNIA*, call 0990 168748.

8.2

Being Aware of Commercial Risk

Eleanor Lewis
Corporate Affairs Manager, Trade Indemnity

Most growing businesses are faced with the normal environmental challenges of sociodemographic, technological, economic, environmental and political change. These are the risks which they can do little to influence or control. In addition to these are those risks which are inherent in everyday trading activities which are more accurately described as commercial risks.

The risk of non-payment of debts caused by protracted default or insolvency or arising from political events overseas remains high, despite the current period of economic growth. Past experience of customers' payment records and of markets is no guarantee of future performance. Some 25 per cent of bad debts suffered by medium-sized and large UK business are from long-established, previously prompt-paying customers.

Very few companies would fail to protect fixed assets against fire and theft, while other business risks such as business interruption, fraud and product liability are insured. Yet trade receivables, which can constitute a high percentage of a company's current assets, are mostly left unprotected against diminution of value. The repercussions of this can be serious. Not only does a bad debt reduce the balance sheet strength of a company, it affects working capital and has a dramatic effect on profitability.

On a bad debt of £10,000, Table 8.2.1 indicates the increased turnover required to recover a company's position.

Table 8.2.1 Recovering from a bad debt

	Proportion of net invoice value to net profit				
	1%	2%	5%	7%	10%
Increased turnover required	£1,000,000	£500,000	£200,000	£142,857	£100,000

Moreover, a survey conducted by Trade Indemnity has highlighted that companies spend a huge amount of time collecting overdue accounts. The survey revealed that on average credit management time is broken down into 15 per cent gathering credit information, 15 per cent evaluating it, 30 per cent monitoring accounts and 40 per cent collecting overdue accounts. This is a large drain on resources, particularly in smaller companies where one person normally performs a number of functions.

While companies are often well aware of and much affected by the impact of late payment and bad debt, they are often unaware that there is an efficient and cost-effective solution available through credit insurance to transfer these risks.

Credit Insurance

Credit insurance brings with it:

- help in strengthening the credit management function;
- protection against bad debt as a large proportion of insured invoices are covered;
- help to target sales efforts by avoiding financially weak customers;
- a credit opinions service and help in setting credit limits;
- assistance in risk control by providing an early warning that a customer is in financial difficulty;
- assistance with meetings of creditors and help to enforce rights of ownership to goods supplied;
- optional cover for legal costs;
- optional debt collection;
- using the policy as security against extra borrowing.

Increasingly these services are available on-line, which improves the efficiency for both the credit insurer and its customers.

The databases of credit insurers allow them to monitor risks more efficiently than can an individual company. Also their unique position in the trading environment often means that the information they hold is more up to date and goes beyond that which is publicly available. For instance, Trade Indemnity monitors over 100,000 companies on a daily basis and has active information on over 750,000 companies.

When trading overseas the dynamics of doing business change considerably as new cultures and different trading practices are encountered. The services of the larger credit insurers extend to advice on and cover in respect of overseas-based companies, as well as the risks associated with the political environments of the countries concerned. Again, credit insurance can help target sales efforts by avoiding politically weak or unstable export markets and financially weak buyers.

Thus, credit insurance helps in the assessment of existing and potential customers, protects against loss and represents a cost-effective outsourcing of part of the credit management function. Moreover, the presence of a credit insurance policy can improve the ability to raise finance to support increased or new business opportunities, as financial institutions are secure in the knowledge that the funds they are advancing are to a large extent protected.

Traditionally credit insurance has been the preserve only of the larger companies at the top of the corporate pyramid. Increasingly, however, as insurers' costs are driven down through more effective technologies, credit insurance is becoming an attractive proposition for the smaller and medium-sized enterprise. A company with a turnover of £500,000 will probably find that its premium is well under half of what it may have been 10 years ago.

Collections Agencies

Using a professional collections agency is another affordable solution which can release valuable management time and resolve payment difficulties without recourse to legal action in a discreet manner. Like credit insurance, it is relatively underused, with only about 20 per cent of businesses in the UK using an agency to outsource the collection of debt, despite its effectiveness. In 1996, for example, over three-quarters of the debts collected by Trade Indemnity Collections were without recourse to law. A small number of collections agencies can also provide an effective and discreet international collections service.

Credit Management Tips

The following are some credit management tips from Trade Indemnity, the UK's leading international credit insurer. More can be found in its interactive credit management seminar, available on disk from the address below.

Terms of trade

- Make sure that terms of trade are clearly defined and agreed before despatching goods or providing services.
- Review terms of trade from time to time with a solicitor who understands your business and industry sector.
- Where appropriate, include a retention of title clause which will help you stake your claim over unpaid stock should your customer fail.

Credit limits

- Set and agree limits with all your customers and review these at least twice a year.
- Grade your customers by risk levels and treat their accounts accordingly. Pay particular attention to those that are growing very rapidly and be wary of companies that have emerged from the failure of another company.

Invoicing and collection

- Ensure that all customers are invoiced promptly and that each invoice is accurate and contains all the information needed by the customer, such as order numbers.
- Follow up the invoice with a phone call to check that it has been received by the right person and is correct.
- Before agreeing any repayment plan, determine whether the customer's situation is likely to improve. Do not agree to repayment plans that would take more than six months to clear a debt.

Staff, systems and procedures

- Give credit management a high profile in your business. Invest in specialist, experienced credit management staff.
- Establish a credit management information system that gives an accurate up-to-date picture of cash flow and outstanding credit situations and of the status of individual accounts.
- Check the status of each account before despatching goods. Do not continue to supply if the account is overdue.

General rules

- Do not let your business fund another's expansion.
- Do not accept that there is nothing you can do to avoid bad debts. With careful credit management, many incidences of bad debts can be avoided.
- Never assume that a long-established, previously prompt payer cannot possibly fail.

Founded in 1918, **Trade Indemnity** is the UK's longest-established and leading international credit insurance company and part of EULER, the world's leading credit insurance group. The company provides insurance of trade debt for UK and overseas sales against the commercial risks of buyer insolvency and protracted default, as well as political risks. In addition, it offers a variety of tailored-add on services and credit management advice.

8.3
Health and Safety for Growing Businesses

Craig Lydiate
Director, Aon Risk Services Ltd

The management of health and safety has to be seen as an essential part of an organisation's strategy to ensure continuing future value. Therefore at the operational level, it must be seen as part of every manager's daily responsibilities, along with others such as sales, production, cost control, quality, profitability and morale (see Figure 8.3.1).

Management can shows its commitment to safety by:

- applying a high priority to safety performance in the planning and evaluation of all projects and operations, and other business activities;
- setting a practical, enforceable and acceptable policy on health, safety and the environment which is a practical working strategy and not just a piece of paper hanging on the company noticeboard;
- monitoring performance via a programme of audits and inspections;
- allocating sufficient resources for the safety programme;
- having recourse to expert advice;
- Setting a good example: any disregard by managers of company safety standards will condone non-compliance in others;
- taking a personal interest in accidents: managers down the line need to take an interest in all accidents, their investigation and follow-up;
- actively participating in inspections and audits;
- including safety considerations, when issuing day-to-day instructions;
- discussing safety at management meetings.

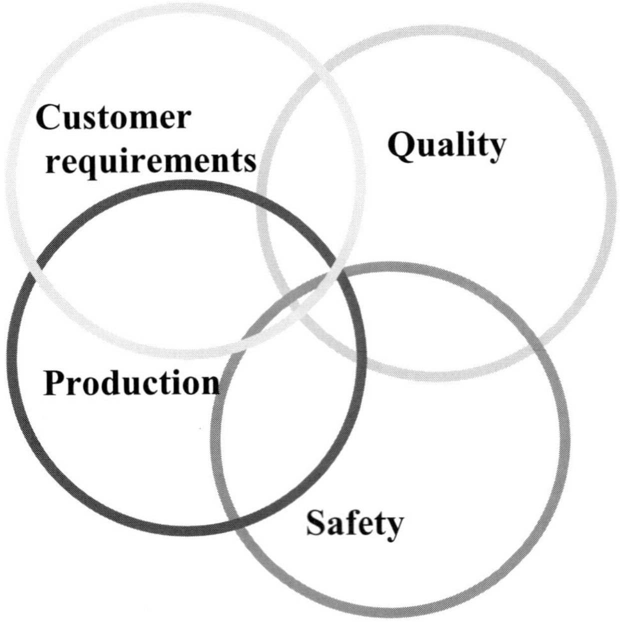

Figure 8.3.1 The role of health and safety

Indeed, many of the features of effective health and safety management are indistinguishable from the sound management practices underlying general business excellence, and those fundamental to the management of quality. The key elements of successful health and safety management are:

- set your policy (strategic);
- organise your staff;
- plan what you're going to do (tactical);
- do it;
- assess how you have performed (operational).

There are three principal reasons why health and safety needs to be properly managed.

Moral

No one can put a price on the pain and suffering involved in accidents and ill-health caused at work. This is not simply confined to the injured person — relatives and friends form part of the equation. It goes without saying that employers (and employees) have a moral duty to see that health and safety is taken seriously.

How Would Your Health & Safety Arrangements Stand Up In Court?

Ark HEALTH & SAFETY

By Rosalind Benjamin - Managing Consultant

Auditing Health & Safety Management - why it's so importanr

Recent years have seen an increase in Directors being found personally liable for shortcomings in their health and safety management systems

The Management of Health & Safety arrangements are under law required to be properly documented. Regulation 4 of the Management of Health and Safety at Work Regulations 1992 places a duty upon senior management to ensure that adequate health and safety arrangements i.e. management systems are in place for the effective planning, controlling, monitoring and reviewing of health and safety within the organisation.
The Health and Safety Executive guidance document "Successful Health and Safety Management" (HS(G)65) is a practical guide for the establishment of an effective health and safety management system.

However, Health and Safety Management is not a once and for all exercise, organisations need to continuously audit their management systems to identify gaps that require attention so that they can review and plan for continuous improvement.

Ark Health and Safety have delivered the solution. Through providing an audit service, using the HS(G)65 guide, Ark have developed an audit based on questions sets that measure the organisations' performance against the HS(G)65 guide. From this, a report is produced identifying strengths and weaknesses including quantifiable evaluation.

Benefits to the organisation.

The audit process comprises measures to test the performance of organisations in how they manage health & safety, against the requirements of :

- **Verification through a third party**
- **Health and Safety at Work etc. Act 1974**
- **Management of Health and Safety at Work Regulations 1992**
- **HS(G)65 Successful Health and Safety Management**
- **Documented Proof**

Organisations managing health and safety successfully display;

- the ability to control their health and safety risks and,
- the ability to demonstrate continuous improvement in their health and safety record.

Organisations undergoing 'due diligence' can have an independent third party audit which means that health and safety liability can be verified, or where the organisation needs to prove it has acted with due dilligence.

Documentation Requirements

A qualified consultant trained in audit procedure carries out a detailed analysis of the following, where available;

"Organisations undergoing 'due diligence' can have an independent third party audit which means that health and safety liability can be verified"

- Company Health and Safety policy (including statement, organisation and arrangements)
- Sample format of a general risk assessment
- Minutes of any health and safety meetings
- Documented safe systems of work
- Procedural Manuals, log book and schedules
- Accident, incident reports and historical documents of non-compliance
- Records of health and safety training instructions
- Induction packs for employees/contractors
- Details on health and safety audits and inspections

Finally a report is produced by the qualified consultant to present the quantified and qualified findings and recommendations using the latest computerised audit package. From this the qualified consultant can then, where required, formulate a tailored programme according to the principles of health and safety management practices, which form the foundations of success and intergrating with the organisations' existing management dynamics and systems.

Contact:
Enquiries administrator

Tel: 0171 582 5497 Fax: 0171 582 3496
E mail info@arkhealthandsafety.com
Internet http://www.arkhealthandsafety

HEALTH & SAFETY, WHY BOTHER?

Ark

HEALTH & SAFETY

By Rosalind Benjamin - Managing Consultant

The unstoppable eurocrats keep on churning out Health & Safety Directives on their member states. These directives lead to legislation which makes new far reaching demands upon enterprises large and small where existing legislation is insufficient.

For the hard pressed owner managers, senior executives whose remits might extend to set-ups, administering existing enterprises or turn around situations, health and safety legislation can present a daunting minefield of compliance problems, together with common law duties (the basic law of the land).

"Health and Safety legislation can present a daunting minefield of compliance problems"

But why comply?

Apart from the moral obligations every employer has to his or her workforce, there are many other issues to be considered when weighing up the downside of non compliance against the cost and investment required to comply.

Firstly, Owners, Directors and Managers face fines, criminal records, suspended jail sentences and in more severe cases imprisonment. The courts might go further to disqualify a director.

Not only that, today's British workforce is only too clear on the duties their bosses have in regard to health and safety, civil claims against companies and their officials are increasing dramatically, compounded by ambulance chasing legal practices and HSE advertising campaigns. These ubiquitous claims are more often settled out of court running into the thousands and sometimes hundreds of thousands.

Business Insurance rates are nowadays calculated on risk history including health and safety of those at work as well as how well the enterprise is seen to manage health and safety.

The softer issues also have to be considered, such as poor employee morale and productivity where workplaces are seen as risky and uncomfortable to work in, resulting in inflated absenteeism and poor performance.

If you are still not convinced, then how about if you decide on a merge, buyin, buyout or raising development capital etc. Enterprises undergoing 'due diligence' post offer are now being subjected to rigorous health and safety audits which may highlight deficiencies that will turn off the prospective acquirer or encourage a negotiation down in price.

How do you comply, and to what extent?

Once senior management are genuinely committed to managing health and safety, the issues surrounding how to comply cover the complexities of legal interpretation, business integration, total quality and competency of health and safety practice, and advice is a tricky one.

Unless health and safety is tackled on a holistic level, running horizontally and vertically through an organisation, with equal merit being given to the legal, quality, business and health safety issues, implementing and ongoing management will be faulted.

"Health and Safety should be seen as a business process"

Health and safety should be seen as a business process, like any other, first identify the aims and issues then plan, organise, monitor performance, and review to achieve the aims.

Apart from this approach being common sense it is law under the Management of Health & Safety at Work Regulations 1992 which in addition requires that employers appoint a 'competent person' to assist in undertaking the measures necessary to comply with the relevant legislation. Competence means where a person is regarded as having sufficient training and experience or knowledge and other qualities to enable him/her to properly undertake the measures needed to comply with the requirements of health and safety legislation.

For many companies the cost of employing a health and safety practitioner at middle management level can be costly, especially as more often their capabilities do not extend beyond health and safety and enforcement.

All to often their approach leaves deficiencies on complex points in legal interpretation, total quality and business integration especially re-engineering issues.

About us.

Ark Health & Safety as leading health and safety consultants provides the total approach by using well defined methods on legal interpretation, business integration, total quality and health and safety practice.

"Ark Health & Safety has developed consultancy services aimed at helping at any level in any organisation"

Ark Health & Safety has been helping organisations nationwide over the last 10 years to reduce their risks and comply with health and safety legislation with a strong focus on client service. Health, safety and environmental management has become an intergral part of operating any organisation and working together, using well defined and reliable methods. Our consultants align people, processes and the workplace with the clients health, safety and environmental management requirements. Whether clients require assistance to establish a firm foundation on which to build, or measures to monitor and control their existing systems and procedures, Ark Health & Safety can deliver services to meet a broad spectrum of needs. Recognising that company officers are facing greater responsibility and liability placed on them by demands of a wide range of legislation concerning fire, health and safety. Lack of health, safety and environmental management can have a far reaching impact on business including increased insurance premiums as a result of claims; litigation, prosecution and fines; loss of confidence by shareholders and financial institutions; as well as loss of business and poor public image of the company and its officers.

Scope of the service.

Ark Health & Safety has developed consultancy services aimed at helping at any level in any organisation in fire, health and safety and environmental management, from senior management and policy makers to planners and implementers and multi-nationals to small owner-managed businesses.

We will assist our clients towards compliance with health & safety requirements, which sets out requirements that encompass how the business is managed; improved; how its goods and services are distributed; how its purchases are made; how contractors are engaged and how its employees are managed and trained.

"Ark creates the most up to date, easy to implement solutions systems, which are both practical and cost effective"

Details of the service.

Ark creates the most up to date, easy to implement solutions and systems, which are both practical and cost effective for small and large enterprises. Through one of its executives, Ark will offer a complete solution to managing fire health and safety throughout a company's organisation and properties throughout the UK. Ark's flexible approach and wide range of services means that we can tailor a programme around clients individual requirements. Whether these are to establish, implement, monitor and review health and safety plans within the clients business and across its premises, or at a specific level, on a building or even on a process by process basis.

Our services include; adhoc advice; consultancy and training; auditing and accreditation development of health and safety policies and management; corporate health and safety manual; site operational health and safety procedures; general health and safety inspections, risk assessments; specific audits/surveys/assessments; helplines; advice and representation; health and safety training. A wide range of fire safety related services are provided including fire safety advice and representation; fire certification and updates; fire compliance surveys; fire safety training; fire evacuation drills; and emergency procedure manuals.

Contact:

Enquiries administrator

Tel: 0171 582 5497
Fax: 0171 582 3496

E mail info@arkhealthandsafety.com
Internet http://www.arkhealthandsafety

Legal

There are two areas of the English legal system which are important in health and safety — criminal law and civil law. As will be seen later, the consequences of not fulfilling the duties set out under each area of law can be financially crippling. A company may be literally stopped in its tracks, and individuals as well as the body corporate may be prosecuted. Neither the size of the organisation nor its state of development will mitigate its legal liabilities. The Health and Safety Executive in January 1997 secured its first immediate custodial sentence for offences under health and safety legislation (previous custodial sentences have been suspended).

Financial

The costs of accidents and ill-health can be split into two:

- the direct (or insured) costs;
- the indirect (or uninsured) costs.

The direct costs include the insurance premium (the employer's liability premium).

Direct costs

Employer's liability insurance claims and costs are escalating and it becomes more and more important to contain these costs. A critical eye is now being turned by insurers not only on the past experience (claims made) of a company, but also on a company's ability to manage health and safety effectively and hence contain future potential claims. The result of this change has been an unprecedented increase in premiums, even for low-risk companies, and, with the increasing awareness and willingness for the general public to initiate claims, the future does not look promising for companies who fail to take accident prevention seriously.

It should be considered that the increased premiums forced on companies can indeed place them in a correspondingly treacherous trading position in that costs must be passed on, reducing competitiveness and profitability.

While the most important consideration is not to have accidents, it is important that, once an insurance claim has been submitted, the company has adequate information and control of the system by effective accident investigation and good working relationships between the company and insurance personnel.

If you have an accident at work...

Sort it... report it

SORT IT HSE's new code of practice, *First aid at work* is aimed at all industries in the UK, setting out the aspects of first aid that employers need to address under the law. It shows employers how to comply with their legal duties and how they can offer practical and realistic first-aid support to their workforce.

First aid at work L74 ISBN 0 7176 1050 0 £6.75

First aid training and qualifications ISBN 0 7176 1347 X £8.50

First aid at work - your questions answered
Priced packs of 15 for £5.00 ISBN 0 7176 1074 8

Basic advice on first aid at work
Priced packs of 20 for £5.00 ISBN 0 7176 1070 5

REPORT IT You also need to report the incident by law - under the RIDDOR regulations. RIDDOR 95 is the Reporting of Injuries, Diseases and Dangerous Occurrences Regulations 1995, which came into force on 1 April 1996. The new RIDDOR replaces five sets of previous Regulations and makes things easier, simplifying what you should report and how to do it. They require the reporting of work-related accidents, diseases and dangerous occurrences and apply to all work activities (though not all incidents).

If you are an employer, self-employed or in control of work premises you will have duties under these Regulations. For most businesses a reportable accident, dangerous occurrence or a case of disease is comparatively rare but it pays to know what to do if something does happen.

A guide to the Reporting of Injuries, Diseases and Dangerous Occurrences Regulations 1995 L73 ISBN 0 7176 1012 8 £6.95

Everyone's guide to RIDDOR 95
Priced packs of 10 for £5.00 ISBN 0 7176 1077 2

F2508/2508A Reporting forms ISBN 0 7176 1078 0 £5.82 inc. VAT

First aid saves lives and prevents minor injuries becoming major ones

HSE priced and free publications are available from:
HSE Books, PO Box 1999, Sudbury, Suffolk CO10 6FS
Tel: 01787 881165 Fax: 01787 313995 or from good booksellers.

HSE BOOKS

Indirect costs

It has been estimated that the direct (insured) costs of an accident make up only about one-fifth of the total cost in some cases. The indirect or uninsured costs can include:

- safety administration costs;
- first aid/medical costs;
- cost of lost time of injured employee;
- cost of lost time of other employees;
- cost of replacement labour;
- cost of payments to injured employee;
- cost of loss to production;
- cost of repair to damaged plant;
- cost of damaged material;
- other costs etc.

A company should, realistically, spend 90 per cent of its safety effort on prevention. Therefore the safety adviser (part-time or otherwise) must learn to measure the total cost of the accident problem. This is not just the cost of major injury accidents, but those which are often left out — minor injuries, damage to property, plant, tools and equipment — which is normally 15 times greater. Unless the latter is taken into consideration, the company's final 'accident cost' figure represents only a fraction of the turnover that the company has actually been losing.

The Accident Pyramid

Most organisations still measure safety performance in terms of a reactive approach by recording accident statistics. The problem with this approach is that it ignores the vast majority of data available for measuring the effectiveness of safety programmes (for every serious or major injury there are up to 600 incidents with no visible injury or damage).

Following on from this concept of the accident 'pyramid', it is possible to define three categories under which measurements of safety performance can be made.

Measurement of consequence

These are measurements of accidents that have occurred and, as such, are reactive in nature.

Measurements of cause

These measurements allow an appreciation of the causes of accidents and can either be reactive in nature, such as accident investigation, or proactive by determining unsafe acts or conditions that may lead to a subsequent accident.

Measurements of control

These are measurements of the degree of control that is being applied by management in its safety management programme and are entirely proactive in nature.

Thus, to progress to a truly proactive safety programme, it is necessary to move away from reliance solely on accident statistics to the collection of measurements of consequence, cause and control, with emphasis primarily on measures of control.

Safety Audits

Safety management auditing constitutes the best means of obtaining a measure of control of an organisation's safety programme, by providing an independent assessment of the validity and reliability of management planning and control systems. Auditing provides managers with information on the implementation and effectiveness of plans and performance standards. It also provides a check on the reliability, efficiency and effectiveness of the arrangements for policy making, organising, implementing, measuring and reviewing safety performance.

Aon Risk Services Ltd is the UK insurance broking and risk management consulting operation of Aon Corporation. Over 3000 staff in more than 25 offices throughout the UK provide a full range of consulting and insurance services to all sizes of companies.

8.4

Product Liability in Europe

Trevor Cook
Partner, Bird & Bird

Product liability has a variety of legal bases. In Europe these take three general forms. There are the two traditional forms — the contractual relationship with the supplier of a product, and the fault-based liability of manufacturers or intermediaries with which one will typically not have a direct relationship sufficient to found an action in contract, and which is manifested in England by the tort of negligence.

However, for the last decade the countries of the European Union have had in addition a third basis of product liability, that of strict liability for defective products, established at a harmonised level by Council Directive 85/374, and implemented for example in the UK by the Consumer Protection Act 1987. This latter measure has been back in the news recently as an action brought by the European Commission, against the UK government alleging that the Directive had been incorrectly implemented in UK law, was thrown out by the European Court of Justice at the end of May 1997.

The dispute concerned the manner in which the UK had implemented the so-called development risks defence, which serves to mitigate some of the severity of a product liability regime which does not depend on a showing of fault. The Directive allowed member states to give a manufacturer of a defective product a defence if it proves 'that the status of scientific and technical knowledge at the time when he put the product into circulation was not such as to enable the existence of the defect to be discovered'. Most member states, among them the UK, have included this defence in their national implementation of the Directive. The UK, however, was criticised for having departed from the strict wording of the Directive in such a way, so the Commission argued, as to impose a subjective, rather than an objective, standard on the manufacturer. The European Court of Justice, apart from rejecting the Commission's complaint, took the opportunity of observing that the 'knowledge' referred to in the defence must be 'accessible'.

The development risks defence has particular application in high-technology industries where knowledge is not static and especially in that sector which has for long been a target of the product liability lobby — the pharmaceutical industry. But the defence has in practice been little used, perhaps because the effect of increasing regulation in industries such as pharmaceuticals has been successful in far reducing the risk of drugs with dangerous unknown side effects getting to market. Neither, irrespective of the application or otherwise of the defence, has there been the plethora of product liability litigation which it was once feared would follow the implementation of the Directive, considering the experience of strict liability laws in the USA. The reasons are largely matters of legal procedure, rather than of substantive law.

The first is a simple matter of proof. The introduction of strict liability has served merely to remove the need to demonstrate fault on the part of the manufacturer. In practice this was not the main problem with negligence, as fault would often be presumed, once a defect and causation had been established, and it would be left for the manufacturer to undertake the uphill struggle of proving that it had not been negligent. What the introduction of strict liability has not done is to remove the need to prove causation — a link between the defect and the damage — which has over the years proved and remains the great stumbling block in actions brought against pharmaceuticals manufacturers.

But the wider procedural factor at work is that Europe lacks the jury awards and punitive damages of the USA. Juries have a natural inclination to assume causation, and to favour individual plaintiffs against what they see as large corporations with deep pockets. In Europe the relatively low level of damages (damages are compensatory rather than punitive), coupled with restrictions on the ability of European lawyers to take cases on a contingency basis, has restricted the scope for the speculative actions seen in the USA — the ability that UK solicitors now have to take personal injury cases on a 'no win, no fee' basis is but a pale shadow of the latitude allowed to their colleagues in the USA. Still, however, in the UK the number of such actions has steadily increased, fuelled by the availability of legal aid, the absence of costs sanctions against legally aided plaintiffs, and a greater interest on the part of many solicitors, denied traditional sources of income from conveyancing, in looking to other sorts of work and the freedom that the removal of the restrictions on advertising has given them to do this. The economics favouring the bringing of such actions can be improved by combining actions in respect of a single type of defect suffered by numerous individuals into a single multiparty claim, and the English courts have developed procedures to facilitate such actions.

Even so, product liability has not yet proved to be the growth area for lawyers which one might have predicted several years ago, compared for example to professional liability for bad advice, where the sums in issue have been so vast and the developments such that the scope for insurance to cover the risks is limited, and where the pressure is now on governments to pass laws enabling defendants to such actions to limit their liability.

In contrast, insurance has effectively served the needs of those faced with risks in product liability. The bottom line for business is that if one makes products there is no legal fix which will lift the risk of an action in product liability. Such risk cannot be excluded by the use of contract terms, even though between those involved in designing and manufacturing products appropriate terms and conditions apportioning liability and imposing obligations to conduct proceedings and to indemnify do have their place. The best defence is to be able to demonstrate adherence to proper standards within the business, and to insure against the inevitable risk.

Trevor Cook is head of intellectual property at Bird & Bird. **Bird & Bird** has an international reputation for its work with leading-edge and technology-based businesses. Widely recognised as one of Europe's leading intellectual property practices, the firm has one of the largest departments dedicated to this field.

8.5
Boosting Windows NT Productivity and Security

John Wakeman
Sales and Marketing Director,
Symantec Northern Europe

According to research group IDC, sales of Windows NT are predicted to grow almost 700 per cent by the year 2000, giving the operating system a huge 40 per cent market share. Businesses migrating to Windows NT are looking to software companies to develop products to support the new operating system. One of their key concerns is in the area of data security and the main requirement is for faster and easier communications.

The Virus Threat

In the UK, analysts estimate that as much as £1.2bn is wasted in lost productivity each year by computer viruses. Dataquest predicts that nearly two-thirds of companies using computers have suffered virus attacks — and of those, over 60 per cent have resulted in lost productivity. The recovery time for an average local area network is 30 days, with the cost as high as £10,000 per network.

Viruses for Windows NT have been relatively slow to develop, this is largely due to the sophistication of the operating system. The cost of the higher-configuration PCs required to run NT is another factor. With the majority of virus writers thought to be teenagers and home PC users, limited access to this higher-cost equipment is slowing down virus production.

However, we can be certain that the deterrent effect of these factors will be overcome in the near future, in which case the numbers of NT viruses will escalate dramatically.

Symantec has invested heavily in developing a secure antivirus solution for the Windows NT environment. Norton AntiVirus 2.0 for Windows NT has been developed to protect both servers and workstations operating under Windows NT 4.0 and Windows NT 3.51. The system protects from viruses whether they are transmitted over the Internet, through intranets, attached to electronic mail, hidden in compressed files, or on floppy disks, hard drives, CD-ROMs, network drives and drives shared between peer machines.

A further threat to all computer users is the fast-growing number of operating system independent macro viruses which infect documents, spreadsheets and templates generated by Microsoft Word and Microsoft Excel. Norton AntiVirus automatically detects and repairs all known macro viruses, as well as providing the most advanced solution to help combat the ever-changing, chameleon-like polymorphic viruses.

The Need for Utilities in Windows NT

While antivirus software is designed to stop lost productivity due to virus infections, PC utilities are designed to enhance productivity by ensuring that computers consistently run smoothly, anticipating and fixing potential problems before they cause system crashes or data loss. There has been a growing demand from customers for a utilities solution that provides a safe, stable and robust environment for Windows NT. In response to this need, Symantec recently introduced Norton Utilities for NT.

Norton Utilities has two main components, Disk Doctor and Norton Speed Disk. Disk Doctor guards workstation files by protecting underlying resources such as memory or disk space, while monitoring the hard disk for problems, viruses or fragmentation. It monitors for impending problems and fixes them automatically before any damage is done. The user does not even need to know which utility to use — System Doctor automatically runs the programs as they are needed.

Speed Disk improves system performance by defragmenting files and free space on the hard disk and provides smooth multitasking, optimising the hard disk in the background while allowing the user to continue to work.

Another valuable part of the system is Norton Protection/UnErase. This keeps Windows NT files safe even when overwritten by other applications or deleted from the DOS box. It continuously monitors all file deletions, moving deleted files into a protected recycle bin from which they can be recovered as needed.

The Changing Face of Business Communications

Business communications are changing fast. The PC is increasingly being used as a communications tool, whether for e-mail, Internet, computer telephony or fax. The growing power and sophistication of notebook computers and the trend towards teleworking make PC communications ever more important.

Many Windows NT users need to access their PCs, applications and information remotely from home, from the office PC or network. Symantec's market-leading remote access solution for Windows NT, pcANYWHERE 32, enables quick and easy connections via modem, a network or even the Internet to check e-mail, support clients remotely, download files or run remote applications.

The communications software takes full advantage of the multitasking capabilities of Windows NT 4.0, allowing simultaneous remote control, file transfer and chat capabilities.

The Operating System of the Future

The development of software to safeguard data and facilitate leading-edge communications will be an important factor in the success of Windows NT, which looks set to become the backbone of the computer systems of the next decade. Symantec will continue to address customer needs, helping to make business systems more productive, cost-effective and, most importantly, more secure.

Symantec Corporation develops, markets and supports a complete line of application and system software products designed to enhance individual and workgroup productivity as well as manage networked computing environments. Platforms supported include IBM personal computers and compatibles, Apple Macintosh computers and all major network operating systems. Founded in 1982, the company has offices in Europe, the US, Canada, Australia and Japan.

Part 9
Financial Management

9.1

Knowing who you are Doing Business with is the Key to Credit Management

Peter Brooker
Associate Director, Experian

The new Labour government took a major step forward in its early legislative programme with its proposals to tackle late payment. The effect a late payment has on cash flow, particularly for a small, growing business, can sometimes make all the difference between survival or failure. When a major customer delays payment, the effect can be felt all the way down the line; invariably, it is the small business that suffers.

But the right of interest on overdue accounts only applies to payments that are already late. The objective of every business should be to minimise late payment and bad debts, which is why a well-managed credit control and management function is an essential management tool.

The CBI's prompt payers' code set out best practice and identified companies adhering to it, but in the end these are only guidelines and responsibility still remains with individuals and businesses. It is up to them to ensure they know exactly who they are doing business with and when, or indeed whether, they are likely to be paid.

Even if customers prove to be financially sound on an on-going basis, it does not mean that they will pay their debts on time. Many companies have a deliberate policy of holding on to cash as long as possible. However, research shows that nearly half of late payments are unintentional, suggesting that more rigorous credit management could reduce debtor days by as much as half.

What is clear is that, in general, the larger the customer, the longer it will take to pay its bills. Research from Experian shows that, on average, large companies take 72 days from date of invoice to pay, while small businesses are squeezed down to just 53 days.

In addition, whereas large companies tend to negotiate terms that require payment at the end of the month following the month of invoice, small companies are forced to accept 30-day terms from their larger customers. In effect, small businesses are providing their larger customers with as much as 15 days' free credit. Experian estimates that just 45 per cent of large customers pay their bills to terms. Effective credit management identifies those companies and gives the growing business the opportunity to negotiate more advantageous terms.

So how does the growing company avoid doing business with poor payers?

Effective credit management is all about knowing your customers. And not just new customers — as many as half of all bad debts are the result of the failure of long-standing customers.

Credit management is not just collecting payments. In fact, it is a measure of failure if the credit manager is spending all his or her time chasing payment. The critical time for credit management is before the sale is even agreed.

To be effective, credit management has to take precedence over many other considerations. Salespeople need to refer new customers to the credit control manager before accepting orders or negotiating credit terms, so that potential problem customers can be identified and weeded out before they become late payers.

In the past, credit checks often took the form of a bank reference and two trade references. Banks now charge heavily for this service and it requires the written permission of the customer to approach its bank. This causes lengthy delays and often leads to a sale being lost. It can also damage an existing customer relationship when there are concerns about the finances of a long-standing customer.

Before accepting a new customer or a repeat order from an existing customer, three questions have to be answered:

- Is the customer in a position to pay for the goods or services provided?
- How long does the customer take to pay its bills?
- How much credit should be extended?

The first step towards answering these questions is to analyse the company's trading performance and balance sheet to provide a credit rating and a credit opinion with a recommended limit to the value of goods or services

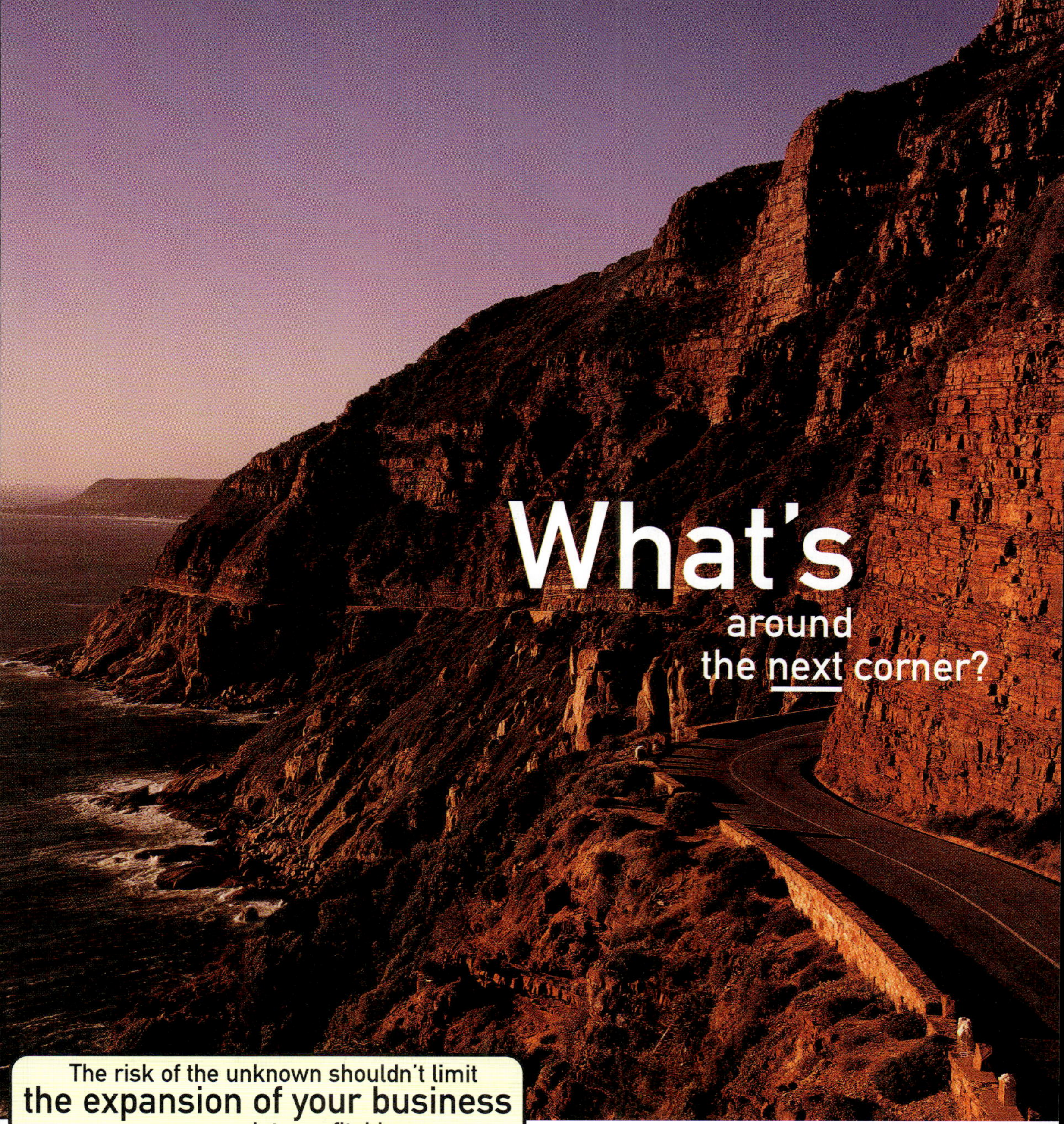

Why limit your business?

When you travel with NCM there is no such thing as the unknown. We have the most comprehensive knowledge of the countries, markets and sectors you might wish to expand into. To help you drive your business ahead, let our knowledge become your knowledge.

NCM not only provides for full credit protection, at home and overseas. We also have the wider range of business assistance and support to prevent you worrying about debts and claims. This comes from our having the experience of being the world's leading private credit insurer, supporting trade worth more than £ 75 billion annually.

We have unique services to supply credit insurance and market information to companies of any size from an instant On-Line service to a tailor-made service for multi-nationals. For your peace of mind, call NCM, 0800 - 801024, today. And get way ahead of the competition.

ncm credit management worldwide

the customer should be allowed on credit. Credit ratings on businesses are based on sophisticated scoring techniques to ensure that the credit managers can make sound decisions on whether and how much credit to extend.

With new companies or small businesses which have reduced reporting requirements, making it more difficult to analyse the company from financial information alone, it is often necessary to examine the people behind the company. This requires examination of alternative sources of information: on the directors of the company, to see whether they have a background of failed companies; on the company's record of paying its invoices; and on any adverse data such as County Court judgements, insolvencies or loan defaults. Armed with this information, the credit manager will have the answers to the three key questions regarding the creditworthiness of customers.

Inevitably, no manager of a busy, growing business has the time or resources to locate and analyse all the information themselves, which is why credit reference agencies have such an important role to play.

Many businesses now turn to credit reference agencies to provide the information they require to assess the risk of trading with a company. The major agencies are Experian (formerly CCN Group), Dun & Bradstreet and Infocheck.

With all the necessary information available on-line, over the telephone, fax or even the Internet, comprehensive reports are delivered in an easy-to-use format, enabling credit managers to navigate through the data, locate the desired information and interpret the findings easily.

Despite the well-documented economic recovery, it is just as important to be absolutely certain about a customer's creditworthiness now as it was in the height of the recession. Late payment is still endemic and there were still over 40,000 company failures in 1996.

While many failures affect new companies, many well-established companies hit trading difficulties, often as the result of late payment and cash-flow problems among their own customers. Subscribing to a business-monitoring service which keeps track of the financial fortunes of major customers will ensure that the growing business is alerted to any critical changes in a customer's financial status, whether positive or negative.

With early warnings of 'negative' information, appropriate action can be taken to ensure that any outstanding payments are collected early. On the positive side, should current financial information on an existing customer indicate a recent strengthening of the balance sheet, this could be taken as an opportunity to develop more business.

Ultimately, prevention is better than cure and well-disciplined credit management as the cornerstone of the customer management cycle is critical to the survival of the growing business.

Experian, formerly CCN Group, is the world's leading supplier of information on consumers, businesses and property. Experian's databases are supported by advanced software and analytical services for targeting new customers, building successful customer relationships and managing financial risk.

9.2

The Prevention and Cure of Bad Debts

Gerard P Barron
Managing Director, Commercial Division, Intrum Justitia Ltd

Any growing business can be killed in its infancy by the lack of control of its sales ledger. Bad debt can lead to the untimely decline of a growing business through lack of knowledge of credit control and the lack of understanding of the dynamics of the process of credit management.

Most growing businesses are, by their very nature, sales oriented and tend to ignore simple, but effective, rules for setting up their sales ledger management. These fall into two simple categories, as highlighted in the title of this chapter.

Prevention

Ensure that you have proper terms and conditions for conducting your business. This should include an 'all sums due' clause for retention of title of goods, so that in the event of the failure of one of your customers you can at least have some prospect of recovering your manufactured goods. Within the terms and conditions, onerous interest payments for late payment can be set out and agreed.

You should have a written credit policy to sit alongside the strategic plan of the business. It is important that the credit policy is relevant to the changing needs of the business as it grows and that there are mechanisms within the management of the policy to ensure that your DSO (days to sales outstanding ratio) is maintained at a level which is reflective of the industry and reflective of the stage in the business cycle that the growing business is in.

There is no point having a credit policy if it is not applied properly. You must, therefore, have the necessary resources to apply the credit policy and the procedures laid down and executed as a matter of course in running the business.

Before granting credit to customers it is always wise to take out credit information. This may seem expensive at first and on occasions be irrelevant if you are dealing with larger, stable businesses. It is often the case, however, that growing businesses tend to take more risk in their sales strategy, and if this risk is not tempered by making an objective view as to whether you will be paid, or paid on time, then the influence of sales over credit control may be so dominant that eventually the business becomes unstable.

The credit management policy should be backed up by procedures for implementation. You should also establish, at an early date, a referral mechanism to third-party collectors for the debts which are not able to be collected in-house by your procedures.

A procedure of allowing the third-party collectors to have some delegated authority to negotiate on your behalf is wise, and you should also ensure that their policies, documentation and approach to the debtor mirrors your wishes. It is often the case that a developing relationship with a potentially good customer could be strangled by inept collection techniques.

What About Cure?

If an invoice is paid late, you, rather than a bank, are funding your debtor. You should therefore develop initial contact procedures, post-sales, to ensure your invoices are sent on time, that they are not capable of dispute and that you have the necessary documentation to back up the invoice, such as proof of delivery. The invoice should then be followed by a statement and, where necessary, a 'Dunning letter' which reminds the customer that payment is required. Fair, polite but firm persistence is required for collecting debt.

Knowledge of the options available to you as manager, and indeed to your staff responsible for credit management, should be a priority. Training is provided by most large credit organisations to give credit control staff the basic knowledge of the options available to them. This will obviously include the limitations of legal proceedings if they become necessary, which will in turn clarify the expectations of the growing business in referring matters to collection or for legal proceedings.

For example, few businesses know that individuals and partnerships can be subjected to the threat of bankruptcy for debts as little as £750 by a process called a statutory demand. Also, currently, limited companies who owe an undisputed debt of £750 or more can be threatened with winding-up proceedings by way of a letter. The letter can be sent out by your third-party collectors for as little as £1.50 with no commission.

Where your systems fail, you will have to spend money to recover your debt, but you must remember that there is a realistic investment in the process to be considered. Many a small company has taken umbrage at the fact that its efforts have not been rewarded by payment and the owner/proprietor/manager of the business has taken the issue personally and spent an inordinate amount of time, effort and, very importantly, cash investing in debts which were clearly not collectable. This only leaves the growing business bitter and disenchanted with credit management, but it often fails to see what the causes of the dispute were rather than the effect.

Your third-party collectors should have good collection techniques and qualified staff to ensure that their efforts are simply not duplicating your efforts already invested in the process.

It is clearly evidenced in credit management that the intervention of a third party in the relationship between the supplier and the customer does send a message to the customer that you are prepared to put the effort in to manage your credit control. The threat of legal proceedings as a stage before the last resort sends a clear message to the customer that you mean business.

Any third-party debt collector is looked on by small businesses as a distress purchase. The anticipation of the small business is to have a fault-free, flowing process between sales, payment and cash control. Regretfully this is not the case.

A recent European-wide survey on late payment revealed that the UK is one of the worst countries within the European Union for prompt payment. The payment culture in the UK has developed over decades and it will require a substantial change in our attitude to the granting of credit and the collection of debt before this alters. Knowledge of the options available to you, and good preventive measures, will at least give the growing business the best possible opportunity for continuing growth.

Gerard Patrick Barron is the Managing Director of the Business to Business Division of Intrum Justitia in the UK. He is a Fellow of the Institute of Credit Management, a Fellow of the Institute of Licensed Debt Practitioners and holds a Master's degree in Business Administration. Working initially in the legal profession for 22 years, he now lectures widely on all aspects of credit management, but particularly legal actions and insolvency throughout the UK.

Intrum Justitia is Europe's largest credit management and debt collection provider, operating in 19 countries and with a network of agents throughout the world. Established 75 years ago in Sweden, Intrum Justitia has grown into one of the largest and most sophisticated collection businesses in the world.

9.3

Cashflow — Check you're Getting it Right

David Singleton
Lloyds Bank, Commercial Service

Vital to Help Your Company Grow

Cashflow management can make the difference between the success and failure of a business — good management gives a strong indication of the health of the company according to which strategic decisions can be made. Poor management can mask financial problems.

Cashflow forecasts are vital for the strength of the company and can be used for setting future strategy and buying stocks.

Good systems also minimise the negative effect of external forces, such as economic changes or the loss of a major account. Protection comes from being able immediately to assess the impact and to manage and limit any adverse effects.

A good cashflow forecast should set out all expected payments and receipts in a given period. In addition, a checking process which allows you basic control over the system should be in place to help ensure it works efficiently. A fundamental check is to monitor actual income and costs against the forecast.

Data from the Small Business Research Trust shows the majority of larger companies (turnovers of more than £1m per annum) update their forecast annually, although one-quarter said they updated them monthly.

However, despite knowing the importance of accurate forecasts, there is also evidence that growth businesses can be particularly vulnerable to weak cashflow management. One of the greatest risks is letting rapid expansion lead to overtrading. Danger arises when a business does not have enough money for new stocks and schemes because it is waiting for payment from previous orders.

While cashflow forecasts are crucial to the health of the company, they are a working tool which should not be used in isolation. There can be a danger of companies with weaker cashflow management becoming so focused on it that they lose sight of strategy and profitability.

Benefits of Good Cashflow Forecasts

Greater control

Good cashflow allows you to have greater control over your business. Bad practice can be fatal for your business if estimates are widely out or if it is in fact trading at very much lower levels than expected.

Increased profits

Knowing exactly how much money is available at any given period will allow you to make sound financial decisions on what to do with the cash. Decisions on where money is invested to help the company grow are crucial. Long-term commitment to areas such as staff training and updating equipment are vital to the health of the company, although evidence suggests that many growing companies fail to set aside enough time and money for training.

Secure discounts

Having funds at hand or knowing when they are likely to be available will also help to secure discounts on offer from suppliers for prompt payment which can have a substantial effect on profit margins. On the other hand, it can minimise the need to give discounts sometimes offered as an inducement for prompt customer payment.

Reduced bank charges

Knowing what money is in hand — and being able to make accurate forecasts — can lead to less reliance on bank borrowing, which will cut the cost of running your business.

How Cashflow can be Improved

Check your pricing policy

Money from sales is likely to be the largest single income to your business. Price levels should be set to give you the highest possible profit, reflecting a realistic assessment of the competition and the marketplace. Review pricing strategy regularly.

Scrutinise all costs

Many costs will have grown up with the business. It is important to ensure that all are justified. Review suppliers annually to see whether there is room for renegotiating your contract or whether you are still using the best source.

Payment authorisations

Monitor payment authorisations within the business. Make sure you know who is authorised to make payments and for how much. An outgoing from an unexpected source can unbalance the books.

Analyse stocks and build up a database

This will give you an immediate indication of what is selling well and will be a useful tool for deciding future sales strategy.

Operate a just-in-time stock system

Surplus stocks mean that money has been spent which is not working for you and will have reduced the capacity for stocking items which are faster moving.

Work smarter

Look at work patterns — improving work efficiency can reduce salary costs.

Electronic banking

No longer a luxury for growing companies, electronic banking allows you to see what is happening to your account at the touch of a button and means that you can keep close tabs on payments in and out.

Avoid late payment

This is crucial for good cash management. You need to get the money in so it can be working for you. Credit checks and your own credit scoring for customers are ideal ways of spotting potential problems before they arise.

David Singleton is business development director for **Lloyds Bank Commercial Service**, which serves businesses with turnovers of between £1mn and £100mn. His responsibilities cover strategic planning and marketing for the unit, which includes acquisition finance.

9.4
Managing Financial Risk

David Singleton
Lloyds Bank, Commercial Service

The Value of Financial Risk Management

Recognising and controlling business risk is a vital ingredient in management success, and interest rate risk is no exception.

Interest rates have traditionally been unstable in the past decade and movements erratic, with base rates averaging 10.9 per cent in that period. Movements can damage profit margins which are eroded by higher borrowing costs and can have serious implications for cashflow forecasts which in turn hit business plans. Hedging against uncertainty is an option to minimise the adverse effects on your business of strong interest rate movements.

Accurate cashflow forecasts are vital when considering financial risk management, so businesses should identify their interest rate exposure and then decide the likely impact on the business if rates go up. They also need to decide the duration of any cover and weigh up all these elements against the cost of the cover.

The Advantages of Financial Risk Management

Financial risk management gives certainty to the costs of borrowing which can help make long-term business plans achievable.

Accurate pricing strategy can also be drawn up to cover the costs of hedging. Hedging will also help give businesses the financial edge over competitors.

The Options

Fixed rate loan

These can enable a business to budget accurately as costs are stable, providing peace of mind. Various flexible repayment options include capital repayment holidays, stepped repayment structures and interest-only loans, with capital being repaid at maturity. However, one note of caution: break costs may be payable if for any reason you should decide to repay before maturity.

Base rate caps

If you believe that interest rates are likely to remain stable or even go down, you may still want to protect your business against the possible risk of an unexpected increase, whilst enjoying the benefits of a rate fall. Base rate caps are available for larger transactions (often upwards of £100,000) and are like an insurance policy. A pre-agreed rate is established (strike price) for a set period; if base rate goes above the strike price, you receive a refund of the difference. A premium is usually payable up front with the costs dependent on the strike price and length of cover.

Base rate caps, while fixing a rate ceiling for a set period, are not tied to any particular form of borrowing.

LIBOR caps

These are linked to the London Inter-Bank Offered Rate rather than base rate and are available to those who borrow on LIBOR. They are also available from a minimum of £500,000. LIBOR is a rolling average of the previous three months and offers greater stability from base rate changes.

Swaps

An interest rate swap is an alternative to using a fixed-rate loan, and allows the business to convert its variable rate into a fixed rate. Its greatest appeal is its flexibility; the business can protect itself while retaining the ability to repay all or part of the underlying loan. Generally, swaps are available from £500,000 for periods of between one and ten years and can be cancelled at any time.

Forward rate agreement

When planning ahead, perhaps predicting your seasonal borrowing or preparing a tender, it may be possible to fix the cost of finance in advance with a forward rate agreement (FRA). The rate is set at the prevailing market rate providing protection up to a maximum of two years forward. If rates at the chosen time exceed the FRA rate, you are reimbursed the difference; if rates are below you pay the difference.

Exchange Rates

The rapid appreciation of the strength of UK sterling in the first half of 1997 shows the importance of being able to manage exchange rate risk. Fluctuations in currency markets can play havoc with pricing and payment which can affect the profitability of business plans. If there are adverse movements, it can knock the health of importers who will see the cost of their payments rise — if the strength of sterling appreciates, it can hit the competitiveness of exporters whose goods can be bought cheaper elsewhere. For companies dealing internationally, whether as importers or exporters, protection against fluctuations is vital.

The Options

Forward contract

This is a commitment between you and the bank which means that the bank is obliged to buy or sell a foreign currency on your behalf at a specific rate for delivery at a future date.

Currency options

For larger amounts, currency options may provide security. If the rate moves in favour of the business, the option can lapse. Otherwise the business buys the currency at the designated price.

Currency accounts

These are vital for many businesses. If interest rates in the currency are less than those for sterling, businesses have the option of borrowing in currency at the lower cost.

9.5

Tax and Growth

Dr Andrew Jupp ACA BSc(Hons) PhD,
KPMG Tax

For a growing business, particularly one managed by its owners, there are few areas of taxation that do not require consideration at some stage in its lifecycle. Planning for succession, remuneration extraction, motivation and retention of staff and pension planning are all vital considerations, and owner-managers who do not give them due attention do so at their peril.

These are huge subjects in themselves, and outside the scope of this chapter, which concentrates on the taxation of the profits of the business. Of course, there are occasions when what is most tax effective for the company will not be most tax effective for the owners, and compromises will be required. But if we start from the premise that what drives and motivates an owner-manager is the creation of wealth within the business, then effective tax planning at the corporate level is paramount to growth and success.

The well-known and often overused phrase 'don't let the tax tail wag the commercial dog' is undoubtedly true; decisions should never be taken purely to save tax. But tax is a real business expense. What other single cost to the business — other than perhaps payroll costs — has such a direct effect on the profits available for growth? After all, the funds available for future spending, and hence future growth, are those remaining *after* tax. Therefore, while decision making based purely on tax strategy can never be advocated, decisions taken without due regard to the tax consequences are short-sighted in the extreme. In the space available it is impossible to do more than highlight some of the key areas in which the successful owner-manager will seek to minimise tax; each area could be the subject of a whole book. As well as mentioning the purely domestic considerations, it is the author's experience that sooner or later the growing company will encounter the complexities of overseas tax regimes — either by accident or design. Simply dealing with an overseas customer or supplier — and getting it wrong — can in a stroke wipe out the benefits of all your careful tax planning.

So what are the main areas with which the growing business should be concerned?

Structure

What is the most appropriate structure — sole proprietorship, partnership, company, group? This will be determined partly by size, partly by the personalities involved, and partly by commercial factors such as customer perception. But most businesses sooner or later will incorporate. When there is more than one line of business, is a group most appropriate? Consider this carefully: moving from one to two companies not only increases the administrative burden but immediately introduces a restriction to the availability of the small companies' rate of corporation tax. Get it wrong and your tax rate increases from 21 per cent to 31 per cent, and if you are in the marginal rate even higher. Maximising the use of the small companies' rate can provide a simple but very effective tax saving over a number of years.

Funding

The possibilities are covered elsewhere in this volume, but what about the tax effectiveness? Will interest on debt be tax deductible? Is the debt in the company best able to use the deduction? Can longer-term finance be provided tax effectively, maybe via the Enterprise Investment Scheme or a Venture Capital Trust?

Withdrawal of Funds

How can funds be withdrawn most efficiently to reward managers and investors? This must be determined by the company's cash flow and working capital position. Should dividends be paid or would remuneration be more appropriate? Dividends can be more tax effective if the company can use the ACT and pays at the small companies' rate of corporation tax, otherwise remuneration may be better. Where there are conflicting requirements, such as outside shareholders where the company would not obtain tax relief for 'remuneration', consider different classes of shares so that dividends can be paid on some but not others, or consider dividend waivers. Time the payments of dividends to minimise delay between paying the dividend and recovering the ACT, and to maximise the time before shareholders pay the higher-rate tax liability. Consider payments in kind so that the company saves employer's national insurance — effectively another tax. Remember that remuneration must be paid within nine months of the year end to obtain tax relief.

Reorganisations

For a trading company an expense will be tax deductible only if it is incurred wholly and exclusively for the purpose of carrying on the trade. The rules for investment companies are different; consider whether there should be a group holding company which should bear the expenses incurred on corporate acquisitions, disposals and reorganisations. Not all expenditure will be deductible, but more will be than in a trading company. When acquiring a business, consider whether it should be an asset purchase or shares. Asset purchases usually permit greater tax relief, especially if the purchase price is allocated to qualifying assets, but consider whether there are any benefits in a share purchase such as brought-forward ACT or unused tax losses.

Overseas Issues

The UK currently has one of the lowest corporate tax rates of most of its main trading partners. Sooner or later most growing businesses do business overseas. Simply sending a salesperson to another country for a few days can inadvertently create an overseas tax presence. Consider overseas tax strategies at an early stage; moving from one structure to another months or years down the line can create significant tax costs. Is a formal overseas presence required, and if so, what should it be? Branch, subsidiary company, or perhaps some form of commissionaire structure? Are there overseas tax-filing requirements? Consider how the overseas operation should be funded to maximise tax relief, set transfer prices to be defensible but as tax efficient as possible, and think about profit repatriation to minimise withholding taxes and to maximise cash flow.

Don't Forget the Basics

The most effective ways to minimise tax and maximise retained funds for growth are often the easiest. With an increasing trend towards profits for tax purposes being computed on the basis of the accounting profits, consider your accounting policies and the effect they have on tax. Consider capital expenditure, whether assets should be leased or bought, and time the expenditure so that tax relief is obtained sooner rather than later. Are provisions sufficiently specific to be tax deductible?

In conclusion, this chapter highlights the importance of tax strategy in assisting growth. Tax is a major cost to growing businesses. Both absolute savings of tax and the timing effects in terms of cash-flow advantages are vital in providing owner-managers with funds for growth and reinvestment.

Andrew Jupp is a tax senior manager with chartered accountants and business advisers **KPMG**. He leads the owner-managed business tax group in KPMG's Reading office and specialises in advising companies expanding both in the UK and overseas.

9.6
How to Unlock your Hidden Assets

Stuart Parker
Chairman, Factors and Discounters Association

Many small businesses are wasting valuable assets. Their unpaid bills, which they spend valuable time chasing and which go unpaid for several months, could be turned into cash immediately. The key to unlocking this precious resource is provided by invoice discounting and factoring.

How does Invoice Discounting Work?

In an invoice discounting relationship, companies send out their invoices, duplicating them to the discounter. On receipt, the discounter makes an immediate cash payment of typically 80 per cent of the approved invoice value, with the balance due when the customer pays.

Formally, the small business sells its unpaid invoices on a continuous basis to the discounting company. These provide the security for the discounter to provide the cash.

The client maintains full control over the sales ledger and is responsible for chasing slow payers.

Invoice Financing For The Discerning Business

A bold statement, but one that can justifiably be made by **Credit Lyonnais Commercia Finance**. As part of our European heritage, we adopt a longer term, relationship-based attitude towards our business partnerships. We believe this attitude generates a more flexible relationship and allows a mutually beneficial solution to all aspects of invoice financing.

We use Invoice Financing as a generic term for all forms of Factoring and it's derivatives, which represent one of, if not the, UK's fastest growing forms of finance. Based on statistics released by the Bank of England the industry accounts for about 7% of lending to small businesses in Britain. To speak of the demise of the traditional bank overdraft may be a little premature, however the raising of cash against a business's invoice offers a flexible, non-demand facility based on the future potential of a business, rather then the historic past trading.

Within the industry it is still the high Street banks-not traditionally seen as friends of the small business - who control as much as 80% of the market, through their factoring subsidiaries. The main reason seems to be inertia, given that our own research shows that around 70 % of business who factor only look as far as their bank introduced subsidiary.

We believe there is an alternative for those discerning businesses who wish to control their own future.

To this end Credit Lyonnais have developed a range of ***OPTIONS*** which allows a business the ability to choose the level of administration and cost it wants, potentially halving factoring costs.

OPTIONS includes:

Agency Factoring - a business manages it's own credit control.

Single Invoice Factoring - ideal for businesses dealing with large single orders or peak season trading conditions.

Full Factoring - involving full credit control, administration and optional credit insurance.

Selective factoring - business handles credit collection for major customers.

Export factoring - a full factoring service for businesses who export some, or all of their turnover.

Invoice discounting - a business manages it's own credit collection and administration.

This range of ***OPTIONS*** highlights our flexibility and approach to our business relationships.

Your relationships with CLCF will be handled by an experienced Client Manager who only has approximately 25 businesses to look after.

Your credit collections will be handled by an experienced credit controller dedicated to your customers, not a computer sending out letters and a pool of clerks telephoning from a list.

We can be flexible because we know our business partners, the discerning ones!

Want to know more, then contact Les Brown at Credit Lyonnais Commercial Finance Ltd at Icon House, Selsdon Way, Docklands, London E14 9GL or telephone 0171 712 4888 quoting ref: LBScbi

How does Factoring Differ?

Factoring provides the same financing facility. The firm sells, on a continuing basis, all its invoices to a factoring company which immediately gives it up to 80 per cent of the agreed value in cash. However, the factor then collects the debt itself. The remaining 20 per cent of funds is returned to the company when the invoice has been settled with the factor. The factor also takes over responsibility for the administration of the sales ledger and credit management.

In addition, it offers the option of credit protection. With this arrangement, the factor provides 100 per cent credit cover against bad debt losses, thus protecting profit margins. Alternatively, companies may prefer not to take credit protection if they have a large spread of customers or alternative arrangements for credit insurance.

For companies with a large spread of customers or those which already have credit insurance, recourse factoring, where credit protection is not provided, may be more suitable.

Both factoring and invoice discounting are growing rapidly in popularity as mechanisms for companies to improve their cash flow and sharpen their sales administration.

Today, more than 19,000 growing companies use factoring or invoice discounting services provided by members of the Factors & Discounters Association (FDA). FDA members currently factor around £40bn of debts for British firms each year and that volume is rising at an annual rate of more than 20 per cent — making factoring one of Britain's fastest-growing forms of finance.

In the past, expanding businesses may have turned to their bank for an overdraft, but many banks are now far less welcoming than they were in the 1980s. Banks were generally battered by bad debts as a result of the fall in property values in the early 1990s and the business failures which accompanied them. They now tend to be highly cautious about increasing lending to small and medium-sized companies.

What is more, banks will rarely lend more than 35 per cent of the value of trade debts and impose limits on their lending based on historical criteria — usually the value of property owned by the company or its directors. These tend to remain depressed long after a recovery in business activity. A business dependent on an overdraft facility, therefore, may be unable to capitalise on a potential increase in orders because it is constrained by external borrowing limits.

By contrast, finance from factors and discounters is automatically linked to today's and tomorrow's debts and is therefore able to keep pace with a company's working capital requirements. As business grows, factoring and discounting can offer a far more flexible and growing source of finance than the traditional bank overdraft or loan. Uniquely, they offer companies finance linked to their *current* levels of business, so that as a company increases sales, the more money the factor or discounter is able to advance against unpaid invoices.

Late Payment

Concern about the damaging effects of late payment has focused many companies' attention on both factoring and discounting over the last few years. Only around half of all firms in Britain are now being paid on time and most wait at least 75 to 80 days for customers to pay up, compared with normal business terms of 30 days.

With bad debts spinning out of control, it is hardly surprising that factors and discounters have been besieged with enquiries from potential customers. They can offer not only immediate cash payments of typically 80 per cent of the value of approved invoices, but also much speedier debt settlement, now down to an average of just 59 days. For the multitude of companies plagued by illiquidity, the attractions are obvious.

SALES LEDGER FINANCING BRANCHES OUT

Small and medium-sized businesses need an easily accessible source of cash to fund working capital and finance growth. For many UK companies, especially businesses which are growing quickly, overdrafts or bank loans may not be flexible enough to help them face the challenges of today's economic climate. Research by Barclays Commercial Services (BCS), the sales ledger financing subsidiary of Barclays Bank, shows that the use of factoring and invoice discounting has grown by 280 per cent in the last decade - suggesting that sales ledger funding is now a key cashflow solution for expanding businesses.

Sales ledger financing is a simple method of releasing the cash tied up in a customer's unpaid invoices, providing working capital within 24 hours of a business issuing an invoice to its customers. Using a sales ledger service will also reduce the collection period for outstanding invoices from 75 to 80 days, down to an average of below 60 days.

Unlike traditional funding solutions, sales ledger financing promotes natural business growth. Factoring and invoice discounting facilities accommodate a growing business by providing extra funds automatically linked to increased sales. In almost every case substantial additional more cash is available through sales ledger financing than through more traditional bank lending.

Barclays Sales Ledger Financing has over 30 years experience of providing a full portfolio of factoring and invoice discounting facilities and fully understands the challenges facing growing businesses.

If you feel your business can benefit from unlocking the working capital tied up in unpaid invoices to fuel business growth, please contact your local Barclays branch or call

Barclays Sales Ledger Financing

Sales Support Team on:

0800 227 222

Costs

The factoring and discounting solution is a highly cost-effective one. The charge for finance secured against sales is normally equivalent to the prevailing overdraft rate, and has recently in fact tended to be lower.

Administration charges for full service factoring range between 0.5 and 2.5 per cent of gross annual turnover, and for invoice discounting between 0.2 and 0.5 per cent. But in most cases, these costs are comfortably covered by savings, from a reduced administrative burden and lower bank charges to the flexible provision of finance, and by the additional growth that the facility can fuel.

The Factors and Discounters Association comprises the majority of factoring and discounting firms operating in the UK and Ireland. The Association exists to promote flexible forms of finance to a wide public of users, potential users, trade associations, professional bodies and government.

Stuart Parker, Chairman of the FDA, is also Managing Director of NMB-Heller Commercial Finance Ltd, a member company of the FDA.

9.7
Business Finance: Which Route to Take?

Martin Hall
Director General, The Finance & Leasing Association

Choosing the best way of financing assets is a vital, if somewhat daunting, feature of running a business. You often know your requirements and what you have to spend. But do the two tally and, if so, what is the best way to finance the asset to suit your present and future business needs?

In this chapter the Finance & Leasing Association (FLA), whose members fund over a third of all UK fixed investment through a number of different finance schemes, maps out what the various business finance options have to offer.

Outright Purchase

Paying cash is generally the easiest and least expensive option. It does, however, carry quite a high risk, with the possibility of encountering cash-flow problems in the long term. It is also the case that your money could be more profitably employed elsewhere in your business. Due to high administration costs finance houses tend not to consider financing anything under £2000–£3000, thus limiting the choice available to you.

Pros

- The transaction is interest free if you fund out of reserves (bank or finance house borrowing will incur interest).
- You can sell the asset at any time.
- You can claim back VAT.

Cons

- It could cause you cash-flow problems.
- Maintenance costs require budgeting and can be expensive.
- Your capital could be put to other uses.

Hire Purchase

Hire or lease purchase is the only option (except outright purchase) which will eventually result in you owning the asset. It is therefore important that you ascertain the value of the asset at the end of the agreement.

Pros

- You can claim back the VAT on the capital — up front.
- Interest is allowable against profits.
- Your working capital remains intact.
- You eventually own the goods.

Cons

- You take most of the risks of ownership.

Finance Lease

Although the finance lease is similar in economic effect to hire purchase, the ownership of the asset remains with the leasing company. The finance lease agreement can consist of two periods, primary and secondary. The primary period is the lease period that was initially agreed and during which the rentals, consisting of capital and interest, are repaid. If the asset turns out to have a longer working life than expected, the agreement may enter a secondary period at nominal cost.

Pros

- You will not have any ownership worries.
- Rental charges are allowable against profits.
- VAT can often be reclaimed on the full amounts of the rentals.
- You may be able to decide when and if the asset is sold.
- If sold you may get a rebate in rentals from the proceeds.

Cons

- It is the leasing company which claims capital allowances — you cannot claim them.

Operating Lease/Contract Hire

This is basically a long-term hire agreement where the asset remains owned by the leasing company. Rentals are payed over an agreed period.

In the case of an operating lease, rentals only cover the depreciation on the asset and the finance charge. With contract hire the agreement will also include maintenance.

These agreements are usually more common with assets which have a strong second-hand value and market as well as a determinable working life.

Pros

- You do not have ownership worries.
- You do not have to dip into your working capital.
- You don't usually have to worry about resale values on the asset.
- You can set rentals against profits.
- The agreements are classed as 'off balance sheet'.

Cons

- Equipment needs to be well maintained as this is linked to residual values.
- It is the leasing company which claims capital allowances — you cannot claim them.

Before you Sign

Once you have investigated which finance option best suits your needs, remember to make the following checks before entering into any agreement:

- Is the finance house or leasing company reputable? Does it belong to an organisation such as the FLA which operates a code of practice to which all its members adhere ?
- Have you chosen a finance house/leasing company which can offer the best deal on your requirements, as some specialise more in particular asset types?
- Is the agreement flexible to account for any future changes in your business requirements?
- Does the length of the agreement realistically match the life of the asset?
- Do you understand your responsibilities and those of the finance house/leasing company for any maintenance contracts?

The **FLA** is the principal representative body of the UK finance and leasing industry. Members' outstandings currently total £82bn. FLA members are drawn from merchant banks, high-street bank subsidiaries, leasing companies, leading finance houses and the finance arms of manufacturers and retailers. Collectively, they finance over one-third of all UK fixed investment, 30 per cent of all consumer credit and over 50 per cent of all motor finance. Adherence to the Association's Code of Practice is a condition of full membership.

9.8

VAT Planning

George Michie
KPMG Tax

Why Plan for VAT?

Value Added Tax (VAT) is a tax that is of vital importance for every business, regardless of the stage of its growth or evolution. As a self-assessed tax, the burden of compliance is laid on the business itself and it increases in its complexity and scope with each passing budget. Add to that the European dimension (whereby each EU country's domestic VAT system must conform to a common ideal), and it is not difficult to appreciate why VAT is assuming a heightened profile in every company's tax affairs.

In this context, it is vital for every business, and particularly *growing* businesses, to make the greatest use of all the various VAT facilitation measures that are available. VAT planning of this kind is not to be confused with VAT avoidance, which is very much in the news at the moment. This is because VAT planning is no more than sensible housekeeping: making sure that nothing more than the correct amount of VAT is accounted for to HM Customs & Excise (Customs), no earlier than it needs to be paid over.

Over the years since VAT was introduced in 1973, Customs have come to recognise that the compliance burden impacts disproportionately severely on smaller and growing businesses, so they have introduced a number of measures to make life easier for the busy entrepreneur. The aim of this chapter is to highlight what benefits are available and how to make best use of them.

VAT Registration

Registration for VAT is the first step that any business should consider. Many, however, do not consider it soon enough and incur penalties. Others, particularly those that are incurring substantial start-up or pre-stocking costs, do not appreciate that registration can be applied for (as an 'intending trader') in advance of making taxable supplies. This can mean valuable cash-flow benefits, which can be very useful when substantial costs are being incurred. Similarly, where a business is incurring costs over a protracted period before any income is received (such as with a property development or refurbishment project), a monthly return facility at this stage enhances input VAT recovery.

For a business expanding by acquisition, there are two important issues to address: if the business being acquired is a 'going concern', ensuring that VAT is not incorrectly charged by the vendor; and considering the benefits of VAT group registration, particularly to avoid having to charge VAT on inter-company invoices.

Cashflow Issues

Other than those mentioned above, a number of other facilities can improve cash flow. Where taxable turnover does not exceed £350,000 (VAT exclusive), use of the 'cash accounting' scheme can eliminate all bad debt worries, as VAT does not have to be paid to Customs until it is received from the customer. The downside, however, is that VAT incurred on purchases cannot be reclaimed until they have been paid for.

Two other measures can spread the pain of accounting for VAT. Where payment is made by credit transfer, the due date can be extended, subject to Customs' prior approval, by up to seven days. However, care should be taken when weekends or bank holidays intervene; and larger VAT payers —£2mn + pa— are not eligible. The 'annual accounting' scheme is available for use by businesses whose VAT-exclusive taxable turnover does not exceed £300,000. Where turnover is between £300,000 and £100,000, nine monthly payments are made on account of the estimated turnover (the first payment not being due until the last day of the fourth month of the accounting year). At the end of the year, the single annual return is submitted, together with a payment to satisfy the actual liability. For businesses whose turnover is £100,000 or less, the benefits are even greater, as only three (quarterly) payments on account have to be made.

Late or non-payment by customers is a perennial problem, especially for growing businesses. Under the bad debt relief scheme, VAT accounted for on supplies that remain unpaid for six months or more after the date payment was due can be reclaimed, even though it may be expected that the customer will ultimately settle his bill. However, a provision in this year's Finance Act means that a VAT-registered debtor must be notified of a claim, which could lead him to assume that the debt itself had been written off.

Property

Every business, regardless of the sector in which it operates, is involved with property, whether as occupier, landlord or investor. Especially where it is not a core business activity, the complexity of the VAT rules affecting property transactions can easily be overlooked. It is not within the scope of this chapter to analyse these rules in depth. Suffice to say that Customs have reclaims of VAT on property costs very much under the microscope at the moment and, although their focus is on what they perceive as tax avoidance, the rules potentially affect many legitimate commercially driven transactions and there are expensive pitfalls for the unwary.

Disputes with Customs

It is perhaps inevitable that even the best-organised business can come into confrontation with Customs. This is especially the case with a growing business, where the increase in turnover will result in increased scrutiny by the local VAT office. There are certain guidelines that should always be followed. If an officer on a visit to your premises expresses a view on any issue of importance, make sure that it is confirmed in writing. This is because Customs will only treat themselves as bound by a written ruling. If an officer indicates that he intends to raise an assessment, seek to negotiate before it is actually issued. This could avoid a situation where positions become entrenched. Once an assessment has been issued, there is a valid alternative to an appeal straight to the VAT Tribunal. Under the informal 'local review' procedure, an officer senior to the one who issued the assessment will conduct an internal review. However, it is vital that your case has been well prepared, to ensure that it is properly reviewed.

The Way Forward

Successive governments, regardless of political hue, have recognised the need to reduce the public borrowing requirement. Indirect taxes which, pound for pound, are perceived as the most cost-effective to collect (by the Treasury at least, notwithstanding the immense administrative cost to the taxpayer) are the obvious target to help achieve this aim. The 'Spend to

Save' initiative, currently coming into full operation, is a signal to every growing business that VAT is going to be increasingly relied upon as a source of central government revenue. However, for the taxpayer, as has been highlighted above, VAT planning makes good business sense. It is vitally important to recognise not only that the VAT pitfalls must be avoided but also that VAT can, by careful planning, actually be made to work *for* a growing business.

George Michie joined **KPMG** in 1989 and is the partner-in-charge of the firm's Indirect Tax Services Group. He is also chairman of the KPMG International VAT Committee and a member of the Institute of Taxation VAT Sub-Committee. Previously, Michie spent three years in the Fiscal Policy Unit at HM Treasury, where he acted as tax adviser to Peter Lilley, the then Economic Secretary to the Treasury responsible for indirect taxes.

Part 10
Making the Most of IT

10.1

The Future of Networking: Global Networked Business

Paul Mountford
Managing Director, Cisco Systems

Traditional business philosophy dictates that companies keep customers, partners and employees outside their information bases. Information and internal systems have been seen as strategic assets to be shared only on a selective basis in order to minimise risks. When they have been shared, it has often only been through expensive, cumbersome technologies and interfaces such as electronic data interchange (EDI).

Market research company IDC predicts that the entire electronic commerce market, including consumer sales, will grow to $117bn by the year 2000. They also predict that business-to-business transactions will be 95.6 per cent of that market. But electronic commerce is just one part of what we see as the 'opening up' of companies in the future.

To be competitive, businesses need to maximise revenue, contain costs, build scalable, controllable business transaction systems, and foster close relationships with their customers, partners, prospects, suppliers and employees.

Businesses who have not yet realised that they are competing in a global, networked market are both missing opportunities and allowing competitors to gain important economic advantages. Cisco believes that being connected is not enough; electronic commerce is not enough; you need to be networked to all your important constituencies.

The way forward is to move to a *global networked business* environment — an open, collaborative way of working which transcends traditional barriers and sets new standards for relationships with customers, partners, prospects, suppliers and employees.

A global networked business allows its various business constituents to define and control the manner by which they access information, resources and services. This must be done in a reliable, secure and efficient way. Once enabled, global networked businesses can expect to reach new markets; maximise revenue growth; process customer transactions more efficiently; reduce the cost of sales; improve productivity; deliver customised support; improve product quality and time to market.

Companies can enable this new business model by simplifying their network infrastructures and deploying a unifying software fabric that supports end-to-end network services.

Open access to information, resources and services through a networked business environment sets new standards for relationships with customers, partners, prospects, suppliers and employees. The global networked business represents a new business model, removing barriers to relationships and ultimately ensuring mutual success.

How the Internet can help your business

The Internet has quickly become one of the most significant developments in the Information Age. It is currently estimated to consist of 45,000 networks worldwide, connecting an estimated 30 million people. It is growing at an astounding rate. In 1992 the volume of data moving over the Web was 500 megabytes. Just two years later, data volume was 20 times as much each day. One industry source is predicting that the Internet user population will exceed 100 million by 1998. And every day, thousands of companies are joining the Internet, either to use it for communications or to use it for marketing and real commerce.

By applying Internet technology to dozens of its business areas with customers, prospects, business partners, investors and employees, Cisco is predicting that it will save approximately $250 million in the next 12 months and that number continues to increase. Cisco's global networked business is demonstrated by the Cisco Connection family of services. Using these systems, Cisco leverages networking to conduct interactive, engaging business relationships with its business constituents. Through networking, Cisco provides immediate, open access to its information and resources — at any time, anywhere.

The use of Cisco Connection Online (CCO) has grown explosively. By 1993 there were 5000 logins to Cisco's Web site per month — now there are more than 400,000 per month. In fact, more than 75 per cent of registered customer requests are now handled on-line. A natural worry would be that customer satisfaction would suffer due to lack of personal contact, but Cisco's satisfaction rating has increased 30 per cent over the past few years.

The benefits of this are many:

- By using the Internet, information is available at any time and anywhere.
- Ordering products over the Internet means that there is less chance of human error and improved delivery times (now down to two or three days). The number of customers who choose to order in this way is continually increasing and is now over 25 per cent.
- Downloading software files over the Internet eliminates any wait for upgrades, new features, bug fixes and other enhancements. More than 70,000 Cisco software files are currently downloaded by customers each month.
- Improved and faster technical support is offered to customers in a way that is cheaper for Cisco. Approximately 70 per cent of all technical support enquiries are resolved through Web-based applications. This frees up Cisco's technical support staff and gives them time to devote to the most difficult questions which need to be dealt with by phone.

Cisco believes that its intranet adds significant value to internal processes by improving employee productivity, enhancing internal communications and collaboration, and reducing costs. The site has dozens of applications that touch almost every aspect of the company's international operations, including registration for training classes, submission of expense forms, computer and telecommunications support, human resource forms and procedures, employment opportunities, events planning, facilities management, sales tracking and competitive analysis.

Cisco has used the Internet to achieve tangible business benefits. By using it to make many of its processes more efficient, it has freed up its employees for other tasks where their skills are of most value. Cisco's success as a global networked business can be attributed to three key factors: expertise gained through historical networking marketplace leadership; ability to scale with tremendous growth by leveraging its network; and its commitment to the needs of customer, partner, prospect, supplier and employee success.

Paul Mountford has 14 years in the IT industry and prior to joining Cisco ran an independent channel business advising UK companies on international channel and distribution strategy, as well as setting up US technology companies' European channel operations. **Cisco Systems** is the worldwide leader in networking for the Internet. A 1995 study by The Yankee Group, a Boston consultancy, reported that more than 80 per cent of the routers that form the backbone of the global Internet are from Cisco.

10.2

Use of IT to Support the Global Supply Chain

Geoff Robb
Business Systems Manager,
Hi-Tech Logistics Ltd

Changing Face of Logistics

Logistics has been steadily changing, with companies having a need to maintain their competitive edge by looking further afield to find reductions in costs and improvements. Having the best products does not always guarantee success or profitability.

Traditionally, organisations tended to concentrate on getting products to the retailers at the lowest cost. Now more and more companies are concentrating on improving customer satisfaction. In this way they are putting pressure on the ability to meet customer requirements with products at a price that they are willing to pay while at the same time achieving the required level of growth that is the lifeblood of any company.

A current problem with a number of businesses today is that they still operate using yesterday's technology and processes, which are usually labour intensive and inefficient. One way in which this can be improved is through more efficient use of IT to provide increased control of the supply chain through automating stock and order processes.

At the heart of each company, therefore, is a need for software which will allow the business to be able to provide cost-effective solutions, in essence using technology more accurately to control and automate the supply chain, eg to automate the planning and generation of new supply orders to fulfil current demand.

The Supply Chain

Figure 10.2.1 is a supply chain model which can be applied to many industries and/or companies.

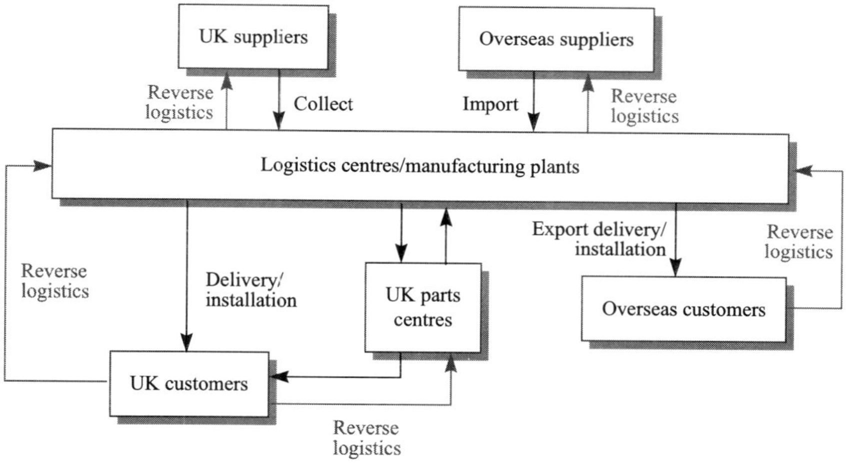

Figure 10.2.1 Total supply chain management

Typically the supply chain covers the collection of raw materials, components and product from customers and business suppliers. These are delivered to logistics centres/manufacturing plants where various added-value activities may be carried out. This can mean order consolidation, customisation, configuration, cross-docking, software loading and testing.

Delivery can be on a scheduled, urgent or emergency basis, either within the UK or overseas, direct to customers or to customers' customers. Added value can be carried out through product installation or, in the case of parts distribution, stored close to where they are eventually used by customers' engineers.

But that is only half the picture. The model covers support for reverse logistics, whereby material can be collected from customers and delivered back to logistics centres for inspection, repair or consolidation. Some product may be returned to the original manufacturers under warranty, some repair work may be carried out at logistics centres.

A global logistics network and infrastructure will enable the provision of any combination of managed logistics services/manufacturing plants. The use of IT is key to enabling all or part of the supply chain to be tailored to suit individual or specific logistics requirements.

What can be Done?

In order that the best use is made of IT in providing a solution, the basic requirements need to be evaluated with a view to the provision of a business management system which will provide the level of control desired.

Software solution

The software solution must provide a high degree of control with certain basic functions. Additionally, it needs to be future proof well into the twenty-first century if it is to provide the financial investment and return on what will be a sizeable investment.

Flexibility is key to the success of the application. It will have to be parameter driven to accommodate changes in business direction and customer needs without having to change the basic code of the application (something that is costly and time consuming).

The basic functions required by such a system would typically include:

- accounting;
- marketing/customer care;
- delivery load planning;
- order scheduling;
- MRP II;
- stock movements;
- manufacturing, ie bill of material, works order processing, job costing;
- inventory management, ie status, accuracy, order profile, visibility, asset control.

In defining the total requirements for an integrated package, it must encompass a function to support the total supply chain and thereby link all the organisational business groups, from purchase of raw material through to delivery of finished products, and also return of products for scrap after the lifecycle is complete.

The vital question that needs to be addressed is the type of software and the level of investment that should be made. There are three main avenues/solutions that could be used.

Bespoke

The perfect answer would be to develop a solution which encompasses all the functionality that would be required specifically to suit one's own business needs. Starting with a blank sheet of paper may be utopia for the developers; however, this is often a costly solution and the time lapse will in the majority of instances be too protracted.

Best of breed functionality

Another possibility would be the purchase of individual best-of-breed applications which cover all the functions required. Although this would provide, at an individual level, the functionality required, it should be noted that integration of disparate applications is usually difficult to achieve and often very expensive when one has to consider connectivity.

Integrated application

Another alternative is to match the requirements against industry standard integrated software, ie off-the-shelf applications, particularly as there are now many vendors who will provide specific software for a particular marketplace. Usually these packages are parameter driven and can therefore be finetuned to suit almost any business.

There are many benefits of using such integrated packages:

- immediate availability, ie off-the-shelf;
- implementation support is usually available from the supplier;
- ability to view the product at a reference site;
- the stability of product can be demonstrated and it is not necessary to go through a protracted test period;
- products are kept current and up to date by the supplier, who will upgrade to make use of new technology and additional functionality.

As you would expect there are drawbacks to integrated packages:

- unlikely to achieve a 100 per cent functional match;
- where there is 'missing' function it will mean installing a base product and bespoking only the 'missing' functions deemed to be vital.

As companies look for the magic factor that will give them a competitive edge, it must be recognised that whatever formula is found, it must be able to fit seamlessly into the supply chain or it is doomed to failure.

Solutions implemented must be flexible, robust, easy to use and cost effective. It should be remembered that IT is a tool that will allow companies to gain competitive advantage and is not a toy for the technical whizzkids to play with.

Geoff Robb is a senior business systems manager who has spent many years in distribution and logistics, providing IT solutions using a focused approach to customer needs in order to provide quality solutions to changing business needs and processes. **Hi-Tech Logistics** is owned by employees, Tibbett & Britten and IBM. Although the company only came into being as an independent entity in 1993, it has over 35 years' experience in the worldwide distribution of high-technology products, starting life as the distribution arm of IBM.

EXPAND YOUR HORIZONS

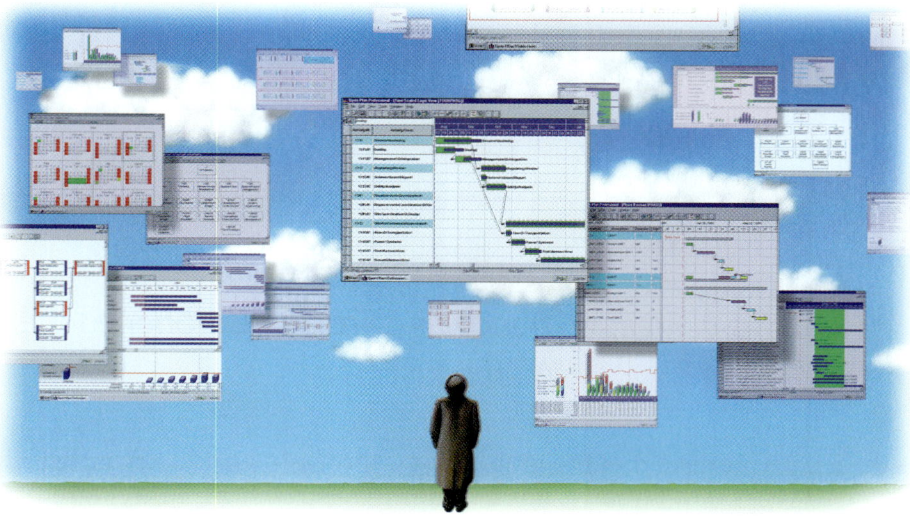

Integrated scheduling and cost from Welcom provides you with a unique, scaleable solution of powerful project management with the full functionality of a cost management system. What could be more simple?

Open Plan Professional™ supports multi-project analysis and resource scheduling and is designed for the professional scheduler and planner.

Open Plan Desktop™shares projects seamlessly with the Professional edition and its ease-of-use makes it ideal for deployment to team members.

Cobra® provides flexible cost management that utilises schedule information from within Welcom scheduling applications.

Expand your horizons and call Welcom today for more information and free demonstration software!

Welcom Software Technology International

South Bank Technopark
90 London Road
London SE1 6LN
Tel +44 171 401 2626
Fax +44 171 922 8865
email: info@wsti.co.uk
www: http://www.wst.com

WST

Welcom Software Technology International

10.3
Mobile Communications

Charles Dunstone
Managing Director, Carphone Warehouse

It is difficult to believe that the mobile communications industry is just a little over 10 years old. Equally, it is beginning to stretch credulity to remember that until just four years ago, mobile phones were strictly business tools, found only in the boardroom or BMW. Market growth has been underestimated time and time again as communication on the move increasingly becomes the norm for people in all areas of business and across all social sectors.

Mobile phones are an important step on the communications evolutionary ladder. Fixed-line telephony, fax and e-mail, mobile phones and now mobile communicators have played a vital role in increasing managerial flexibility and expanding business horizons.

While there is no precise measure of their value, mobile communications have made a considerable impact on business, through increased control, contact and geographical flexibility in working practices.

The senior manager, who needs to stay in control of all areas of the business, is no longer confined by distance. He or she can be reached by phone, anywhere in the world, can receive and amend documents via e-mail and check up on the company's share price or sales figures through data links to the appropriate source.

Salesforce efficiency is also improved, allowing staff to collect messages, make and confirm appointments and transfer information back to head office while still on the road.

In fact, while mobile phone ownership is still a relatively new phenomenon, most businesspeople cannot imagine doing business without one.

A quick look back will show how far and how fast the industry has moved. The first mobile phones of the mid-1980s were hardly mobile, being the size of an average house brick, with batteries of such weight and magnitude that in-car use was really the only option. There were two networks, Cellnet and Vodafone, operating on the analogue system and offering simple voice communication.

The next few years saw dimensions decrease and portability increase. However, the real advance was brought by the introduction of digital networks and the start of a new era of global communications. Vodafone and Cellnet created new networks adopting the GSM standard, while new entrants to the market, One 2 One and Orange, opted for an alternative standard, PCN.

As digital communications work on a binary system, the computer protocol, the capabilities of the mobile phone increased to allow both voice and data communication. The new technological advancement prompted the development of handsets which, with the addition of a PC card attached to a computer or laptop, were capable of sending and receiving data. Products and systems have been upgraded constantly, as new, more technically sophisticated solutions are found. While these developments have helped make the mobile office a reality, the amount of equipment required is a definite move away from the neat portability and simplicity of using a pocket-sized mobile phone; that is, until the launch of the new communicators.

The first communicator was launched in 1996, combining a mobile phone with self-contained Internet, e-mail and faxing facilities, in addition to a convenient electronic diary and address book. Its development has allowed businesspeople even greater flexibility and freedom to work when and where in the world they want, while remaining in touch with the workplace.

The new communicators feature a full keyboard, which for practical purposes requires the unit to be about the size of a personal organiser. However, as before, handsets are becoming smarter while their size becomes smaller, and early 1998 will see the launch of the next-generation smartphone, with a touch-sensitive colour screen, which will negate the need for a keyboard.

And the next step? The future lies with mobile and computer integration. There are a growing number of alliances between computer and handset manufacturers, working to increase the technical capabilities of mobile phones, and they will continue to get smaller.

What of communications in general? Before too long, we will see the convergence of fixed and mobile telephony. You will have one handset, which will operate as a fixed-line phone in your home and office while working as a mobile elsewhere. You will have one number, possibly for life, on which you can be contacted, wherever you may be. Once again, strategic alliances between fixed and mobile network operators, satellite service providers and handset manufacturers are being formed to research and develop the communications tools of the future.

Charles Dunstone set up the **Carphone Warehouse** in 1989 and it is now the UK's leading independent communications specialist retailer with over 100 branches throughout the UK and Eire. In 1996, the Carphone Warehouse was recognised by a major national survey in the *Independent on Sunday* as Britain's fastest-growing private company.

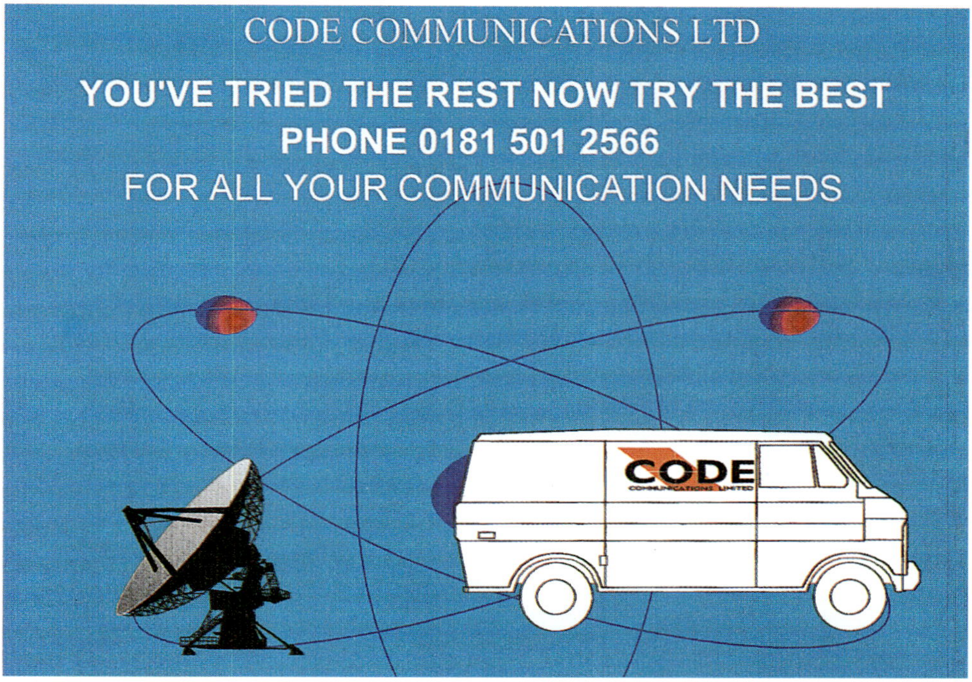
CODE COMMUNICATIONS LTD
YOU'VE TRIED THE REST NOW TRY THE BEST
PHONE 0181 501 2566
FOR ALL YOUR COMMUNICATION NEEDS
CODE

OUR
KNOWLEDGE
IS YOUR
BUSINESS
• Telephone Systems
• Voice and Data Processing
• Low Cost National & International Calls
• ISDN Solutions
JUPITER
COMMUNICATIONS
TELEPHONE 01708 869436

10.4
The Value of Teleworking

Alan Denbigh
Executive Director, Telework Telecottage and Telecentre Association

Teleworking is working at a distance from your employer, either at home, on the road or at a locally based centre. Teleworkers use computers, telephones and faxes to keep in contact with their employers or customers.

In 1985, the Institute for the Future predicted that 40 per cent of employees in the US would be teleworkers by the year 2000, yet the teleworking revolution hasn't happened yet. According to the 1993 BT manual *Teleworking Explained*, 'Teleworking is not a new idea. Nearly 25 years ago, during the 1970s oil crisis, it struck American academic Jack Nilles that instead of people commuting to work, the work could commute to them by telephone — telecommuting'.

But teleworking has failed to live up to the grand, expansive predictions made in the 1970s. AT&T predicted then that 'all Americans could be homeworkers by 1990. What is more likely is an evolutionary change in working practices . . . Teleworking will increasingly be absorbed into the mainstream of normal working practice . . . the distinctions will begin to blur and it will become accepted practice for people to spend part of their time working outside the traditional office.'

The recession of the late 1980s and early 1990s didn't help, dampening all economic activity and removing one of the main drivers for teleworking — the need to expand organisations without crippling increases in overheads.

The 1996 *TeleFutures* report takes up the story: 'Despite the slow take-off, in 1994 the European Union placed the adoption of telework at the top of the Bangemann Report list of actions to make Europe more competitive. The EU even set a target of 10 million teleworkers in Europe by the year 2000. Meanwhile, our screens and magazines are full of lifestyle articles on how to convert your spare bedroom into a home office, which Internet provider gives the best service, comparisons of mobile phone costs and announcements of high technology job creation.'

A variety of interchangeable terms are used to describe the new forms of work, including teleworking (the catch-all term for workers who use teletechnology), telecommuting (often used to describe those who work for just one employer and who spend only part of their time working from home), distance working and remote working.

Sources disagree on the precise number of people teleworking, but a rough figure of between 1 and 1.5 million UK teleworkers is the most often used, when both self-employed and employed people are taken into account. This figure puts the UK together with Scandinavia as the leaders in Europe in the numbers of teleworkers.

There are a wide variety of different reasons for adopting teleworking, many of which are listed below, but overall the drivers for increased teleworking fall into four main categories:

- *Improved competitiveness* — large companies can keep down costs and overheads in comparison to non-teleworking competitors. Productivity increases of up to 60 per cent have been recorded. Small companies that are growing fast can expand without major capital investments.
- *Better lifestyles for workers* — more flexibility, less commuting stress, better balance between home and work lives.
- *Environmental considerations* — reduced commuting means less pollution, better use of office space, less traffic congestion.
- *Improved technologies* — developments in the use of ISDN (videoconferencing, fast file transfer), the Internet (e-mail and World Wide Web) as well as increased interoperability of IT systems make teleworking a practical alternative.

Two sectors, other than those in the technology industries, where teleworking seems to be on a roll are financial services and local authorities. In the financial services industry, which has been revolutionised by the direct telephone-based service approach to customer service, the methodology has influenced the way the business is run. One of the banking pioneers is Lloyds Bank which began teleworking as part of a move to help retain staff and reduce training costs. Others in the industry include the Co-operative Bank as well as the Britannia Building Society and the Nationwide.

Pensions and insurance company Scottish Widows, having revolutionised its business operations, has also taken up teleworking. Teleworking enables the 'pensions by phone' company to widen the net when it comes to recruiting good staff. A recent recruiting campaign looked for new staff to join 20 existing homeworkers who provide support to the Edinburgh call centre and 50 financial advisers who also telework from their homes. The jobs are within the direct sales arm of the company which, since September 1995, has operated 24 hours a day, 7 days a week. In April 1996, the last of the high street branches was closed and the business transferred to the 'invisible office', with advice being given and sales made over the phone.

A number of local authorities are also taking up teleworking. The reasons behind the move include their status as large employers, their large property portfolios, and their responsibility for environmental planning such as highways management.

The pioneers include Surrey, Oxford, Hertfordshire, Cambridgeshire, Kent and Stoke City Council, also recently disbanded authorities Dyfed and Grampian. Another recent convert is Birmingham City Council. Many of the councils are applying the new working method to peripatetic areas such as trading standards and social services.

Surrey County Council recently officially opened a telecentre which will enable a sort of halfway house approach to teleworking. Its report from the first few months of activity concludes that there has been good feedback from staff using the facility, productivity has increased and there had been an improvement in service to clients. A reduction in travel times had also had a beneficial effect on the environment. The report stated that the number of staff members using the telecentre is growing steadily, from 147 when the centre first opened in September 1996 to 236 in November. In the rest of the country a network of 150 telecottages and telecentres provides the basis for many other companies to adopt a similar approach.

With the ever-increasing onslaught of remote access technology coupled with environmental pressures, skill shortages and the need for increased flexibility, there is little doubt that teleworking is likely to become a well-established way of working in the next few years.

The Telework Telecottage and Telecentre Association (TCA) was set up to spread the benefits of teleworking — working for a remote employer or customer and using computers and telecommunications to bridge the gap. Members include self-employed and employed people working from home, but also the companies introducing teleworking into their organisations. The Association has over 2000 members and 140 telecottage members who offer facilities to teleworkers. Telecottages offer public access to computers and other IT equipment, training facilities and supply services to assist other businesses.

COMPUTER MANUALS

TOMORROW'S COMPUTER BOOKS TODAY

ANSWERS FOR NEW TECHNOLOGY JUST A PHONE CALL AWAY

WITH OVER 5000 TITLES, FROM SAGE TO SOFTWARE TESTING, COMPUTER MANUALS HAS A BOOK TO SOLVE EVERY COMPUTING PROBLEM!

SPECIAL EDITION USING MICROSOFT EXCEL 97
Best-selling author Ron Person shares his invaluable insights and time-saving tricks in an all-purpose, one-stop reference guide. In addition to the basic features, you'll find complete coverage of creating charts, managing lists and analysing worksheets. Learn how to build complex formulas and master pivot tables to unleash the full power of Microsoft's spreadsheet tool! Using Excel 97 also covers the use of Excel in a workgroup environment and in conjunction with the rest of the Office suite of applications.
Publisher: Que Ref: 254411
Price: £32.49

HOW NETWORKS WORK BESTSELLER EDITION
Part of the best-selling 'How it Works' series, this book takes you on an exciting and visual journey down the highways and byways of networking and communications. Whether you build and maintain networks or are simply curious about their inner workings, How Networks Work will take you through topics such as ISDN, the connection of LANs and how the network can become an indispensable business resource in easy to understand stages, each section supported by full-colour illustrations.
Publisher: Ziff-Davis Press Ref: 212866
Price: £26.95

LAUNCHING A BUSINESS ON THE WEB - 2nd EDITION
Unsure about how to place your business on the Internet to reap maximum benefits? Launching a Business on the Web will show you how! Written by experts, this title provides quality advice on issues such as choosing a service provider, advertising effectively, taking orders and security. An indispensable resource for all those interested in Web commerce and marketing.
Publisher: Que Ref: 235923
Price: £36.99

WINDOWS 95 FOR DUMMIES - 2nd EDITION
Windows 95 for Dummies is a light-hearted, no-nonsense guide designed to help you get the most from this popular operating system. Packed with handy tips and reminders, this book cuts through the technical jargon to appeal to the most inexperienced of computer users. Learn how to customise your desktop, make old versions of DOS and Windows programs work under Windows 95 and save time with the new Windows 95 features. There's even a Top Ten list of aggravating things about Windows 95 to use when things go wrong!
Publisher: IDG Books Worldwide
Ref: 272602 Price: £18.99

MS WINDOWS NT SERVER RESOURCE KIT
The Windows NT Server 4.0 Resource Kit contains official technical information and tools for the support professional administering this powerful operating system. In three volumes, this kit covers the topics of deployment, configuration, networking and connecting to the Internet. It's also packed with general troubleshooting tips to enable you to deal with all rollout and support issues surrounding Windows NT Server 4.0. The companion CD-ROM contains more than 190 tools and utilities and the complete text of the Windows NT 4.0 Workstation Resource Kit. This kit is must for all those involved in supporting the NT platform in your organisation!
Publisher: Microsoft Press Ref: 234480
Price: £140.99

RUNNING MS OFFICE 97 FOR WINDOWS -SELECT EDITION
Learn how to use each of the Office applications - Word, Excel, Powerpoint, Access and Outlook - then discover the advantages of sharing data between them to increase your productivity. Hundreds of screen illustrations, real-world examples and advice from the experts combine to provide you with a clear, easy to navigate reference that you'll keep by your computer and use every day. The enclosed CD-ROM provides you with an electronic version of the book and the ability to get answers on-line by searching Microsoft's huge KnowledgeBase.
Publisher: Microsoft Press Ref: 234333
Price: £37.49

CALL OR E-MAIL NOW FOR A COPY OF OUR FREE COMPLETE BOOKLIST

PLEASE QUOTE CODE: 685 WHEN ORDERING

AMERICAN EXPRESS Cards Welcome · SWITCH · VISA · Access

0121 706 6000 · E-MAIL INFO@COMPMAN.CO.UK

FAX 0121 606 0477 · HTTP://WWW.COMPMAN.CO.UK/AD.CGI/685

ALL PRICES INCLUDE VAT WHERE APPLICABLE. E & OE. ALL DETAILS AND PRICES ARE SUBJECT TO CHANGE WITHOUT NOTICE

The Future of the future

People are finally starting to realise that the world is changing, but it is changing in quite an alarming and uncontrolled way and much of this change has been brought about by the developments in communications and network technology.

Perhaps the most noticeable and well publicised innovation in Networking has been the Internet. This remarkable technology, which people have already started to take for granted, has brought with it innumerable benefits, especially for business. The World Wide Web and e-mail have, in the words of many a good telecommunications company, "brought people together" and provided a low cost, instant means of global communication. But as we look to the future there are many other areas which will provide even more assistance to the business man.

In 1996 the Internet brought you the world, in 1997 the Intranet promises even more. The Intranet may well become as commonplace as Windows and its use of Internet technology within the secure confines of a private network can save companies both time and money, for example with internal process, administration and training. The projected growth of Intranets far exceeds that of the Internet, which portrays a scenario for the future with business on the Internet not being thousands of individual sites vying for attention, but secure company LANs communicating and doing business with each other. This will allow unheralded levels of immediacy meaning business to business operations will be instant. No more waiting for couriers or confirmations by return of post; goods can be ordered, dispatched, invoiced for and paid for in one transaction.

Real advancements in network infrastructures will also help to achieve this global-localisation. Already hardware is available to create virtual LANs, allowing your home, your office and the office in Hawaii to effectively move into the same building. This will have far-reaching effects for both employer and employee. What will matter is the employees skills, not the employer's location. Furthermore, location will no longer effect target markets. Instead of researching twenty competitors who operate in your area, you will be competing with a thousand businesses across a hundred countries. These advance-ments mean that the transfer of knowledge will become much simpler and power will move more and more toward the user, meaning a one man organisation can be as effective as any multi-national.

As the real "global village" develops, technology will provide ever increasing ways to reduce some of the current problems that afflict network communications. The current infrastructures have largely been developed on an ad hoc basis and for that reason are slow and unreliable with a lack of organisation that reflects the Internet's origins. These problems will undoubtedly be solved and there are numerous options open to telecommunications providers: more pipes, satellites dedicated to information transfer or optical cables. But as the available bandwidth grows, users will undeniably want to have phone, television, video and Internet access via one unit and this will become one of the greatest challenges, to be always one step ahead of the insatiable user who always wants more and more and more.

So is there no hope left? Will we all be out of business in ten years time? Some sources have ventured that up to 100,000 UK businesses will fold due to digital business from other countries. This seems slightly extravagant, but if there is a lesson to learned from these spirited predictions, it is to be prepared.

Yet change need not be feared, so as the third millennium approaches, business must take up arms in readiness.

Giles Guest
Director – 4MAT Digital Publishing – www.4mat.com – 0171 721 7811

…making your business swim in the internet age…
4MAT
The Internet is the ultimate business tool. The Intranet is the ultimate communication tool. Together they represent the ultimate opportunity.
4MAT is now offering a free consultancy to find out why.
www.4mat.com
info@4mat.com
0171 721 7811

10.5

Growing Business in Darlington with Orange

Andrew Glover
Group Director, Customer Services, Orange

For Orange, the concept of 'telebusiness' — using communications technology to support widely distributed business centres — has been familiar from day one.

The company was established in 1994 to offer a full person-to-person communications service, determined that its technology would become an integral component of an overall system rather than an isolated gadget. Part of that ideal is providing a service which recognises that customers and their requirements are vital to the company's success, and responding to them accordingly.

The Orange customer base, now over 900,000, comprises sophisticated and demanding users. Many of them work with and depend on an extensive and complex communications system, of which Orange is just one element. As a provider of this key communications element, Orange must respond swiftly and effectively when customers call for support — wherever in the world they are. As a grass-roots supporter and driver of technology-supported business practice, Orange has sought to establish its own business centres in locations which combine the best and most cost-effective solution for its customers. Irrespective of geographical location, Orange customer service operations combine knowledgeable, friendly staff who have access to a range of computer-based information at their fingertips to ensure that every query can be dealt with straightaway.

One of the company's most important customer service operation sites is at Darlington, an area which represents the perfect setting for Orange. The town is a development zone, meaning that it welcomes and supports new businesses by providing training grants and seeking to stimulate opportunities for local people. Its appeal is doubled for a communications company like Orange, whose technological infrastructure enables it to take advantage of the best Darlington can offer without the problems normally associated with a major move away from traditional business centres. As a supplier and user of mobile communications technology, the Orange customer service centre in Darlington is as closely connected to its customers as it is to other Orange centres, using software, networking and intelligent systems to create a single, comprehensive information resource.

The enormous uptake of mobile telecommunications also poses a management challenge for the company, which now deals with some nine million support calls a year. Darlington offers Orange the facilities and resources to grow its operations in a controlled manner, adding the best skills and resources without the penalty of enormously increased overheads. The company's business success worldwide has led to the construction of a further, brand new Darlington site; an innovative design scheduled for completion in 1998 which will accommodate the current complement of 300 staff plus the anticipated increase in numbers by then and in the future. It also represents an opportunity for Orange to become more involved in the Darlington community and establish links with local groups and activities, building on a solid present to ensure a cooperative and prosperous future.

Darlington is, of course, an attractive business region for companies other than Orange, making part of its appeal the chance to build entirely new business communities. Its location makes it particularly relevant to other telecommunications and high-tech companies and many of these are connecting with each other to cooperate and grow. For Orange, Darlington offers significant opportunities to forge major new business relationships in Darlington with companies who share the telebusiness philosophy and who want closer links with other businesses, with their customers — and with their own staff.

Telebusiness is very much a reality for Orange. Its own technology is a cornerstone in the company's growth plans; and this, combined with the desire to provide a first-class service to its customers, means that there is a genuine impetus to improve its offerings all the time. Business zones like Darlington are a tremendous opportunity for technology companies to demonstrate how effective a carefully planned, managed and supported business can be, irrespective of where it actually is.

Orange entered the market in 1994 aiming to become the first choice in wirefree communications. It has built a strong, fresh and clear identity that has set it apart from the confusion that previously characterised the market. Orange innovations like simple Talk Plans, 12 months' free insurance and a 14-day money-back guarantee offer real value for money and have changed people's attitudes towards wirefree communications. Orange covers 92 per cent of the UK population and is still growing. The new Orange 'dual band' phone will allow customers to 'roam' freely in 50 countries by the end of 1997.

Part 11
External Relations

11.1
Investor Relations

Brendan McNamara
Senior Executive, Dewe Rogerson Ltd

How do you find new investors and how do you keep them happy? At the simplest level, these are the issues addressed by 'investor relations'.

Normally, these responsibilities fall to the company's broker — finding investors, placing stock — and to the financial public relations company, which facilitates the process of communication between company and investor. There will also be a need to employ lawyers to provide objective advice and ensure that the company is not caught out by statute or regulation.

Education

Education is repeatedly stated to be the nation's number one priority for the new millennium. It is equally important for business finance — ensuring that investors and those who influence investors' decisions have a level of understanding that allows them to do so knowledgeably. This group of influencers encompasses financial media and stockbroking analysts.

Planning

Planning is essential. Many of the key components of any investor relations programme will have already been developed around the boardroom table when drawing up the business plan. But it is essential that investors are presented with a clear picture of the company, its management and its prospects. The basic information may be available, but do its language and format meet investors' requirements?

Strategy

Declaring that the company's aim is 'to be the world leader' indicates ambition. It does not in itself give investors any confidence in the company. So it is essential that the company defines its strategy to achieve its aims. This will include a clear statement of the company's position — in its business sector, in its geographic marketplace and in relation to its peer group, its competitors. It will be an honest assessment of strengths and weaknesses, opportunities and actions necessary to achieve credible objectives.

Addressing the strategy will clarify the key messages that the company wishes to promote. This process will assist in the construction of a presentation to investors — both existing and potential —- and to influencers of investor opinion, which answers the key investment issues of security and return. And, of course, no matter how good the presentation, how solid the prospects of the company, they will serve no purpose if it is not directed at the most relevant target audiences. Identification is the responsibility of the financial public relations consultant and the broker.

Targeting

Not every venture capitalist, banker, analyst or journalist will be interested in the company. Few companies attract front page attention from the media — except when they go wrong or are big enough to be followed by the major investment banks. So targeting communications activity will save management time and money. The approach will also vary. A significant potential investor will deserve, and expect, attention from the company's senior management, to be dealt with on a one-to-one basis. For sectoral analysts and journalists, group briefings may be more appropriate. In each case, however, individuals will want contact with senior management[1] — the quality of the management is the most important criterion in making investment decisions.

Measurement

Measurement and monitoring will also provide further information for the company. Research among target audiences will help identify both familiarity and favourability. If conducted early, benchmark figures can be set, against which the effects of a company's communications can be tracked.

1 Dewe Rogerson CityScan

Moreover, regular contact will help identify problems and concerns at an early enough stage for remedial action to be taken and to make sure that the perception matches reality.

Clearly, investor relations is a two-way street involving that sometimes forgotten aspect of communication — listening. If the company does not know what its investors, its *owners*, feel, then it cannot form a reasonable judgement about the commitment and stability of their investment. How often are takeovers successful because the target company has failed to keep its shareholders informed?

Normally, the results of this activity feed into the valuation debate, the determination of a fair rating relative to the market that reflects the security of sustainable long-term growth against the risks.

One side effect of ensuring regular contact with investors is that there is likely to be a greater level of support for the company should the unforeseen arise. When dealing with a crisis, rather than taking down the carefully prepared manual, it is more important to have a few key individuals who can react quickly. One of the first actions is to ensure the support of the investors and with that solid base address the problem.

A properly managed investor relations programme requires commitment from management and a consistent approach. A company cannot choose to stop communicating if it has bad news and, indeed, to do so would almost certainly cause a worse reaction than admitting to a problem. But even bad news can present an opportunity — perhaps to show how management is meeting the difficulty and taking advantage of changed circumstances to refine or retune the corporate strategy.

Marketing the product or service is necessary for the company to succeed. But marketing the management of the company is essential to maintain and secure investors. This reflects the importance of investor relations.

Dewe Rogerson is the UK's largest specialist financial business and corporate communications agency working in public and investor relations, advertising, corporate design, market research and editorial and production services for employee and customer publications. Dewe Rogerson has its own offices in London, New York, Hong Kong, Warsaw, Hungary, Germany, The Hague, India and Tokyo and trusted affiliates across continental Europe, Latin America and Australia.

11.2

Managing the Bank Relationship

Richard Parkinson
Director, The Bank Relationship Consultancy

For all businesses, the bank is an essential supplier, providing such vital services as basic money transmission and finance, yet few companies spend time maintaining or improving their relationship with the bank.

The Banking Relationship

There has been a great deal of theoretical analysis about how the banking relationship has changed over the last few years, but for a growing business the fundamentals are still much the same. Every business needs a bank to handle its money transmission requirements and most need the bank to finance business expansion.

What has changed in recent years? Certainly, the easy profits in the banking industry have disappeared and banks are trying to reduce costs. This is most obviously reflected in the closure/consolidation of branches and reductions in staff levels. At the same time banks are trying to offer a greater range of products and services and face increasing competition from each other and new providers of financial services. Nonetheless, companies that take time to develop a good relationship with their bankers benefit in the good times as well as the bad. A company that works at its bank relationship gets the most out of it.

Money Transmission Requirements

Every company needs to move money, known in banking circles as a company's money transmission requirements.

Few companies properly understand how their commission charges for these services are calculated and many do not try to negotiate them. A business may be offered free banking in the first year of its existence, but for many companies bank charges then become a significant expense. As a first step, a company with a growing business should establish the basis of its existing bank charges and then consider whether some sort of special arrangement can be negotiated. It must be noted that the banks' standard commission charges are only appropriate for very small businesses. Other businesses have the opportunity to negotiate the charges to a more realistic level. For most businesses this means seeking a breakdown of the charges for each type of transaction. As a rule of thumb, the bank's standard tariff can be halved with little or no difficulty, but further reductions will depend on the nature of the business and numerous other factors.

Incidentally, there is no such service as free banking, so if a company is not incurring any explicit commission charges or finds them to be particularly low, the bank will be receiving excessive compensation from some other aspect of the business.

If a company is importing or exporting, the banking charges become much more significant. Prices that were previously pence become pounds as payments are made to foreign suppliers or funds are received from customers based abroad.

The European Commission has been trying to encourage the banks to introduce a low-cost money transfer system in Europe, but the services that have been introduced can only be used for very small value transactions.

A company incurring significant charges for foreign transactions should ask its bank how it can make more effective use of the banking system. Such a company may find it worthwhile to employ someone with the appropriate banking and treasury skills either as a full-time member of staff or as an adviser to the company.

Cash/Liquidity Management

Managing bank charges is only part of managing the bank relationship. Banking services can also be used to manage the cashflow and liquidity of the company. Managing the sales ledger, chasing outstanding debts and taking the appropriate credit terms are basic cash management. However, there is also a need to ensure that funds are remitted to the bank promptly and that the most effective payment methods are being used.

Any credit balances should be invested. Most banks will offer automatically to invest credit balances in a deposit account at little or no cost, and this can be a very effective way of ensuring that the money is working for the company at all times. If larger surpluses are seen these should be invested in the money market.

Most growing businesses will require funding from time to time. This need not just be by overdraft. Short-term borrowing lines, factoring or other forms of finance may be better for a growing business.

Borrowing Facilities

A business that is expanding must establish in the early stages what the effect on its balance sheet will be. Many growing businesses fail to understand the amount of working capital that will be needed to fund an expansion, let alone the additional fixed assets that they might have to purchase. This fundamental piece of analysis must be an essential part of any business plan.

Having established the amount of borrowing required, the appropriate funding structure must be put in place. Most companies use overdrafts. This is certainly the most frequent form of bank debt, but is often abused by both borrower and bank. It is supposed to be used for short-term working capital finance; for example, finance to cover the purchase of stock for a peak sales period. This form of finance should bridge gaps in a company's cashflow. This allows the company to pay suppliers and employees pending sales proceeds being received.

An overdraft is also a very flexible form of funding. There are no formal restrictions placed on this type of borrowing, although an adequate limit should be agreed and respected. There is also no formal repayment schedule and as a result companies often start buying fixed assets using an overdraft. This leads to 'hard core borrowing', which is the term used by bankers to describe the portion of debt on the overdraft which is never repaid. Banks can and do worry about the emergence of this sort of permanent debt and this can lead to a deteriorating relationship with the bank.

In these circumstances a more permanent form of debt is appropriate. The bank should be asked to provide a loan provided that the company can demonstrate that the funding can be repaid within a reasonable period. Banks can and will lend for up to five years and longer periods are available when a suitable case is made. If the company cannot demonstrate that the loan can be repaid within an agreed period, a more permanent form of funding is required and this should not be bank finance. In other words, more equity or some other sort of venture capital should be sought.

When approaching the bank, remember that a banker is primarily interested in obtaining repayment without difficulty. It is therefore essential that the company submits a realistic proposal with all the relevant information. Different banks use different methods of analysing the credits. Why not ask your bank what information it would like to see and how it analyses your case? Then you can work with your bank manager or account officer to ensure that your case is well represented within the bank and the faceless person who makes the credit decisions approves the credit.

To summarise, the relationship with the bank is like many others in life. The more you put in, the more you get out. A growing business must take time to manage the bank relationship if it is to get the best out of this external relationship.

Richard Parkinson is a director of **The Bank Relationship Consultancy** which provides independent advice to companies on all aspects of banking finance and treasury management.

11.3

Growing Relationships for the Growing Business

Mark Goyder

Director, Centre for Tomorrow's Company

Linford Christie stood by the trackside, a dismal spectator in the Olympic 100 metres final. After two false starts he was out of the race. Years of preparation and months of fine tuning were at an end. He was now a spectator, not a participant.

For the business, especially the growing business, competitiveness is a race. But it is a race without a finish. And as with Linford Christie there are two kinds of preparation.

The first is the more obvious and the more urgent. It is about equipping the business to increase sales, reduce costs, use cash more efficiently and position itself right. The second is less obvious, and may seem trivial until it goes wrong. It is about risk management, reputation, trust and goodwill. When you are handling these things well, nobody notices them. When you get them wrong your entire business may be in jeopardy, because you lose what has come to be called your licence to operate.

Have you thought about your licence to operate? Have you worked out who can stop you doing business? The most obvious examples come from the big companies — British Gas, Camelot, Ratners.

But let's take a more local example. A friend of mine was a GP, a brilliant innovator. He had a marvellous concept for a comprehensive new health-care centre where his patients could go not only for GP and nursing services but for a pharmacist, aromatherapist, physiotherapist and a range of complementary offerings, all provided in a part of town which lacked even the most basic GP surgery. He identified the site, lined up the health authorities, got his bank finance in place . . . and yet his proposal was rejected by the planning committee of the local authority.

Thirty residents whose property adjoined the proposed site disliked the idea. They were hostile to any building — even this one — being put on what was previously agricultural land. They campaigned against it on the grounds that the increase in traffic would represent a road safety hazard. A local councillor backed their campaign, and the local authority planning committee ruled against the new health centre. My friend had not thought hard enough about his licence to operate. Only after months of lobbying and rescue work did he win the case on appeal.

Think of the licence to operate as a space within which you are free to move. Manage the space well, and you win trust and expand your room for manoeuvre. Manage it badly, and the forces that can stop you doing business close in on you.

Anglo-Saxon business is full of oversimplification. We all love to say that there is only one bottom line. But this can lead to a fatal single-mindedness. It can cause us to miss relationships which are crucial to our survival. The Tomorrow's Company Report – the work of business leaders, not academics – showed that in the future an *inclusive* approach will be crucial to competitive success. The Centre for Tomorrow's Company (created growing businesses that are committed to the inclusive approach) is now helping businesses to plan their own route to success through relationships. The key point to remember, in our experience, is that there is no common formula. Every business has to work out which relationships are crucial.

For a small chain of licensed premises, the police and the magistrates are a crucial part of the licence to operate. The local paper, by the tone of its reporting, can in a few incautious words destroy months of careful reputation building. A casual employee who happens to be rude to some particularly influential local families can also dent the reputation.

It pays every business to be clear who can stop it doing business. Attending to each and every relationship that makes up the licence to operate is not an alternative to controlling costs or promoting sales: it is complementary.

A clear focus on relationships is crucial to risk management. But it is also crucial to taking opportunities that others will miss. The Centre for Tomorrow's Company is only a year old. We are growing fast, and have plenty to think about. When asked whether we would be willing to take someone to do work experience with us it was tempting to say no: we needed to focus; things hadn't settled down; the issues we dealt with were less easy to explain to a school sixthformer. But we said yes. And our particular sixthformer proved to be a fast learner, and has become a regular stand-in during holiday periods. At Christmas, when our regular staff was much reduced by sickness and holidays, he was on his own in the office handling the issuing of a crucial press release. He didn't let us down: so far the relationship has been a winning one for him and the centre.

It can sound so trite and feeble to say that business is ultimately about relationships. But it is one of those truths that are so obvious that we forget to live by them. Every month your business has a board meeting or equivalent. It certainly reviews financial outcomes: and monitors the return being earned on the investment being made by its investors. How often does it review the health of some of its key relationships? How do you know what progress is being made in the training and development of some of your key people? Are you better or worse than your competitors at the skill with which you manage your supplier relationships?

Once in a while we come across that rare company in which the reality is as good as the words on the mission statement. Cynically, we ask people working there questions like, 'I know what it says on the mission statement, but it's not really like that is it?' And to our amazement, the response is not one of cynicism but of conviction. 'Yes,' people reply, 'in this company the words are lived, not mouthed.' 'We all know what the company's values are, and we all try to live up to them.'

Shareholder value is inextricably bound up with business and human values. In the best companies values can pervade the bloodstream. Leaders feel a true confidence that people are striving not to deliver an acceptable result, but to exceed expectations.

Just as athletes like Linford Christie have won their medals in the past through a triumph of mind over matter, so winning companies achieve lasting success because they develop a powerful corporate mind that is stronger than any policy manual, any incentive scheme.

The evidence is there already, particularly in the US. Companies with a strong sense of purpose and values outperformed the stock market average by 15 times over 70 years.[1] In another study, researchers picked companies with strong cultures. They found that simply having a strong culture was not a predictor of success. On the other hand, having a strong culture which emphasised leadership, and relationships with customers, employees and shareholders (in that order), was a strong predictor of success. Companies with this emphasis increased their share price over 10 years by over 400 per cent; companies with a strong culture but without this emphasis increased share price by 100 per cent.[2]

Values and relationships are crucial to long-term success. It isn't enough to pay lip service to this statement of the obvious. As the Centre for Tomorrow's Company is now demonstrating, values can be monitored; relationships can be measured; leaders can find out whether the people who are supposed to be following them believe in what they're being told and want to go where they are being led. Your own corporate fitness depends on how well you ask these questions and act on the answers. Continue to build the bone strength that comes from financial robustness, but never ignore the muscle strength that come from values and the faster reactions that come from well-tuned, well-measured relationships!

References

[1] *Built to Last, Collins and Porras,* Century, Random House, 1995.
[2] *Corporate Culture and Performance,* Kotter and Heskett, Free Press, 1992.

Mark Goyder is Director of the **Centre for Tomorrow's Company**, a business-led organisation which exists to inspire and enable British business to compete with the world's best through the inclusive approach. His book *Living Tomorrow's Company* is published by Gower in 1997. The *Tomorrow's Company Report* was produced in 1995 by the leaders of 25 businesses and can be obtained by telephoning Gower on 01252 317700.

11.4

Winning Business with Public Relations: Communicating with your Audiences[1]

Jeremy Weinberg
Public Relations Manager, Institute of Public Relations

For public relations read communications — no mystery, end of story. And what are companies communicating? Reputation.

The Institute of Public Relations defines public relations practice as 'the discipline which looks after reputation — with the aim of earning understanding and support, and influencing opinion and behaviour'. It also adds that the practice must be 'planned and sustained'.

Good PR and reputation do not just happen, however. They have to be fought for and require constant maintenance and nurturing — messages need updating and then they need communicating.

A public relations strategy can ensure that business objectives are met. PR can:

1 This chapter is an extract from the IPR publication *Winning Business with Public Relations.*

- influence shareholders and share prices;
- change legislation;
- increase profitability;
- improve staff retention and morale.

It can also encourage higher prices for products and services. It can mean that a company stands out from its competitors.

But a business needs first to decide what it wants people to think of it. The quickest service? The lowest prices? The latest model range? And if that business is not sure what it does best, its customers won't be sure either. All organisations need to be clear on who its audience (or public) is. Existing and potential customers, investors and employees spring readily to mind. Others are less obvious: if you can identify them it may be necessary to reexamine them in the context of the business plan.

PR frequently involves changing negative or apathetic attitudes into positive and favourable opinion, helping people feel involved and consulted. It starts with a detailed knowledge at the outset of how publics regard an organisation. This might involve conducting market research in some situations, but may just mean starting an honest dialogue with key customers, suppliers or the workforce.

Properly planned and implemented, public relations is a two-way process, feeding back reactions and opinions from all audiences so that strategies can be redefined. PR is not about spreading good news; it is about understanding the whole business and making sure that the right people have the right information to correct misunderstandings and enable them to contribute to the company's success.

In practical terms, public relations covers many techniques from newsletters, exhibitions, meetings and letter writing, to lobbying, customer care programmes, media relations, employee communications and investor relations. This diversity means that public relations can often convey messages more effectively than other media.

The 1995 Royal Society of Arts (RSA) report *Tomorrow's Company* clearly identified the important role that communications plays in business practice. It suggested that those companies with a solid communications programme would be the ones to succeed in the next millennium, as there was an increasing demand on the part of all publics for more information. Companies could no longer hold back information at will, as perhaps they had done in the past.

People increasingly care about the values of those behind the products and services on offer — witness the numerous media reports of organisations fighting to defend their reputation. Feelgood factors are less important than successful trading. Customers boycotted Shell's filling stations during the Brent Spar problems, making a significant and measurable dent in the company's trading performance.

Reputations are too important to be left to their own devices. All major organisations use public relations extensively and continuously. Marks and Spencer is always quoted as an example of a business that has got it right, having built an enviable reputation for fairness and understanding, allowing it to trade successfully without the use of extensive advertising budgets. Fortunately, public relations techniques are not just for the lucky few or the biggest organisations; small groups — and individual traders — can benefit considerably and economically from using some or all of them in their daily work.

By following a few basic guidelines any company can start thinking about the importance of public relations:

- Define the publics, understand their views and why they think and do what they do.
- Be clear on what you, as a company, would like them to think about the company.
- Make sure employees know why they are working for the organisation and how they can help.
- Convey the company messages in a way that suits its audiences.
- See the media as a way of achieving the company objectives.
- Understand the people who can affect business success. Do not assume that they automatically know what the company is trying to achieve.
- Create an atmosphere of sharing and trusting as the background to your communications. Don't just tell people what you want them to think.
- Be clear about company objectives. Measure progress throughout the project, adjusting the programme and redirecting resources as the results suggest.
- Do not leave the company image and reputation to fate. Plan ahead, and see improving communications as a continuous process, involving everyone involved or dependent on its success.

The Institute of Public Relations is the only professional organisation for public relations practitioners in the UK. Its 6000 members are involved in all aspects of the public relations industry. The largest professional body of its type in Europe (with rigorous qualifications for membership) the IPR stages over 500 meetings, seminars and key note events throughout the UK each year.

11.5

Competitive Tendering in Advertising

John Storey
Joint Managing Director,
Media Audits Ltd

Of all the dictums in advertising Lord Leverhume's must be the most famous. The sage old Lord knew that only half of his advertising expenditure was effective; his problem was knowing which half. According to the latest figures released by the Advertising Association, advertising expenditure last year in the UK amounted to £11.99bn so the waste could be significant.

For senior executives, managing the growth of business brings new challenges, one of which may well be managing an advertising budget and wondering if the talented team of advertising and media-buying personnel appointed to his account really are delivering value for money.

Advertisers now face an increasingly complex and dynamic media market where the decision of how to employ advertising budgets can create real competitive advantage, a factor increasingly recognised at board level. After all, the advertising expenditure is a significant proportion of most companies' variable expenditure. A capital investment such as a new item of machinery or in a building would involve careful consideration at board level, discussions with financial backers and would have to be justified on a commercial rate of return for the business. Why then is expenditure on advertising so rarely given the same scrutiny?

My advice is that it should be, and the first step is to pick your media buyer as carefully as you would select your bankers. Selection is usually done through a process of competitive tendering and while it may not be rocket science, there are a few simple pointers to help you draft a short list to both help reduce management time taken, and reach the best decision.

Creating a Short List

If you are unfamiliar with media agencies, the first step should be to contact a trade organisation like the IPA or a fee-based service such as the Advertising Agency Register that will put you in touch with a 'long list' of possible suppliers who meet your basic criteria. This should lead to a credentials presentation, possibly with around five or six potential suppliers. When short-listing agencies from the credentials presentation for a more detailed 'pitch' presentation, the following points should be considered:

- Does the media agency have specific experience of your market sector and does it understand your business?
- Does the agency already represent any current or potential competitors to your company?
- As with other areas of business, personal chemistry is important. Will the team who come in and pitch for your business also be the team who will carry out the work?
- What are the ranges of budget size handled by the agency? Beware of being the small fish in a big pond, as you are unlikely to get the best personnel on your account.
- Try and assess the 'cultural fit' of the two organisations — important if you are to build trust and confidence in your relationship.
- Ask if you can contact current clients for their opinions.
- Do provide the agency with a detailed, written brief.
- Do make time available to address their questions.

From the credentials presentation and the answers to that above you should be able to draw up a short list of two or three agencies to make detailed and specific presentations as to how they would handle your account.

Once a final short list has been produced it is important to score the agencies presentations objectively. A score card of key requirements helps create a level playing field to aid judging. This should be drafted by senior client executives involved in making the decision process. For example, agencies would be scored out of 100 and judged on five core areas, each weighted according to importance. The score card, along with notes justifying the score, should be completed by each of the executive team immediately following an agency's presentation. It may also prove useful to have the pitch process chaired by an independent consultant who, as well as adding specific media expertise to the client team, can also act as a facilitator.

One further piece of advice; agencies may promise the earth, but the important question is 'can they deliver and can you keep them motivated to go on delivering the best value?' To help focus the agency's mind on reaching and maintaining the desired performance targets it is sensible to introduce a success-related bonus as part of the agreed fees.

Buying the cheapest should not be the sole ground for appointing an agency. What is important is getting the best time and space at the best price to reach your customers cost effectively. One important factor is ensuring your advertising campaign has the correct balance between coverage and frequency; put simply, reaching the right people often enough to encourage action. This ratio will change according to the type of produce or service you are promoting and the impact of the creative execution you are running. Clearly planning the correct coverage and frequency for a campaign will improve effectiveness.

Advertising can be a vital commercial tool to help your business grow, so treat it with the same rigour and analysis you would treat other major investments. If you do, you will reap the returns.

Media Audits is the independent, market-leading consultancy offering advertisers a comprehensive range of media consultancy services from the largest real-price media database. Media Audits acts as a consultant to over 150 advertisers, including 40 of the top 100 UK advertisers and 124 of the top 300 brands.

Part 12

Competitive Purchasing

Founded in 1919, and with more than 100,000 members and students, the ***Chartered Institute of Management Accountants (CIMA)*** is the leading management accountancy professional body worldwide.

The modern business environment and the profession of management accountancy have grown up together during the 20th century. As organisations become increasingly complex and the art of management more demanding, Chartered Management Accountants are carving out a special role as professionals who apply their skills to enhance management decision making. They can do this because the CIMA training and qualification is based upon coupling the best financial and business practices with information management skills. Chartered Management Accountants know how to turn knowledge into profit.

All CIMA students throughout the world study an identical syllabus to become Chartered Management Accountants. The CIMA training and qualification is unique in two respects. No other body offers such a coherent global concept of financial training. No other profession seeks to apply accountancy and other management techniques to the needs of general management through a fully integrated course. The syllabus takes a student through four stages. These call for three or four years of concentration to marry independent study with the Institute's practical experience requirements. At first the emphasis is upon two study streams - basic accounting and management principles. The syllabus then evolves into core streams - financial accounting, management accounting, managerial and quantitative techniques, information technology and marketing management and strategy. All CIMA students therefore receive a broad based, practical and commercially focused financial training for business.

In applying their skills Chartered Management Accountants can be found working in general management roles where financial management becomes a core skill on which they can build. Others grapple with financial and statistical programmes of fearsome complexity. Their settings are many and diverse and in both the public and private sectors. A Chartered Management Accountant may be finance director of a company, executive chairman of an international group, a government official or, further down the chain of command, a junior project analyst.....the list is a long one.

An increasing number of Chartered Management Accountants are in professional practice providing a range of management accountancy and consultancy services to small and medium sized enterprises. Working as sole practitioners or as the members of partnerships or consultancy firms they help solve the problems and realise the opportunities of thousands of businesses ranging from small shopkeepers to multi national concerns.

The CIMA qualification is increasingly a passport to a successful international career. Over 20,000 companies worldwide employ or contract the services of Chartered Management Accountants who are equipped with the skills and knowledge to work comfortably within the business framework of any country.

Professional competence once attained has to be maintained. To ensure that throughout their careers Chartered Management Accountants continue to apply and to demonstrate their knowledge and professionalism CIMA provides continuous professional development and skills training opportunities and services, together with ethical guidance which demands the highest standards of principle and practice. Chartered Management Accountants in professional practice operate within a regulatory professional standards framework which encourages best practice and the delivery of high quality services.

12.1

From Strength to Strength in Facilities Management

John Weston
CBX Management & Consulting

The task of managing facilities grows in direct proportion to the size of an organisation. This chapter looks at the options facing an expanding company in taking a strategic approach to managing the workplace.

As an organisation grows, so does the management time required to manage workplaces and monitor the services required to run them.

Facilities management (FM) means selecting and managing property, maintaining buildings services such as plant and equipment, managing services including cleaning and security, and controlling projects such as relocation and building refurbishment. In a small to medium-sized enterprise (SMEs), these processes tend to have evolved alongside the organisation. However, as an SME grows to a critical point of employing more than 150 people, the burden of creating and managing the workplace becomes significant.

A busy director can find that, without constant attention, rent levels have become excessive, for example, or that maintenance contractors are not fulfilling their obligations to protect the business assets. FM responsibilities are often simply added to a director's existing role. While real estate may represent 25 per cent of business assets, it is often viewed as a cost, rather than a contributor to the business. In the busy environment of a growing business facilities tend to take a back seat. No one considers the 'big picture' — how effectively the workplace, like any other factor of production — is contributing to business progress.

Often, facilities will not be supporting the growing company at all well. The costs will have grown significantly and can be absorbing a substantial proportion of turnover. The quality of the workplace tends to decrease, so that the facilities are not contributing to employees' comfort, satisfaction and productivity. In addition, the business tends to be at risk from poorly maintained assets and non-compliance with health and safety legislation.

The owner-director, conversant with the modern business philosophy that he or she should only be investing in core businesses, is faced with several options. At the heart of these choices is the option to outsource, the objective being to move to a point where support services benefit from the same strategic perspective as core business activities.

Why Take a Strategic Approach?

A strategic approach to facilities management saves a company money. It raises the quality of the workplace. It ensures that the services purchased — from cleaning and catering to maintenance and telecoms — are all working as efficiently and enthusiastically as the core business itself.

The figures speak for themselves. Typically, depending on the nature of the business and the region in which it is located, facilities costs will be between £20 and £40 per square foot occupied per annum or between £2000 and £5000 per employee for basic services. Viewed strategically and managed properly, many organisations can save between 10 and 25 per cent on their existing workplace bills — savings which go straight to the bottom line.

So what are the Options?

Effective FM starts with an objective assessment of a company's strengths and weaknesses, and comparisons with peer group organisations and industry best practice. This appraisal process inevitably leads to the identification of opportunities to enhance service quality; reduce financial, health and safety, environmental and business risk; and identify ways to cut costs over time. Next comes implementation — ensuring that real estate, facilities, project management and technical services are working hand in hand at best practice levels.

In order to reach this strategic position, organisations are faced with three options.

The in-house manager

First, instead of allowing several distracted amateurs to take responsibility for facilities, the director can recruit an in-house expert to take responsibility for FM. But before the company takes on the cost of a full-time facilities manager, a director needs to assess whether there is really a need for a premises manager whose sole responsibility is to manage the performance of service delivery personnel. (As a rule of thumb, an organisation will need to employ around 500 people to warrant a full-time professional.) This is because, although specifying, tendering and procuring contracts takes time, once they are in place the role of the facilities manager should diminish to one of day-to-day monitoring and responsibility for *ad hoc* demands. This takes time, but perhaps not a full working week, and the director needs to ensure that the administration or support roles do not create work. The alternative can be appointing a part-time manager at a lower level — but is he or she going to provide the expertise necessary to provide benchmark levels of facilities costs and quality?

Outsourced management

Secondly, in order to free up the management of the growing company of contract management responsibility and gain access to advanced systems, the director can choose to outsource FM to a specialist facilities management company, with no vested financial interest in the value of service delivery. This is the route increasingly taken by larger corporates — however, the same advantages are available to the SME.

This approach has considerable benefits over the *ad hoc* purchasing of services from a number of suppliers. An independent facilities management company possesses bulk purchasing power to procure services at highly cost-effective levels, which in turn more than compensates for the management fees — the objective being to ensure that the total cost is considerably less than the organisation was paying before. An expert FM company will also have the contract management and monitoring expertise and systems to drive quality upwards.

However, there is again a point in the growth of a business when this full-time relationship begins to make sense. The same criteria apply: does the growing business really need a full-time manager on site provided by its outsourced provider?

Benefiting from the flexibility of outsourcing

The answer to this question depends on the size of the company. However, the beauty of outsourcing as a business process lies in its providing organisations with the ability to purchase precisely the right amount of services to

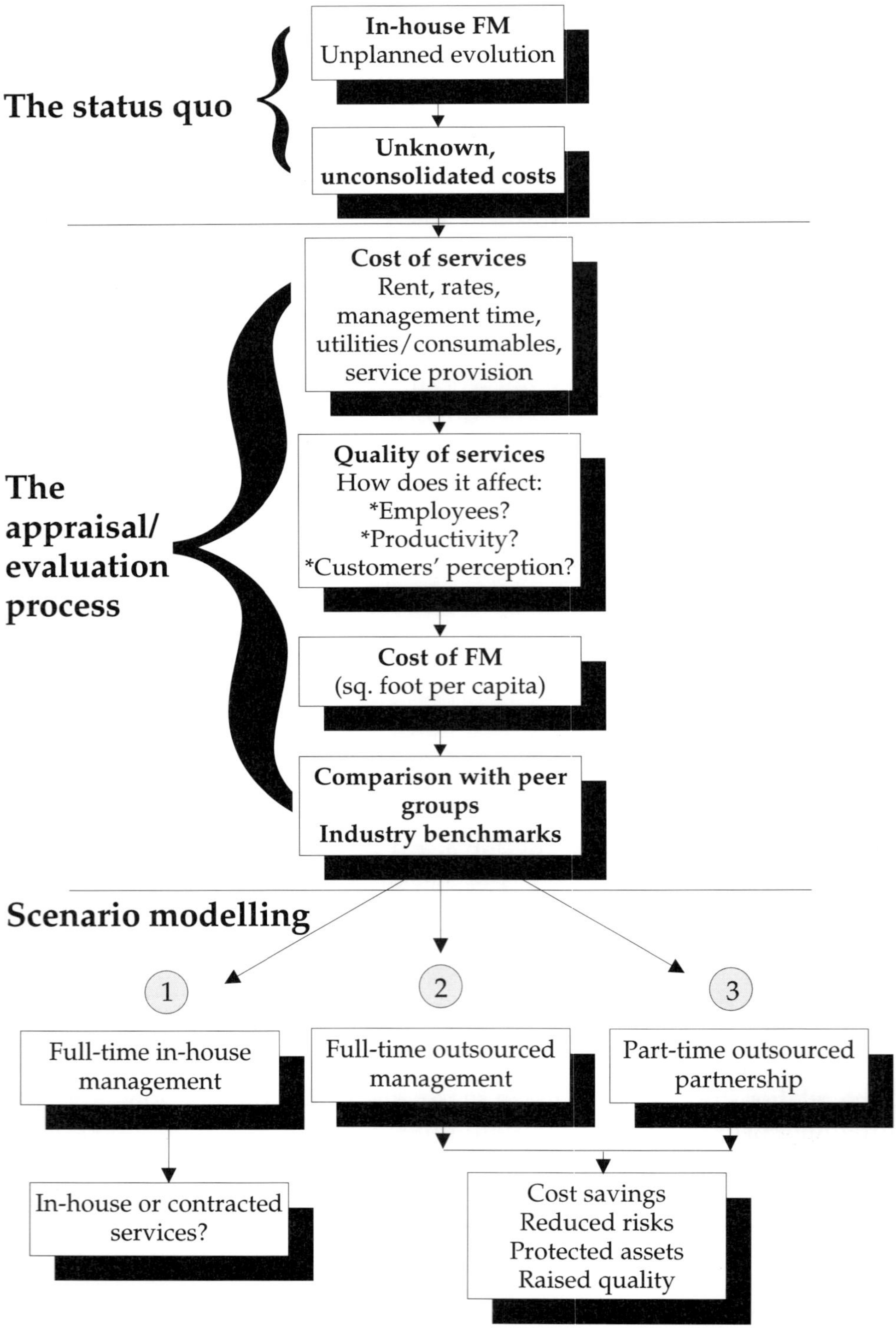

Figure 12.1.1 The facilities management process

It's not just a letter. It's a way to get work done.

The letter is X. The company is Rank Xerox. And the story is all about change.

Change is something we're comfortable with at Rank Xerox. It's what we've been doing since the day we created the first copier, and changed forever the way people work with documents.

Indeed, we've built our business by following the document wherever it takes us. Today, few things in business change as fast as the document. It begins on a computer screen. It moves around the world on interactive, electronic networks. It exists in multimedia environments. It can be scanned, stored, retrieved, revised, distributed, printed and published where, when, and how you want it.

In short, the document is constantly moving from digital form to paper, and back again. Which is why now, more than ever, our mission as The Document Company is clear: to put together the innovative document services you need – the systems, solutions, products and people – to make your business more productive.

It is also why this new "digitised" X is more than a letter to us. It is a symbol of change and vitality in the newly emerging digital world. It represents everything we do to help you get your work done, and make your life at work a little more satisfying and rewarding.

We'll be using this new symbol in many different ways, so keep your eyes open for it.

For us, it signals the next step in a long Rank Xerox tradition of taking the first step into the future. And in a world that won't stop changing, that's still the most productive step anyone can take.

THE DOCUMENT COMPANY
RANK XEROX
Worldwide Sponsor

THE DOCUMENT COMPANY

RANK XEROX

0800 787 787

6085

match the business requirements as and when they are needed, in the process gaining access to expertise and purchasing power which is not available in the core business. Figure 12.1.1 summarises the options.

The growing business should therefore take advantage of this flexibility. Appoint a management company prepared to gain an in-depth understanding of the organisation (since each solution will be bespoke) to carry out an appraisal/evaluation process of the way property and premises are currently managed. Act on their recommendations, which will create a situation tailored to the individual needs of the growing business. Then continue to benefit from a relationship which allows for part-time management of services by the FM company — at the levels appropriate to the organisation.

By purchasing FM in this way — by using outsourcing to effect — an organisation can benefit from the 'big picture' without substituting one inefficient management system for another. As we have seen, the advantages are there to be taken: costs go down while quality goes up. FM, like the company it supports, will go from strength to strength.

John Weston is a member of the **CBX Management & Consulting** executive management team, responsible for the development of customer strategic planning and situation audit programmes.

12.2

Competitive Power Purchasing[1]

Chris Partridge
Editorial Manager,
John Hall Associates

In contrast to the strong position that industrial or commercial buyers held late in 1995, when energy prices had fallen to low levels, buyers now find that they generally have to concede considerably tougher terms. What strategy can buyers adopt to minimise the likely increases?

Gas

The most important move is to conduct a full tender about three months in advance of the new contract. A full tender involves a formal approach for price quotations to about 20 major gas suppliers, the creation of a short list of the four or five most competitive offers and allowing them the opportunity to improve further on their prices — not just a speculative telephone call to one or two suppliers.

Before the tender is compiled, the consumer must decide whether to pay the premium for firm gas supplies, ie guaranteed gas supplies, or to take the cheaper option of an interruptible supply, whereby at times of peak demand on the transmission system the gas supply may be suspended, some-

1 A longer version of this article previously appeared in *CBI News*.

times for a period of days. A minimum annual consumption of 200,000 therms is required before the option of an interruptible supply may be considered.

Interruptions may be implemented at the behest of either British Gas TransCo, up to a maximum of 45 days per year to maintain transmission system pressures within prescribed limits, or at the demand of the individual gas supplier to facilitate its obligation to balance its input and offtake from the transmission system on a daily basis.

To support the tender, the consumer should provide as much accurate data as possible, which should include:

- total annual consumption;
- maximum daily consumption;
- the site postcode;
- the site 'M' number, which identifies the gas input at the site;
- the meter serial number and location.

For sites over 25,000 therms, monthly consumption data for 12 successive months is desirable.

The choice for gas suppliers has recently been widened with the introduction of a 'partial interruptible' supply, in which, at the outset of the contract, a portion of the interruptible supply may be designated as firm, to 75,000 therms per year or 10 per cent of the supply, whichever is the lower.

A further strategic decision that must be made is whether to enter into a short- or long-term contract. Most gas supply contracts are for one year, and this would be the normal recommendation, but contracts for longer periods, such as two or three years, are perfectly acceptable provided that there are suitable review or competition clauses — at the buyer's option of course — at least at the anniversary of the contract, if not more frequently.

The new National Balancing Point (NBP), a gas futures contract from the International Petroleum Exchange (IPE), is a tool that is just becoming available to gas traders and purchasers. The ongoing growth in volume of the spot gas market, combined with the resultant increases in price volatility, prompted the IPE to develop a futures contract based on the delivery of gas at the NBP. The contract offers a mechanism whereby trading and hedging gas price risk is facilitated through the use of a standardised contract of 5000 therms of gas per day during the delivery month. This can offer the benefits of transparent price generation, trader anonymity and speedy market access, through the medium of electronic trading.

A further strategy option for the gas purchaser is for the gas supply contract to allow for a specified proportion of gas purchases on the spot market. The normal seasonal pattern of gas prices might show gas prices in the summer months being lower than the annual contract price, so some spot market purchases at this time, using the contracted gas supplier as purchasing

Switch it on to bring your bills down.

Switching to lighter priced electricity from SWALEC could cut your company's electricity bills by £££'s. Which can help to make you more cost effective, as well as improving your productivity and performance. Even though we're lighter in price than other suppliers, we're heavyweights when it comes to giving our customers the service they demand. Each of our business customers have their own Business Account Manager to take care of things, reviewing and fine tuning our service as it's needed. And our very flexible contracts and methods of billing and payments will suit you down to the ground. Just some of the reasons why companies large and small throughout England and Wales are switching to SWALEC.

FOR FURTHER ENLIGHTENMENT CALL 0800 833 697

SWALEC

A Hyder company

agent and shipper (for a modest administration fee), may prove advantageous.

One caveat: when contemplating a change of supplier ensure that any costs ensuing from a delay in handover, whether due to TransCo or the incumbent supplier, are the liability of the incoming supplier, not the consumer.

Electricity

In the electricity supply industry, similar to the gas industry, it is the duty of the conscientious buyer to ensure negotiation of the lowest price, rather than relying on regulatory reductions to effect savings.

Of greatest assistance in obtaining low prices is the provision of accurate, detailed consumption data for each site with a demand over 100kW. This is obtained from a meter which will record and transmit half-hourly data readings.

Most electricity contracts are placed for 12 months, although in the tendering round for 1 April contract starts — the tendering for this round takes place during the winter months — there is a possible advantage in opting for an 18-month contract. This can be beneficial because transmission charges are calculated on the basis of peak winter demands, so in the case of an 18-month contract starting in April, these charges are spread over a greater period reducing the effective per-unit cost. However, this is a one-off benefit, because an 18-month contract starting in October would involve two winter periods with two sets of charges.

There are many different types of electricity supply contracts available, including:

- pool price-based contracts (the pool may be described as the wholesale electricity market);
- seasonal time of day (STOD) contracts, in which different per-unit rates are charged according to the time of day and the month;
- maximum demand, based on conventional day and night unit rates plus a charge based on the maximum usage, normally in the winter months;
- fixed price based on fixed day and night unit rates.

To maximise the benefits of pool-based or STOD contracts, load management ability is essential — the capacity to reduce consumption of electricity at particular times. Pool prices, for example, can, for particular periods of high demand, reach considerable levels, with prices of 50–60p/kWh not exceptional. Obviously, if electricity consumption can be reduced at such times, the overall cost of power may be cut significantly. If the buyer's concern is for relatively predictable prices through the year with a minimum of

By 2010, energy efficiency has the potential to save nearly 20% of the energy currently used in the UK.

Industry and commerce spend over £10 billion each year on energy costs; much of it could be controlled by energy planning. One depot saved £5000 a year by investing wisely in energy efficiency.

There are 38 energy efficiency advice centres in the UK all willing to give you free, impartial energy advice. Energy Efficiency Advice Centres were set up by the Energy Saving Trust over four years ago and are funded partly by the DETR and partly by regional organisations.

£nergy savings can boost your **profits**

*f*ree advice on energy saving for your business

*f*ree information on cashbacks schemes and grants currently available when you complete our survey

*f*reephone on **0800 512012**

Energy Efficiency Advice Centres

ENERGY EFFICIENCY

MH/GEEAC Designs

Desmond Corporate Services

As independent consultants to the rapidly expanding Facilities Management profession, this company provides organisations of all sizes, and from all industry sectors, with the expert resources necessary to support effective business development.

In addition to providing practical advice, administrative help or managerial expertise in most areas of organisational change, Desmond Corporate Services provides a portfolio of services designed to provide all the best practice outsourcing expertise that organisations require.

In developing a strategy for future growth, a company should maximise its use of limited management and financial resources, which together constitute its ëcoreí expertise. There must be a distinction between those core functions which contribute to its competitive advantage, and the non-core functions which do not. It is in recognition of this distinction that an increasing number of companies are exploiting the opportunities provided by outsourcing and there is now almost no limit to the range and diversity of functions which can be outsourced.

Whilst the prospect of freeing up company resources to concentrate on core business and bringing in specialist expertise is a very attractive proposition, the exercise can present numerous difficulties which may be problematic to all but the most experienced outsourcing organisation. To ensure that it is pursuing the most advantageous strategy; selecting the most appropriate service provider; obtaining the required quality of service at the best price; and complying with all relevant UK and European legislation, companies must give serious consideration to buying-in this specialist expertise. Few organisations have the available time, let alone adequate practical experience, to accommodate this effectively from available internal resources.

A company should also consider the extent to which the provision of its core services can be developed to meet the specific outsourcing requirements of its own clients. More organisations than ever are now looking to benefit from the growth in outsourcing through the development of their own facilities management capability. The introduction of such a capability however, demands a considerable rethink on an organisationís marketing strategy and customer support services as well as the addition of specialist human resource and information technology skills.

With a wealth of practical experience, Desmond Corporate Services provides as much or as little assistance as organisations require, whether in the pursuit of an outsourcing strategy, or in the development of their own facilities management capability.

Organisations must seek the best possible advice to assist them in successfully developing an outsourcing strategy. I am absolutely convinced that there is no substitute for independent advice based upon sound, practical experience and it is to this principle that this company is totally dedicated.

Peter Desmond, Chief Executive

Desmond Corporate Services

Consultants to the FM profession

If your organisation is planning an outsourcing strategy, considering the introduction of its own facilities management capability, or just looking to carry out competitive tendering, there is no substitute for expertise based upon sound practical experience.

Through our independent services you can now benefit from immediate access to an unrivalled portfolio of specialist advice and support resources.

Single-point access to a portfolio of advisory, administrative and management services designed to provide all the best practice expertise necessary to support the FM profession.

- Guidance on TUPE, changing employee terms, service restructuring and pensions transfers
- Review of outsourcing opportunities
- Tender documentation and supplier selection
- Contract drafting
- Project management of service migration
- Contract management

In addition to our contract and outsourcing services we also provide a wide range of development services to assist organisations in the planning and implementation of organisational change.

For more information on how Desmond Corporate Services can support and enhance your in-house capability and to discuss your individual needs please telephone Peter Desmond on 0171-515 2194.

Desmond Corporate Services Limited, 31 Leerdam Drive,
Docklands, London E14 3JJ
Tel: 0171-515 2194 Fax: 0171-515 3001
lEmail: xem44@dial.pipex.com

A member of the British Institute of Facilities Management

Are your home or business telephone bills too high?

No Problem!

Abell has the answer!

Tremendous savings of up to **60%** on all National and International telephone calls

No connection fee
Per second billing
No membership fee
Monthly itemised billing
No minimum spending
Trouble free, easy use

Who is abell?

abell Telecommunications is an established provider of various telecommunication services. Our customers are both business and residential users who have a requirement for competitive national and international telephone calls.

The abell Voice Service was designed to meet the requirements of small to medium size businesses, as well as large companies with multi-site offices. We understand that the most important part of providing a service is **quality and personal attention.**

By 'least cost routing' your telephone and fax calls via a 4 digit number (which can be programmed into your telephone system), all your national and international calls are routed through one of the worlds most advanced fibre optic networks. There is no need to change your telephone number or system. You will then be able to enjoy these incredible savings!

Other products available include:
abell MCI International Calling Card
- Extremely competitive rates
- No surcharges – *you only pay for your calls*
- 24 hour customer service
- Multi-lingual operators – *19 languages*
- Access from over 120 countries worldwide
- Personalised card number

Multicom House,
2 Spring Villa Park,
Spring Villa Road,
Edgware, Middlesex
HA8 7EH

abell Telecommunications Ltd

For a complete brochure and tariff sheet, please contact sales on
Tel: 0181-951 5858 Fax: 0181-951 5588

maintenance, fixed-price or maximum demand contracts would be more suitable.

A further option for reducing electricity costs is for major consumers to install a combined heat and power facility (CHP), whereby the company is able to generate sufficient power for its own requirements and sell surplus power to the local distribution company. Alternatively, a system exists whereby an industrial consumer volunteers to reduce load at periods requested by the National Grid and receives compensation accordingly.

As with gas tenders, do not rely on a brief telephone survey; conduct a formal tender with documents sent to all major generators and distributors. Do not overlook the increasing competition from smaller generators, known as 'embedded' generators, which supply power within a distributor's area. The National Grid system is not used, so transmission charges are excluded from the price.

Considerations common to both gas and electricity purchasing that have recently become contentious involve ensuring that any existing contracts are clearly terminated with adequate notice given. Further, when new contracts are signed, ensure that this is done allowing adequate time before the contract is due to start — not just the statutory minimum period — and ensure that the contract is signed by both parties. On several occasions recently, suppliers have deferred signing contracts for several weeks before withdrawing the offered price in favour of an upwardly revised one.

Chris Partridge is editorial manager at **John Hall Associates**, a leading firm of energy market analysts.

12.3
Negotiating the Telecoms Maze

Andrews Johns
Director, National Utility Services Ltd

Market forces have brought about many changes in the UK telecoms industry and created a plethora of suppliers that are continually fighting among each other to gain greater market share. The sheer number of providers on the market, coupled with the variety of pricing and contract options available, makes it extremely difficult for the uninitiated telecoms buyer to find the best deals.

Around 200 companies now have licences from the Department of Trade and Industry to provide telecoms services. They range from BT and Mercury, the UK's main suppliers, to cable networks and US multinationals.

Faced with such a bewildering number of suppliers and services to choose from, business users can go wrong in many ways. For instance, they may settle for inappropriate call options with unsuitable tariffs. Or they may end up with the wrong capacity for their requirements, buying oversophisticated equipment or paying over the odds for incoming lines. Costly maintenance contracts and billing errors can further compound the problem.

However, those telecoms buyers with market knowledge who understand their requirements and usage patterns stand to benefit from the many discount schemes that suppliers offer.

Although most managers recognise that they are spending considerably more money than necessary on telecoms services, the majority assume that the only way to reduce call charges, whether voice, fax or data, is to reduce their frequency and volume. This is attempted through work analysis and better staff discipline, with many companies conducting periodic blitzes to discourage abuse and encourage prudence.

Personal discipline will continue to be important, but there are many other ways to cut and control telecoms costs. The problem is knowing exactly how to do this.

Many organisations do not have the in-house expertise or information available to deal with the complicated use/cost equations or to undertake the analysis necessary to understand call traffic patterns. And unless a company has access to a vast amount of up-to-date comparative information about telecoms equipment costs, traffic costs, maintenance agreements and the cheapest routing available, it is at a serious risk of overpaying.

With mistakes of £100,000 not being uncommon, thousands of organisations intent on maximising bottom-line profit have opted for professional advice before committing themselves to a potentially expensive and, in some cases, irrevocable course of action.

Utility Cost Analysis

Some decide to employ utility cost analysts who help them save money by comparing thousands of telecoms tariffs, equipment and call options from all over the UK and overseas, and selecting the best deals to match individual business needs.

One such organisation is National Utility Services (NUS), which advises businesses on all aspects of telecoms expenditure, including installation and maintenance agreements, voice, data and facsimile transmission costs, national/international call charges, supplier options, equipment purchase and lowest-cost routing.

Utility cost control analysis begins with an examination of every aspect of the client's telecoms expenditure and activity over the previous year. If the client has been overcharged in the past, the error can be traced back to its source, with the objective of obtaining the maximum refund from the supplier.

This system frequently exposes examples where the invoice does not reflect the lowest charges. In many cases, users do not realise that they are being overcharged or that there are better deals available in the market. The frequent reluctance of suppliers to admit their mistakes highlights the need for experts with in-depth knowledge of operating methods to identify overcharges and obtain corrections.

Making the Right Moves

It is particularly important for new and growing businesses to make the right telecoms choices early on. They must look critically at the various contracts and prices available from different suppliers so that they can find the right deal for them. If they don't do this, they run the risk of being locked into unsuitable cost regimes that raise expenditure unnecessarily and eat into profits.

For growing businesses attempting to gain a foothold in what are often highly competitive markets, the last thing they want is to be burdened by excessive telecoms charges.

In the light of a dynamic telecoms industry offering a variety of ever-changing options, it is important for a company continually to review its telecoms costs against the choices available in the market.

National Utility Service (NUS) provides a telecommunications, energy, and water cost control analysis to 750,000 businesses worldwide. In the UK, NUS services more than 4700 clients, including 430 in *The Times* Top 1000 companies.

12.4
Managing the Purchase of Professional Services

Peter Collier FCA
Group Business Development Director, The Fairmount Group plc

The Answer is Out There!

However successful a business is, to imagine that optimum growth and development will occur without any outside help is at best complacent, at worst arrogant. Yet learning how to benefit from the full range of professional advice on offer is a skill that many UK businesses seem reluctant to acquire. This chapter explores why professional advice is so necessary to the growing business, and suggests tried and tested ways of finding the right adviser.

Feeling Reserved? Keep it to Yourself

If there is one quality for which the British are renowned, it is reserve. In the business world, a degree of discretion is of course essential. But too great an emphasis on secrecy and self-sufficiency can foster a total reluctance to seek outside help — and this can thus hold back even the most successful business.

Of course, there are several other factors that contribute to the general corporate reluctance to ask for help. The 'once bitten, twice shy' factor makes people cautious. After all, a bad experience with a professional

IN BUSINESS,

THERE IS NO BENEFIT

OF HINDSIGHT.

THE INSTITUTE OF
CHARTERED
ACCOUNTANTS
IN ENGLAND & WALES

Chartered Accountants produce results all year round.

For more information contact the Institute on 0171 920 8633.

adviser is not easily forgotten. Then there is the business of finding the right adviser. Many business people are loath to invest time and money with a professional adviser who is a completely unknown quantity, yet they may not be able to find suitable help via their network of contacts.

Look to the Future, as well as the Past

The majority of businesses are prepared to buy in professional advice relating to historic events — the annual audit, commercial lease or tax return completion, for instance. But far fewer organisations seek help with the forward-looking aspects of their business — areas like fund raising, strategies for business development, human resource requirements or pension planning.

This is ironic when you consider that getting help making the next million has to be more constructive than calculating the last one to two decimal places.

How to Make the Right Choice

Once the need to call in professional advisers has been identified, how do you find the right people to help? How do you decide what will be an appropriate investment? And, perhaps most important of all, how can you ensure that those advisers will have a genuine understanding of your business, your needs and your objectives?

It is often assumed that with the relevant professional qualifications, automatically you get the right solution. Such trust in academia is touching, but may be misguided. Factors such as accessibility, quality of service and timing are also important. And it is essential to have confidence that the chosen adviser is not only up to speed with the fast-changing world of business, but preferably at least one step ahead.

Practical Purchasing

The traditional route to finding a professional adviser is through personal introduction. But businesses need to consider this approach with caution. An adviser who fits the bill for one company will not necessarily be right for the next, simply because the objectives, cultures and requirements of those businesses may be poles apart.

If the personal recommendation route does not bear fruit, the net can be stretched wider to include other local businesses and professionals.

A third alternative is to contact the relevant professional body, such as the Law Society or Institute of Chartered Accountants, with a view to acquiring local or national directories.

An Objective View

Pitching has become an accepted way in which to sound out the true quality or suitability of, say, two or three firms. In order to make a sound judgement, it is important to (a) define your objectives, and (b) provide each firm with a comparable brief.

Whether or not you decide to conduct a pitch, the importance of establishing and communicating your objectives clearly cannot be overemphasised. Fortunately, many professional advisers are skilled in helping clients formulate objectives — acting, if you like, as bolt-on strategists as well as problem solvers.

The Meeting of Minds

In addition to being certain that the firm you are considering has the technical expertise and capacity to take on the job in hand, you need to feel confident that those who will be working together will be able to form good business relationships.

You should always take up references before making any binding commitment. References should be willingly supplied. Excuses or attempts at evasion should be viewed with extreme suspicion.

The Transfer of Skills

Many businesses want to buy in not only advice, but the means for implementing it. A fabulous report that lists all the answers to your problems may be inspirational — but unless it is translated into *action*, it could turn out to be an expensive waste of time. To use the classic example, it's not much good knowing you need a sophisticated new computer system if you have not the faintest idea of how to find it, buy it, install or use it!

So it is important to find out whether your advisers will carry out their recommendations, or if they can 'transfer skills' to your company — eg by training your staff to take on all parts of the implementation process — if this would be more appropriate.

You can, of course, seek advice from several different advisers, in order to gain the required degree of specification and/or capacity. And if you reach a situation where your current adviser can't help, has a conflict of interest or

IQM
INTERNATIONAL QUALITY MANAGEMENT

John Dough (Baking) Company is a medium sized enterprise, employing approximately 100 and was suffering from poor performance, without really knowing what it was doing wrong. IQM were called in to assess the situation. Following our unique system of interview and audit we quickly realised that the company lacked any meaningful management structure with many people unsure as to what their role in the organisation really was. We put together a pragmatic programme of management development, and business strategy. The focus was heavily on bottom up staff involvement, tighter business control, process efficiency and increased profits. The company made savings of £5000 within the first week and went on to greatly improve staff morale, and reduced errors and wastage.

With US$55 million turnover per annum, incorporating profit of approximately US$16 million, this aerospace organisation is, by comparison, a large company. As part of a corporate strategy they had to gain registration to ISO 9001. Having worked with many other divisions within the group, IQM were a natural choice for consultancy assistance. First we had to measure their starting position in relation to ISO achievement. Developing excellent relations at all levels is an important part of successful implementation of any consultancy or training. When looking at implementing something as fundamental as ISO 9001, it is crucial.

Whilst we reviewed their systems to identify process proficiency areas, we also prepared the ground to create excellent communication between departments, frequently found to be deficient on a first audit and an area where this organisation made huge strides forward early in the project. Following our project plan, this company now achieves better communication and teamwork and having had specific training on internal quality auditing have become self sufficient in as short a time as possible. Through ongoing internal audits, they still identify areas for corrective or preventive action to fortify their business,

1, Rose Cottages, Rectory Lane, Saltwood, Kent. CT21 4PU

despite having achieved ISO 9001 with zero non conformances or conditions of certification. They understand that quality is a lifelong quest for continuously improving performance levels.

<u>Oakbeam Ltd.,</u> was a company drowning in paperwork. They bought an off the shelf ISO system, along with 75 'non value added' procedures, from a consultant who assured them they would gain registration with it. They did by altering the way they worked to suit the system given to them. Unfortunately, they almost went out of business "because of ISO". After our first visit with Oakbeam Ltd., they were able to make monumental changes to their ISO system, instantly saving time and money on the way they worked. Their procedures were reduced to the 28 they actually found they needed in order to reduce the risk of failure, increase their levels of end quality and to comply with the twenty sections of ISO 9001. Their QA manual no longer fills a ring binder but is 10 pages of material suitable for use as a marketing tool, while still complying with the Standard. Today they have a thriving business. They also have ISO 9001 and don't mind being audited because they know that ISO is working for them, not the other way around!

IQM compare ISO 9000 to a razor blade. Both are very sharp tools and each is designed to do a specific task. But, if you cut your wrists with a razor blade, you will bleed to death and blame the razor! But it's not the razors' fault, it is the way it was used that's at fault. ISO 9000 is a very powerful business tool and if implemented incorrectly, businesses can suffocate. Used the right way, it can help your business become more competitive and more profitable. It can help you produce less waste and make more efficient use of time, making great savings to your overheads.

We have helped many industries over three continents improve the way they work and increase their profit levels. Many corporate clients are happy to give references on request. IQM can help your business. To find out how your company could get 40% assistance towards the cost of improving your business future telephone us on the number below. Your business could be working smarter for you.

International Quality Management
~ better business management for a better business.
Telephone: 01303 266117
Facsimile: 01303 261755

simply seems a bit slow off the mark, then get another firm in. There is no reason why your existing relationship should not continue.

Getting Value for Money

It is up to you to set criteria for success and carry out your own form of evaluation. Fees will, of course, be an issue — but they are not the whole story. Obviously, good advice has to be paid for, but remember to consider the benefits as well as the cost. If, for instance, your pensions adviser charges you £1500 but saves you £25,000 in taxation, you might consider it something of a bargain!

It is important that both sides are clear about the fee basis and that the client understands how additional costs may be triggered. Details such as invoicing frequency should be agreed in advance and in writing, as should the exact scope and timing of the work. You should expect any changes in fees, schedules and so on to be advised promptly and justified properly.

After all, if you are dealing with true professionals, you would not expect to settle for anything less.

Peter Collier FCA is Group Business Development Director with The Fairmount Group plc. From 1987–96 he was Managing Director of an organisation that administered national networks of chartered accountants and solicitors. **The Fairmount Group plc** offers a range of individually tailored financial products and services, including trusts, pensions, investment management, stockbroking and private banking facilities. Corporate clients range from small businesses to household names and the group also acts for many personal clients.

Part 13
Site Selection

13.1
The Problems of Relocation

John Greenwood
Partner, Healey & Baker

Relocation has traditionally been viewed as the inevitable consequence of companies outgrowing existing property by securing new contracts/business, or alternatively a sign of withdrawal and consolidation.

In today's global market a 'competitive edge' can be the difference between success and failure and as such property costs, like others, are under the microscope at local, national and international levels.

A company's ability to switch production or distribution at short notice to maximise efficiency and productivity is often essential in securing new contracts and business. In too many cases property relocation tends to be a reaction to changes in circumstances rather than being pre-planned in line with an agreed strategic business plan.

For many considering this course of action a good starting point is the commissioning of a property and/or lease audit to establish and evaluate both existing property liabilities (which in many cases are not accurately recorded) and future financial liabilities and obligations. With the audit complete, the decision to move can be analysed with the business case criteria and evaluated on a 'weighted matrix'.

The weighting assessment should clearly prioritise the factors influencing the move: whether they be driven through either by consolidation or expansion, or by the ability to effect cost savings through the introduction of automation or changes in labour practices.

Some of the main factors that need to be considered at this stage of the exercise are not directly financially related, but have social consequences that are often overlooked. These would include education and housing availability, but are more often related to a close analysis of the availability and cost of labour (skilled and unskilled) in certain sectors of male and female age groups. The other macro effects that need to be analysed at this stage are more directly related to the business: access to customers, availability of supplies and raw materials, transportation costs and a detailed review of communications, including accessibility to international airports, container ports, motorways and rail link cargo terminals.

The inclusion of specific financial data and the availability of grants and capital allowances are also important — rent and rates are often of secondary significance in the preliminary stages (unless the relocation is that of an overseas investor).

Financial sensitivity should be applied to the second phase of the study to analyse the relative strengths and weaknesses of each option against the economic and financial constraints.

Due to the current shortage of new speculative industrial/warehouse accommodation, many organisations are finding that properties which meet their requirements are not currently available. Companies are being forced to take second-hand, inferior units or are alternatively deferring their expansion by having a bespoke unit constructed.

Timing is therefore critical, and with further possible delays resulting from planning procedures, grant applications, infrastructure works and design modifications, in general a minimum of 24 months should be allocated to the project. This may be triggered to coincide with the determination of a lease, a tenant's option to break or simply the acquisition of an additional facility for expansion.

Traditionally the property market has thrived on the adage 'location, location, location'. Few outside the sector appreciate that this expression is more attributable to the landlord-dominated UK market than to the needs of manufacturing occupiers/tenants struggling to meet shareholders' expectations. In practice, by far the biggest problem is the lack of flexibility in most commercial leases. Tenants have historically been tied to leases for 25 years on full repairing and insuring terms with upward-only reviews.

With commercial rents having peaked in 1989/90, current rents on many industrial warehouse buildings, subject to location, can substantially exceed today's market rental values. Combined with the upward-only reviews and severe repairing and dilapidation obligations, close attention must be paid to the finer points of lease negotiation. This is particularly important in respect of alienation (the ability to sublet or assign), the provision of sureties or guarantors, the handling of tenant's fixtures and fittings and guidance on future rent review clauses.

Far too often companies are so attracted by the initial financial incentives offered that they neglect to structure a more reasonable deal which gives them flexibility to determine or break their lease, to react to future changes in circumstances and to refrain from the temptation of leasing bespoke accommodation with little, if any, use to other commercial occupiers.

With the Labour government's decision to give independence to the Bank of England, there is the hope that the UK can maintain its excellent economic position. While there is the initial risk, as has been seen to date, that short-term interest rates will rise, long-term rates should fall, thus assisting companies to grow and meet their expectations.

Changing circumstances and requirements make it difficult always to follow accepted rules and practices, but prudent steps to produce comparative analysis against pre-determined criteria should always be initiated in what is for tenants a 'perfect market'.

Healey & Baker is an international partnership, established in 1820, providing real estate consultancy and agency advice. It specialises in all types of commercial property and acts for a range of prominent clients across the corporate, public and private sectors. The firm's global network covers over 160 offices in 32 countries.

FINANCE FOR THE GROWING BUSINESS

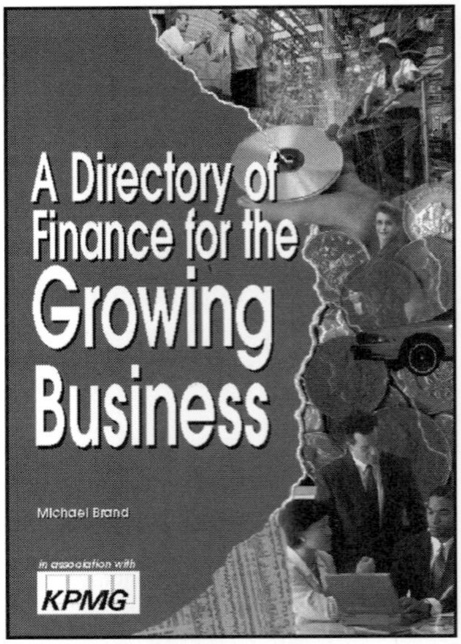

An essential reference for:

CEOs and finance directors of SMEs, owner managed businesses, MBOs and partnerships

- *Unique one-stop guide to business funding*
- *High grade contributors include KPMG, 3i, NatWest*
- *Compliments* ***The Growing Business Handbook***
- *Comprehensive directory of appropriate and reliable sources of finance*

This unique guide and directory provides an authoritative overview of the various sources of finance available to SMEs and a selective directory of reputable providers. It shows how each source works and what it is for, and advises companies how to meet the access requirements and to successfully raise appropriate funding for their particular need. Each chapter relates to one source of funding and combines analysis of that source with a directory of providers.

Author information
Michael Brand is an independent consultant and adviser to SMEs, he has founded buisness angel neteorks in the UK and USA and was previously a vice president of 3I (USA). Contributors include: KPMG, 3i; Evershed; National Westminster Bank; the Association of factors.

Contents

- *Introduction*
- *Early stage capital*
- *Bank finance*
- *Business angels*
- *Venture capital*
- *Leasing and hire purchase*
- *Factoring*
- *Grants*
- *AIM, NASDAQ, EASDAQ,Offex*
- *Deal structure*
- *Bibliography and useful addresses*

Published in association with KPMG

ORDER FORM

ISBN 0799424737 180

This offer is only available direct from the publisher.
• Fax: 0171 278 8198 • E-Mail: kpinfo@kogan-page.co.uk

Qty.	Title and Order No.	Price
	A DIRECTORY...BUSINESS	£30
	Inclusive of postage & packing (Add 10% for overseas delivery	
	Total	

If telephoning your order on: 0171 278 0545, please quote:FIN

Kogan Page Free Information Service
Please send me regular information on new books on:

☐ Business and management

☐ As a service to our customers, we occasionally make our customer lists available to companies whose products or services we feel may be of interest. If you do not wish to receive such mailings, please indicate by ticking the box.

Thank you for your order

KOGAN PAGE
120 Pentonville Road, London N1 9JN
Tel: +44 (0)171 278 0433 Fax: +44 (0)171 837 6348

WHATEVER IT TAKES TO GET IT RIGHT

For development and management of commercial, industrial, high technology and office premises.

AKELER
DEVELOPMENTS PLC

With offices in:
- London
- Leeds
- Glasgow
- Korea

For more information:
Mark Glatman, Chief Executive
Tel: +44 (0) 113 246 0060
Fax: +44 (0) 113 244 8340
Web Site: http://www.akeler.co.uk

13.2
What Price Flexibility?

Joe Valente
DTZ Debenham Thorpe Research
and
Jonathan Paul
DTZ Corporate Real Estate Services

Property is not just a major resource held by companies. It is a resource which is asked to fulfil a multitude of often contradictory roles. Property can be a major asset — often the single largest asset held by a company — capable of nourishing the bottom line. It can act as a vehicle, a conduit through which a company is able to disseminate an array of messages to staff and suppliers as well as the market as a whole. It is a resource that can facilitate operational efficiency, but just as easily act to constrain effectiveness. And when all else is said and done, it is, perhaps, property's role as a liability which most often comes to the fore, as an unexpected and unwelcome weight on the core business.

Against such backcloth, a new role for property needs to be forged which is capable of meeting the rapidly changing needs of growing and mature companies alike. Change is a word that is all too easily bandied about, but no less important for that. As product cycles become ever shorter, competition intensifies and broadens, and as technology opens a myriad of new possibilities, the result is that an entirely different attitude towards the role of property is called for. No company — however small, however dynamic — can afford to waste the value of property and the contribution it can make to competitive advantage.

But in many ways that is precisely what so many companies have done. Because property is not the core business, its role historically has been defined simply in terms of physical envelope, which is rarely integrated into the wider business planning process. Indeed, as business activity becomes driven by the need for greater flexibility, property becomes not less important but more important, as its role of being the most fixed of all tangible assets held by a company becomes paramount and readily transparent. That is not to say that property suddenly becomes central to business planning, nor should it be allowed to drive the core business. On the contrary, that should never be allowed to happen, even though that is precisely what will happen if business decisions regarding expansion or contraction, for example, are taken without an appreciation of the changing relationships between business and property cycles.

The challenge of incorporating property within the business planning process requires a change in the perspective of the resource itself, from a hindrance and envelope to a facilitator of change. Relocation/co-location, an improved working environment and more flexible accommodation can all provide firms with an opportunity to introduce operational reorganisation and the introduction of different working practices. Property also represents a cultural statement for many organisations and again, a change in physical environment can often provide an effective means of stimulating cultural and organisational change within a firm.

This requires an organisation to plan its accommodation needs as part of the business planning process to ensure that the desired level of flexibility is delivered. Property is not as flexible as staff or capital, but that is not where the main problem lies. The issue to grapple with is the cost implication of the requirement for business flexibility. An understanding of this is all too often absent until property begins to impose itself as a constraint on the business.

In other words, the three key questions which all expanding business should ask are:

- How much flexibility do I really need?
- Do all functions within the firm require the same degree of flexibility?
- How much am I prepared to pay above market prices for the desired level of flexibility?

The following case illustrates this point. ABC Inc is faced with an uncertain business cycle over the next five years. The company requires 15,000 sq ft of office accommodation to house its 100 staff and given the uncertainty in its growth forecasts, it does not wish to commit to a lease of more than five years. The company wishes to grow as a single entity and not be forced into two separate locations. However, the property market, in its usual intransigent manner, is only offering 15-year leases at a market rent of £17.50 per sq ft. This presents the company with the prospect of having to relocate to new space after five years and to sub-let its space for the remaining ten years.

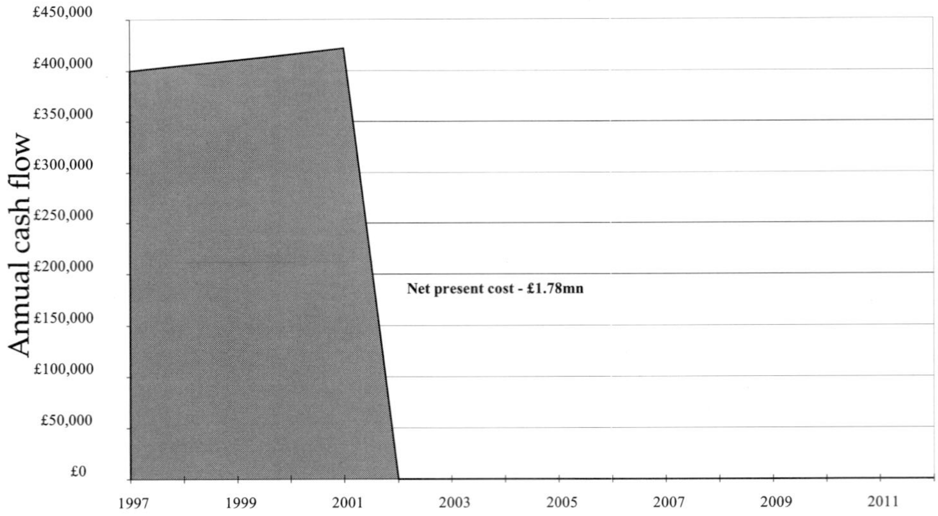

Figure 13.2.1 15-year lease with a break option after 5 years, vacated after 5 years

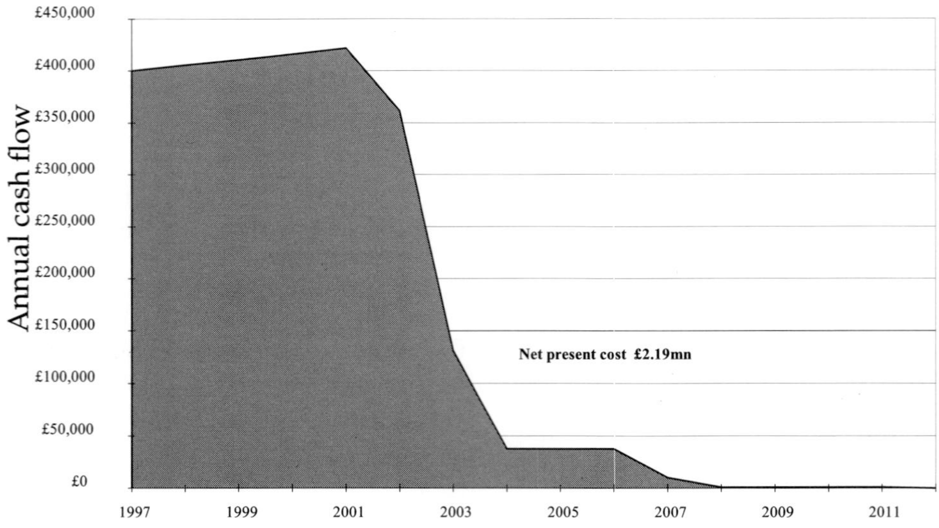

Figure 13.2.2 15-year lease with no break options, vacated after 5 years

However, there are costs and uncertainties with sub-letting. Will there be the occupational demand? How long will it take before a sub-tenant is secured and will they be prepared to pay £17.50, given that the market has declined to £15 over the previous five years?

Figures 13.2.1 and 13.2.2 illustrate the financial impact of this type of scenario, which could amount to as much as £410,000. This sum is significant and when expressed in an annualised form represents an additional £5.40 per sq ft over a five-year period, ie a 25 per cent increase in rent. These potential costs will arise when property is treated as an afterthought. The benefits, on the other hand, can only emerge by tying together business and property cycles.

Organizations need to identify their operational requirements for property in a meaningful and structured manner to ensure that property becomes a responsive resource facilitating change in the business and not hindering it. For many companies this process is left far too late in their evolution, or in the business cycle. It is ignored, or downgraded — until, that is, the legacy of property comes home to roost.

DTZ Debenham Thorpe is the UK's leading firm of property advisers and employs 1200 staff in 14 locations.

The Corporate Real Estate Service team is a dedicated group within DTZ which advises corporate occupiers in the UK and Europe on all aspects of property and its management as an integral element of the client's business. The team concentrates on advice and problem solving as distinct from agency and transaction-related business. It prides itself on being able to develop solutions to the wide-ranging and often complex situations which arise when a client's property portfolio is incompatible with its business needs.

13.3

Breaking Down Barriers to Market Entry

Brian Dudley
Chief Executive, Regus

For any business considering new market entry there is one relocation problem that is not only intimidating, but is likely to absorb a disproportionate amount of time and money to overcome. That barrier is physically locating suitable office accommodation.

Time spent visiting property agents, viewing office after office, checking the small print on lease documents and dealing with numerous service providers — not forgetting the hire of local support personnel — can run into hundreds of hours.

One solution for businesses wishing to leapfrog barriers to market entry, and thus gain a competitive edge over competitors, is to hire fully serviced offices at a business centre. Regus founded the business centre concept in Europe in 1989 and today is the leading worldwide operator of fully serviced business centres, with more than 130 centres in 34 countries. We are planning to open one new centre every week during 1997.

Such centres offer instantly available, fully furnished and equipped offices on short-term flexible leases and they are as easy to access as checking into a hotel. Offices are fully furnished and free businesses from the need to, and the cost of, setting up their own infrastructure. Therefore the financial risk involved in setting up in a new location is minimal compared to committing to a long-term lease or property purchase.

Each office is fully fitted with state-of-the-art telecommunications technology and is supported by multilingual support staff dedicated to customer service. Indeed, many of our centres are equipped with videoconferencing facilities, airport-style business lounges and touchdown areas.

Many of our clients are multinationals who have a need to enter the market quickly and efficiently. Their reasons for needing shorter-term flexible office accommodation vary greatly. Some need to conduct product launches, complete business development programmes or simply fulfil basic overspill requirements.

Many organisations appreciate the instant market access provided by business centres to support their own long-term property plans. For instance, when Marks & Spencer opened its first store in Cologne in October 1996, it not only spearheaded a consumer revolution in German high streets, but also overcame barriers to entry in Germany by using the Regus business centre in Cologne.

'Once we had decided to enter the German market we had to move quickly,' says Mark Bauwens, M&S's general manager for Germany and the Netherlands. 'The six floor store would contain our new office complex, but we needed to have a functional German operations base while the new complex was being built. The instant availability and the flexibility of the centre's terms meant that we were able to move to the business centre in Cologne and be operational from day one.'

Indeed, many blue-chip organisations, such as American Express, BT, Kimberly-Clark, McKinsey, Midland Bank and Sun Life, are already capturing the strategic, competitive, time-saving and cost benefits that our business centres provide.

While location and speed of entry are key factors in the selection of any business centre, cost is also an important issue. A report recently published in the UK by the Chartered Institute of Purchasing and Supply (CIPS) reveals that substantial cost benefits can be gained from using a fully serviced business centre office when compared to conventional office space leases.

The CIPS study evaluates the potential cost advantages of using a fully serviced office at a business centre, rather than having to commission conventional methods of office space acquisition, such as long-term rental, leasing and outright purchase of office space. Comparisons were made between a high-cost city centre and a lower-cost city centre. The figures for a conventional office space lease were compiled with no knowledge of the equivalent figures for business centres, to ensure that the actual comparisons were free of bias.

The comparison also takes into account the full physical cost of establishing a presence in a new market, including cost elements such as floorspace rental, provision of furniture, building services, office administration, electricity, telephone, photocopying and faxing, office cleaning, provision of meeting/boardrooms and actual acquisition costs.

'New' technology is now superseded at alarming speed. In addition, with product lifecycles now being measured in months rather than years, the speed with which new products are brought to market plays a major part in their success or failure. Therefore the use of the fully serviced business centre office is an important factor in allowing companies to concentrate on their core business from day one.

Regus is the leading worldwide operator of business centres with more than 130 locations in 34 countries. It provides instantly available offices on short-term flexible leases complete with multilingual secretarial support and advanced telecommunications. Regus will be opening a further 50 centres during 1997. Brian Dudley is chief executive of Regus and is responsible for the day-to-day running of the company.

Appendix: Contact Addresses

3i Plc
91 Waterloo Road
London SE18 XP
Tel: 0171 928 3131
Fax: 0171 928 0058
Web site: http:\\www.3ics.co.uk
Contact: Patrick Sheehan

Alexander
32 Brook Street
London W1Y 1AJ
Tel: 0171 629 1949
Fax: 0171 629 4002
E-mail: mail@alexco.demon.co.uk
Contact: Graham Alexander

Aon Risk Services Ltd
10 Devonshire Square
London EC2M 4LE
Tel: 0171 680 4000
Fax: 0171 480 6137
Contact: Chris Goodchild

The Bank Relationship Company
17 St Helen's Place
Bishopsgate
London EC3A 6DE
Tel: 0171 256 5657
Fax: 0171 256 5658
Contact: Richard Parkinson

Bird & Bird
90 Fetter Lane
London EC4A 1JP
Tel: 0171 415 6000
Fax: 0171 415 6111
Contact: Trevor Cook

Boult Wade Tennant
27 Furnival Street
London EC4A 1PQ
Tel: 0171 404 5921
Fax: 0171 831 1768
E-mail: boult@boult.com
Contact: Tessa Bucks

BUPA
BUPA House
15–19 Bloomsbury Way
London WC1A 2BA
Tel: 0171 656 2700
Fax: 0171 656 2700
Web site: http://www.bupa.co.uk
Contact: Peter Fermoy

Burton Sweet Chartered Accountants
Cooper House
Lower Charlton Estate
Shepton Mallet
Somerset
Tel: 0117 9738441
Fax: 0117 9733781
Contact: Neil Kingston

Business Links West
16 Clifton Park
Bristol BS8 3BY
Tel: 0117 9737373
Fax: 0117 9745365
Contact: Andrew Stainer

BVCA
Essex House
12–13 Essex Street
London WC2R 3AA
Tel: 0171 240 3846
Fax: 0171 240 3849
E-mail: bvca@bvca.co.uk
Contact: Charlotte Morrison

BZW Equity Ltd
5 The North Colonade
Canary Wharf
London E14 4BB
Tel: 0171 623 2323
Fax: 0171 773 4805
Contact: Tom Lamb

The Carphone Warehouse
Head Office
North Acton Business Park
Wells Farm Road
London W3 6RF
Tel: 0181 896 5000
Fax: 0181 896 5005
Contact: Charles Dunstone

Cavewood Transport Ltd
PO Box 92
Coronation Road
High Wycombe
Bucks MP12 3TW
Tel: 01494 446541
Fax: 01494 447329
Contact: Paul Mainds

CBI
Centre Point
103 New Oxford Street
London WC1A 1DU
Tel: 0171 379 7400
Fax: 0171 240 2651
Central CBI E-mail: cbi-information@geo2.poptel.org.uk
Contact: Fiona Underwood

CBX Management & Consulting
Riverside House
Holtspur Lane
Wooburn Green
Buckinghamshire HP10 0AU
Tel: 01628 643600
Fax: 01628 643700
E-mail: 106003.1543@compuserve.com
Web site: http://www.cbx.co.uk
Contact: John Weston

The Centre for Tomorrow's Company
RSA
8 John Adam Street
London WC2N 6EZ
Tel: 0171 930 5150
Fax: 0171 930 5155
Contact: Mark Goyder

Cisco Systems Ltd
3 The Square
Stockley Park
Uxbridge
Middlesex UB11 1BN
Tel: 0181 756 8000
Fax: 0181 756 8099
E-mail: pmountfo@cisco.com
Contact: Paul Mountford

Dell Computers UK
Mailbank House
Western Road
Bracknell
Berkshire RG12 1RD
Tel: 01344 860456
Fax: 01344 860187
Contact: Philip Vanhoutle

Design Council
Haymarket House
1 Oxendon Street
London SW1Y 4EE
Tel: 0171 208 2121
Fax: 0171 839 6033
Contact: Paul Crake

Dewe Rogerson Ltd
3½ London Wall
London Wall
London EC2M 5SX
Tel: 0171 638 9571
Fax: 0171 628 3444
E-mail: Information@dewrog.co.uk
Contact: Brendan McNamara

Direct Marketing Association
Haymarket House
1 Oxendon Street
London SW1Y 4EE
Tel: 0171 321 2525
Fax: 0171 321 0191
Contact: Martin Bartle

DTZ
44 Brook Street
London W1A 4AG
Tel: 0171 408 1161
Fax: 0171 491 4593
Contact: Helen Basil

Experian (previously called CCN)
Talbot House
Nottingham NG1 5HF
Tel: 0115 941 0888
Fax: 0115 934 4905
Contact: Peter Brooker

Factors and Discounters Association
1 Northumberland Avenue
Trafalgar Square
London WC2N 5BW
Tel: 0171 930 9112
Fax: 0171 839 2858
Contact: Chris Molloy

The Fairmount Group
Fairmount House
Bull Hill
Leatherhead
Surrey KT22 7AY
Tel: 01372 370000
Fax: 01372 376343
Contact: Peter Collier

Finance & Leasing Association
18 Upper Grosvenor Street
London W1X 9PB
Tel: 0171 491 2783
Fax: 0171 629 0396
Contact: Stuart Neill

Healey & Baker
29 George Street
Hanover Square
London W1A 3BG
Tel: 0171 629 9292
Fax: 0171 514 2360
Contact: John Greenwood

Hi-Tech Logistics Ltd
PO Box 145
Rockware Avenue
Greenford
Middlesex UB6 0RZ
Tel: 0181 566 6060
Fax: 0181 575 3814
Contact: Wendy Constantine

Hobsons Publishing plc
Bateman Street
Cambridge CB2 1LZ
Tel: 01223 354551
Fax: 01223 323154
Contact: Chris Letcher

The Institute for Employment Studies
Mantell Building
University of Sussex
Brighton BN1 9RF
Tel: 01273 678322
Fax: 01273 690430
Contact: Peter Reilly

The Institute of Public Relations
The Old Trading House
15 Northburgh Street
London EC1V 0PR
Tel: 0171 253 5151
Fax: 0171 490 0588
E-mail: info@ipr1.demon.co.uk
Web site: http://www.ipr.press.net
Contact: John Lavelle

Intrum Justitia Ltd
PO Box 35
Stratford-upon-Avon
Warwickshire CV37 0BW
Tel: 01789 412081
Fax: 01789 412077
Web site: http://www.intrum.com
Contact: Gerard Barron

ISIS Innovation Ltd
2 Southpark Road
Oxford OX1 3UB
Tel: 01865 272 411
Fax: 01865 272 412
Contact: Dr Tim Cook

Jardine Reeves Brown Ltd
Employee Benefits Consultants & Actuaries
10 Albert Embankment
London SE1 7SP
Tel: 0171 587 0527
Fax: 0171 735 7489
Contact: Thomas Heron PhD MBA FCIS

John Hall Associates Chartered Quantity Surveyors
24 Old Burlington Street
London W1
Tel: 0171 434 0258
Fax: 0171 434 2762
Contact: Chris Partridge

KPMG
1 Puddle Dock
London EC4V 3PD
Tel: 0171 311 2858
Fax: 0171 311 3311
Contact: Peter Mamelok

Kwik-Fit
17 Corstorphine Road
Edinburgh EH12 6DD
Scotland
Tel: 0131 337 9200
Fax: 0131 337 0062
Contact: Sir Tom Farmer

Lex Vehicle Leasing
Globe House
Parkway
Globe Park
Marlow
Buckinghamshire SL7 1LY
Tel: 01628 898000
Fax: 01628 898050
Contact: Steve Carman

Lloyds TSB Group Plc
PO Box 215
71 Lombard Street
London EC3P 3BS
Tel: 0171 626 1500
Fax: 0171 356 1369
Contact: David Singleton

Media Audits Ltd
16 Dufours Place
London W1V 1FE
Tel: 0171 734 4080
Fax: 0171 439 2455
Contact: John Storey

Monks Partnership Ltd
The Mill House
Wendens Ambo
Saffron Walden
Essex CB11 4JX
Tel: 01799 542222
Fax: 01799 541805
Contact: Alison Smith

National Utility Services Ltd
Carolyn House
Dingwall Road
Croydon
London CR9 3LX
Tel: 0181 681 2500
Fax: 0181 688 7229
Contact: Andrew Johns

Orange
St James Court
Great Park Road
Almondsbury
Bradley Stoke
Bristol BS12 4QJ
Tel: 0800 801080
Contact: Doug Walker

PA Consulting
123 Buckingham Palace Road
London SW1 9SR
Tel: 0171 730 9000
Fax: 0171 333 5050
Contact: Jackie Warner

Paisner & Co
Bouverie House
154 Fleet Street
London EC4A 2DQ
Tel: 0171 353 0299
Fax: 0171 583 8621
Contact: David Henry Cohen

The Patent Office
Marketing and Information
Directorate
Central Enquiry Unit
Cardiff Road
Newport
Gwent NP9 1RH
Wales
Tel: 0645 500505
Fax: 01633 813600
Contact: Roland Whaite

Philip Sadler CBE
Shootersway
Farmhouse
Shootersway
Berkhamsted
Hertfordshire HP4 3TY
Tel/Fax: 91442 864400

Pitmans Solicitors
47 Castle Street
Reading
Berks RG1 7SR
Tel: 0118 958 0224
Fax: 01734 585097
Contact: John Hutchinson

Prontaprint Ltd
Coniscliffe House
Coniscliffe Road
Darlington DL3 7EX
Tel: 01325 483333
Fax: 01325 488665
Contact: Jane Gledhall

Regus
Knyvett House
The Causeway
Staines
Middlesex TW18 3BA
Tel: 01784 898444
Fax: 01784 898555
E-mail: 106173.547@compuserve
Web site: http://www.regus.com
Contact: Ian Bayly

Research International
Specialist Units
6/7 Grosvenor Place
London SW1 XSH
Tel: 0171 656 5000
Fax: 0171 235 2015
Contact: Elaine Asbridge

Sanmex International
5–9 Dalmarnock Road
Rutherglen
Glasgow G73 1NY
Scotland
Tel: 0141 647 2244
Fax: 0141 613 1228
Contact: Dr Allan Groden

Sedgwick Risk Services UK
Grove House
Newland Street
Witham
Essex CM8 2UP
Tel: 0171 724 3246
Fax: 01376 500580
Contact: Gary Stott

Springpoint
31 Corsica Street
London N5 1JT
Tel: 0171 704 2878
Fax: 0171 704 2874
Contact: Fiona Gilmore

Stephens & Co
Bridgegate Business Centre
Martinfield
Welwyn Garden City
Hertfordshire AL7 1JG
Tel: 01707 328432
Fax: 0113 2456663
Contact: Steve Pipe

Symantec UK
St Cloud Gate
St Cloud Way
Maidenhead
Berkshire SL6 8AW
Tel: 0171 616 5600
Web site: www.symantec.com
Contact: Richard Saunders

Teamwork
58 Redcliffe Road
London SW10 9NQ
Tel: 0171 376 4479
Fax: 0171 351 4445
E-mail:
100607.2233@compuserve.com Or
teamwork london@compuserve.com
Contact: Lynne Smitham

Telework Association
Shortwood
Nailsworth
Gloucestershire GL6 0SH
Tel: 01453 834874
Fax: 01453 836174
E-mail: 100272.3137@compuserve.com
Web site: http://www.tca.org.uk
Contact: Alan Denbigh

Trade Indemnity
1 Canada Square
London E14 5DX
Tel: 0171 739 4311
Fax: 0171 729 7682
Contact: Eleanor Lewis

Venture Capital Report Ltd
The Magdalen Centre
Oxford Science Park
Oxford PX4 4GA
Tel: 01865 784411
Fax: 01865 784412
E-mail: vcr@vcr1978.demon.co.uk
Web site: http://www.demon.co.uk/vcr1978
Contact: Danny Tomeh

Winkler Marketing International Ltd
6 St Georges Place
Brighton
East Sussex BN1 4GA
Tel: 01273 570144
Fax: 01273 570133
Contact: John Winkler

XR Associates
Myrtle Road
Queensgate
Brentwood
Essex CM14 5EG
Tel: 01277 238238
Fax: 01277 226225
Contact: Nicholas Dalton

Index

Index of Advertisers